DISASTER
AT
D-DAY

GREENHILL MILITARY PAPERBACKS

Anatomy of the Zulu Army
The Art of War
Bomber Offensive
Brave Men's Blood
Disaster at D-Day
Guderian
A History of the Art of War in the Middle Ages (two volumes)
A History of the Art of War in the Sixteenth Century
The Hitler Options
I Flew for the Führer
The Illustrated Encyclopedia of Handguns
Infantry Attacks
Invasion
Long Range Desert Group
The Memoirs of Field Marshal Kesselring
The Note-Books of Captain Coignet
On the Napoleonic Wars
The Red Air Fighter
SAS: With the Maquis
The Sky My Kingdom
The Viking Art of War
War on the Eastern Front
Wellington at Waterloo
Wellington in India
Wellington in the Peninsula
Why the Germans Lose at War

DISASTER
AT
D-DAY

The Germans Defeat the Allies, June 1944

Peter Tsouras

Greenhill Books, London
Stackpole Books, Pennsylvania

This book is dedicated with great affection to the memory of my dear friends,
Bruce W. Watson, Commander, U.S. Navy (retired) and his soulmate and
wife, Susan M. Watson.

Greenhill Books

This edition of *Disaster at D-Day*
first published 2000 by Greenhill Books, Lionel Leventhal Limited,
Park House, 1 Russell Gardens, London NW11 9NN
and
Stackpole Books, 5067 Ritter Road, Mechanicsburg, PA 17055, USA

© Peter Tsouras, 1994
The moral right of the author has been asserted

British Library Cataloguing in Publication Data
Tsouras, Peter
Disaster at D-Day: The Germans defeat the Allies, June 1944. –
(Greenhill military paperback)
1. World War, 1939–1945 – Campaigns – France – Normandy
I. Title
940.5'42142

ISBN 1-85367-411-7

Library of Congress Cataloging-in-Publication Data
Tsouras, Peter
Disaster at D-Day: the Germans defeat the Allies, June 1944
by Peter Tsouras
p.   cm.
ISBN 1-85367-411-7
1. World War, 1939–1945 Campaigns – France – Normandy.
2. Imaginary wars and battles.
I. Title
D756.5.N6 T76   2000
940.54'2142–dc21   00–024669 CIP

Publishing History
Disaster at D-Day was first published in 1994 (Greenhill Books). It is
reproduced now in paperback exactly as the first Greenhill edition.

Printed in Great Britain

Contents

Contents

KEY TO MAPS

General Symbols:

wooded area

flooded area

attack, or
main line
of advance

retreat, or
withdrawal

para-drop

glider
air landing

Military Unit Symbols:

x x x x   Army

x x x   Corps

x x   Division

x   Brigade

| | | Regiment

| | Battalion

Allied unit

German unit

infantry

airborne
infantry

armour,
'Panzer' if
German

self-propelled
artillery, or
assault gun unit

unit size

parent unit

Fiftieth Infantry Division
of the
Thirtieth Allied Corps.

unit numeric
designation/
may indicate
nationality

unit function
or "arms' branch"

© Duncan 1995

Examples:

BR SECOND

x x x x

Second Allied Army, British

x x x
II

Second German Corps

x x
82

82nd Airborne Infantry Division (Allied)

x x
Lehr

Panzer Lehr Division (German)

x x
7

7th Armoured Division (Allied)

x
1
PO

1st Polish Airborne Infantry Brigade (Allied)

x
125

125 Panzergrenadier Regiment (German)

130

130th Assault Gun Battalion (German)

Illustrations

Maps

Tables

Prologue

The rows of American LSTs (Landing Ship Tank) were heading single-file towards the landing beaches, blacked-out and faint against a low quarter moon about to set. It was just after midnight as the entire force stood to General Quarters waiting for the minutes to fall away until H Hour kicked off the landings.

The stillness exploded with the torpedo that burst against the hull of LST 507. She lurched to a stop as fire gushed from one fuel tank to another. Then she blew up. As the horrified men on LST 531 watched, their own ship was struck. She too was swept by flames, exploded, and sank. It was all too easy for the next German E-Boat to make its attack run. The burning ships lit up their sisters all conveniently ambling along in line. Lieutenant von Marwitz chose the one astern of the sinking torch. The boat leapt over the waves as he took it closer and closer before shouting, 'Torpedo, los!' The iron fish plunged into the sea, and he pulled the boat to port. He watched and counted one, two, three, four, five . . . another explosion. He had a kill! Like the others, this ship shuddered to a halt, was engulfed by fire, and blew up. Large pieces of burning debris flew upward and then rained down into the black water.

As von Marwitz and the other E-Boat crews celebrated their good hunting in their favourite Cherbourg bar that evening, the remaining American transports were in flight back to Plymouth. Only small craft remained in the area to rescue survivors in the water. Over a thousand sailors and soldiers had been lost – in an exercise, the D-Day rehearsal of the U.S. 4th Infantry Division staged on that deadly morning of 27 April off the Slapton Sands Amphibious Training Center.

The Allies immediately clamped a lid of secrecy over the disaster so effectively that not even the Germans learned of the extent of their own victory. Among the small circle of Allied officers with a need-to-know, even the most rational man could not but feel the chill dread of premonition. But most soldiers are not rationalists at heart. They are believers, even if down deep, in fate. And this night's omen was evil.

Slapton Sands
1944

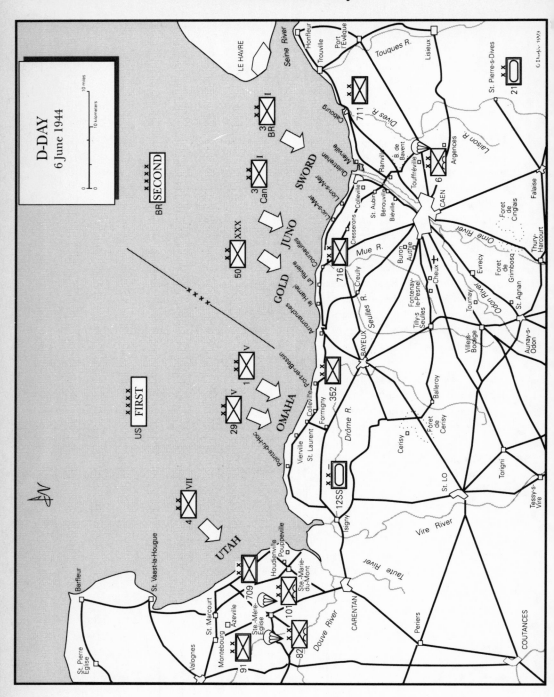

CHAPTER 1

The Chess Pieces Fill
the Board

The Armies

In year of invasion 1066, the English waited nervously all Summer for Duke William of Normandy's invasion fleet to find that necessary but elusive combination of calm seas and fair winds to carry it to England. Almost nine hundred years later, the German conquerors of Western Europe were waiting with equal nervousness for the invasion fleet manned by the British and their Canadian and American cousins to leap upon them through that same rare combination of benign seas and winds. If the settings had a certain reverse similiarity, the fighting men were much the same from one age to another. But now they drove Tigers and Shermans and carried Garands, MG-42s and the Sten and were to fight as Desert Rats, Leibstandarte, The Big Red One, Das Reich, Screaming Eagles, Red Devils, Stonewallers, and Leck Mich am Arsch.

By late 1943 the compass of the war was swinging to the long-promised and often-postponed Allied assault on Hitler's Fortress Europe. For the Allies, the decision to invade into the teeth of Hitler's vaunted Atlantic Wall defences had been fixed. American resolve, made confident by numbers and resources, finally had overcome British attempts to delay the awful moment. For the British, it had not been a lack of courage but experience of bitter defeats at the hands of the Wehrmacht and knowledge that resources were limited. They had but one army to risk. After five years of war, no Army replacements could be obtained without devouring the substance of the Royal Air Force and the Royal Navy.

The Germans

The Germans had also exhausted their resources in the West. The Luftwaffe (Air Force) and Kriegsmarine (Navy) had been broken by the superior production capabilities and manpower of the Allies. The Luftwaffe no longer dared conduct even reconnaissance flights over the British Isles, and the Kriegsmarine's major weapon, the submarine, had lost the Battle of the Atlantic. The once mighty Luftwaffe, increasingly shorn of operational units, transferred more and more idled ground personnel to Luftwaffe Field Divisions, infantry by any other name, and not very good infantry, under Army operational control. At the opposite end of the scale, Luftwaffe resources had been poured into creating more Fallschirmjäger (Parachute) divisions, elite formations of high spirit and skill, equipped even more lavishly than the Waffen SS by Reich-smarshal Hermann Göring's vanity.

As the prospect of the ultimate decisive battle approached, both the Germans and the Allies began to build-up their forces along both sides of the English Channel. Field Marshal Gerd von Rundstedt, Supreme Commander West (Oberbefehlshaber West – OB West), had made his case in November 1943, that significant reinforcements were vital if Germany was to have a chance to defeat the coming invasion. For two years his command had served as a comfortable billet in the sweet plenty of La Belle France and as a replacement pool for the ravenous Eastern Front. Hitler accepted the logic, and reinforcements irregularly started moving West. Coastal defence divisions of over-and-underaged men, the partially unfit, and pressed Soviet prisoners of war (*Ostruppen*) had become a large part of von Rundstedt's command. In the new year of 1944, veteran infantry divisions began arriving. All too often they were burnt-out husks from the Eastern Front, to be rebuilt around their veteran cadres with new conscripts. Such a formation was the 352nd Infantry Division commanded by Generalleutnant (Lieutenant General) Dietrich Kraiss. His veterans, employing that unique German talent for reconstitution, quickly transformed a large draft of Saxon eighteen-year-olds from the Hanover area into a tough, cohesive division.

The arrival of the striking power of the German ground forces, the panzer divisions of the Army and the Waffen SS, was the real proof of Hitler's determination to defend his western conquests. Among them were the greatest of Germany's armoured formations. Pride of place was claimed by the 1st SS Panzer Division 'Leibstandarte SS Adolf Hitler' originally built from Hitler's SS bodyguard regiment. Deadly, ferocious, and utterly ruthless, Leibstandarte was also the mother of unparalleled warriors, sent as cadres for many new divisions. The 2nd SS Panzer Division 'Das Reich' was twin brother to Leibstandarte, both destined to fight in I SS Panzer Corps commanded by SS Gruppenführer (Lieutenant General) Sepp Dietrich. A long-time crony of Hitler since their days in Munich, Dietrich was a veteran of the Freikorps and a veritable Mars. The other major SS formation scheduled for the West was SS Gruppenführer Paul Hausser's II SS Panzer Corps with 9th SS Panzer Division 'Hohenstauffen' and the 10th SS Panzer Division 'Frundsberg'.

From Leibstandarte volunteers, sown like dragons' teeth, the new 12th SS Panzer Division was raised, filled with enthusiastic, fit, and indoctrinated teenagers from the Hitler Youth organization, hence its honorific of 'Hitler-jugend'. Trained to a strange high pitch of soldierly skill, comradeship, Nazi idealism, and brutality, the enlisted men averaged only seventeen-and-a-half years old. Also newly raised was the only panzergrenadier division in the West, the 17th SS Panzergrenadier Division 'Götz von Berchlingen', bearing the name of the grizzled German knight who defied his emperor's new taxes with the defiant taunt, 'Leck mich am Arsch!', in other words the 17th SS Panzer-grenadier 'Kiss My Ass!' Division.

The Army's panzer might was represented with its two best-equipped divisions: 2nd Panzer Division and the Panzer Lehr Division, the latter raised originally from the panzer arm's demonstration regiments. The command of Panzer Lehr had fallen to one of the stars of the Afrika Korps, Generalleutnant Fritz Bayerlein. Another veteran of North Africa, the surrendered 21st Panzer Division, was reconstituted around a core of convalescent veterans of that gallant unit.

The Allies

The Allies were also gathering their armies. The British had kept a number of divisions at home as a garrison for the beleaguered island in case of invasion. If they had seen combat, such as the 3rd Division had, it had been four years before in the short campaign that ended at Dunkirk. Any combat experience had dissipated with time and the endless drafts taken to form new units. The Canadian 3rd Division had a special injury to brood over while it trained. Their sister division, the Canadian 2nd, had been decimated at Dieppe in 1942, in the Allies' experiment to test the feasibility of seizing a great port to support an invasion.

Most of the American divisions quickly arriving in Britain in the early months of 1944 were similarly inexperienced in combat. The first division to land was the National Guard 29th Infantry Division, 'The Blue and Gray Division', from Virginia and Maryland. Its 116th Infantry Regiment was descended from Thomas Jackson's immortal Stonewall Brigade. These 'Stonewallers' from small central Virginia towns were the first to practice amphibious operations at the seaside training centre at Slapton Sands in Devon.

All of this untested metal was to be tipped with six tempered veteran British and American divisions transferred from the Mediterranean Theatre. The 8th Army sent four of its most experienced and effective units. The most famous were the Desert Rats of the 7th Armoured Division, the Red Devils of the 1st Airborne Division, and the 50th (Northumbrian) Division, 'our old friends', as Rommel was to say to Bayerlein later. The 51st (Highland) Division had a more bitter relationship with Rommel. Descended from one of the finest divisions in the First War, the 51st had been cut off from the British Expeditionary Force's retreat to Dunkirk and been forced to capitulate after a desperate struggle at the port of St. Valery. Their conqueror had been a rising general with an uncanny gift for armoured warfare, Erwin Rommel. The 51st Division was raised again from its second line of battalions and served with the 8th Army from Alamein onwards, extracting some payment for St. Valery. These Highland Scots were of a nation of grimly natural fighters and had bided their time in their stoic Presbyterian way for four years to put paid to the whole score.

Joining the British divisions was the pride of the U.S. Army: the Big Red One of the 1st Infantry Division and the 'Hell on Wheels' 2nd Armored Division, the first American armoured division to be raised and the one Patton had trained himself. Both had been blooded and honoured in North Africa and Sicily. The British 50th and U.S. 1st Divisions had been selected for the invasion due to their successes in amphibious operations, a cause of bitterness among the troops who felt they had done enough when others had done nothing.

Aside from the infantry and armoured divisions, the Allies massed two full airborne corps for the invasion, the British I and the American XVIII. The Red Devils of the 1st Airborne Division had won a considerable reputation in North Africa and Sicily as had the American 82nd Airborne Division under commanders like Major Generals Robert 'Roy' Urquart and Matthew Ridgway. Each veteran division was joined by an eager but inexperienced twin: the British 6th Airborne with flying Pegasus on its division flash and the American 'Screaming Eagles' of the 101st Airborne.

The Commanders

Rommel

Hitler and the Allies instinctively chose to command in the great battle two champions whose fates had already intertwined: Generalfeldmarshal (Field Marshal) Erwin Rommel, 'The Desert Fox' and General Bernard Montgomery, 'Monty'. Rommel with his small Afrika Korps had come closer than any man in history to severing the jugular of the British Empire. His first command in the invasion of France in 1940 had seen him carve out a reputation in command of the 7th Panzer 'Ghost' Division as a master of modern armoured warfare. In North Africa he was to make the world his audience, and the British soldier one of his greatest admirers for his brilliance no less than his chivalry. So thoroughly had he won the moral ascendancy over the enemy that British commanders were driven to forbid the common use of the term 'a Rommel' used to describe any action particularly and imaginatively well-done. Even Churchill had recognized the difference when he said to the House on 27 January 1942, with El Alamein still unwon: 'We have a very daring and skilful opponent against us, and, may I say across the havoc of war, a great general.'

Montgomery

Montgomery was to change all that and not by forbidding his men to respect a gallant enemy. Montgomery chose to reestablish the British soldier's faith in himself and his commanders. A thorough professional, he had distinguished himself by commanding the 3rd Division in a demanding rearguard action in the retreat to Dunkirk. He also possessed the uncanny sense of instilling a sense of trust in him, he turned around the 8th Army, defeated Rommel at El

Alamein and chased him across North Africa. His successes in concluding the North African campaign, and in Sicily and southern Italy made him the darling of the British people and their army. After years of shameful defeats, he embodied victory.

The Commanders' Appraisal of the Situation

With an eerie coincidence, both Rommel and Montgomery submitted their first appraisals of the strategic requirements of their new commands to their political masters on 31 December 1943. Both men brought a fresh approach and a master's touch and both rejected the bases of existing plans and assumptions. Rommel had just finished an exhaustive inspection of the fortifications of the so-called Atlantic Wall that ran from Holland to the Bay of Biscay. Rommel's report read:

> We can hardly expect a counter-attack by the few reserves we have behind the coast at the moment, with no self-propelled guns and an inadequate quantity of anti-tank weapons, to succeed in destroying the powerful force which the enemy will land. We know from experience that the British soldier is quick to consolidate his gains and then holds on tenaciously with excellent support from his superior air arm and naval guns, the observers for which direct the fire from the front line.
>
> With the coastline held as thinly as it is at present, the enemy will probably succeed in creating bridgeheads at several different points and in achieving a major penetration in our coastal defences. Once this has happened it will only be by the rapid intervention of our operational reserves that he will be thrown back into the sea. This requires that these forces should be held very close behind the coast defences.[1]

These observations were based on his personal observations of the crippling effectiveness on German operations of overwhelming Allied air power.

Montgomery had just reviewed the plans prepared in London for the invasion at Churchill's personal request. His report read:

> My first impression is that the present plan is impracticable. From a purely Army point of view the following points are essential:
> o   The initial landings must be made on the widest possible front.
> o   One British army to land on a front of two, or possibly, three corps. One American army similarly.
> o   The air battle must be won before the operation is launched. We must then aim at success in the land battle by the spread and violence of our operations.[2]

Advantages and Disadvantages?

Both men were allotted similar roles under a theatre commander. Montgomery was appointed commander of the 21st Army Group which would conduct the Allied invasion. He would personally command the British 2nd Army under Lieutenant General Sir Miles Dempsey and the American 1st Army under Lieutenant General Omar Bradley. Two later armies would follow his army group, and a separate American army group would be formed. His superior was General Dwight Eisenhower who commanded all Allied forces in the European Theatre of Operations and would have overall command of all ground, air, and sea forces in the invasion. Rommel was given command of Army Group B consisting of the 7th and 15th Armies, on a front from Holland to the Loire River. Two other armies in southern France (1st and 19th) were formed into Army Group G. Field Marshal Gerd von Rundstedt, Eisenhower's counterpart, had overall command of all German forces in the West. Neither Montgomery or Rommel would have direct command over the theatre naval and air forces.

The remarkable similarities in their situations ceased at this point. Montgomery worked within one the most cooperative and efficient alliances in history and within a chain of command that functioned rationally. Although he had professional disagreements, some of them bitter, with his peers and colleagues, the system consistently supported his efforts to plan and prepare for the invasion. He was given the widest latitude and initiative. Rommel, on the other hand, worked within a system that had been both morally and professionally distorted by the evil genius of Adolf Hitler. His chain of command theoretically ran from the German High Command (Oberkommando der Wehrmacht – OKW) through von Rundstedt at OB West to himself at Army Group B. The reality was that the unity of command of his army group was badly compromised. He could not move a single division without Hitler's express permission. Hitler involved himself in every detail and muddied the concept of operations to meet the invasion. Rommel did not even control most of the panzer divisions held in reserve to counterattack the landing. That was the domain of the Commander of Panzer Forces West, General Geyr von Schweppenburg, who reported to von Rundstedt.

The great issue that the Germans were not able to resolve before the invasion was the concept and timing of the counterattacks that would drive the invasion into the sea. Rommel was adamant that the operational reserves should be held closely behind the coast. Allied air power would harry and bleed those held deeper inland as they tried to move, so delaying them that they would arrive too late and too understrength to defeat the invasion. Von Rundstedt and von Geyr, having never commanded under conditions of enemy air superiority, tended to discount Rommel's warnings. They maintained that the panzer reserves should be held deeper inland so as to be able to move to any sector of the threatened front. Hitler never endorsed one or the other position decisively. The result was that Rommel was given control of only three panzer divisions: Panzer Lehr, 21st Panzer, and 12th SS Panzer. He wanted to put them all behind the coastal defences in Normandy between the Rivers Vire and Orne. Again Hitler intervened to micromanage affairs, by ruling that Rommel could only move one division, 21st Panzer, directly behind the front. It was not until late May that Rommel was able to extract from Hitler permission to move Hitlerjugend to the Norman coast as well. However, the Führer was adamant that Panzer Lehr remain inland in the area between Chartres and Le Mans.

In divining the location of the invasion, the great question facing the Germans and one the Allies took great pains to keep from them, Rommel was at first convinced by the conventional wisdom that the invasion would come the shortest distance across the Channel, straight at the Pas-de-Calais area. The Pas-de-Calais not only offered a short road into the Reich itself but was site of the vaunted, mysterious 'wonder weapon' that Hitler had promised would make the English weep for peace. Naturally the Allies would strike there. But as the winter turned to spring, Hitler's vaunted intuition seemed to make a comeback. He sensed more than analyzed that Normandy might be the site of the invasion or at least a major diversion. Rommel's increasing familiarity with his sector had also changed his mind to the degree that he thought at the very least the Allies would conduct major airborne diversionary landings in Normandy. Infantry divisions that had been going consistently to reinforce the 15th Army at the Pas-de-Calais now began to be assigned to 7th Army. The 91st Airlanding Division was moved to the Cotentin Peninsula, and in March the 352nd Infantry Division was assigned to the Calvados coast, the area between the Vire and the Orne and the responsibility of Generalleutnant Erich Marcks, commander of LXXXIV Corps. Rommel also specifically ordered that Kraiss' division take over a section of the coastal defences manned by one of the weaker coastal defence divisions. Hitler's interest was the key to approving the move of 21st Panzer and 12th SS Panzer Divisions up behind the coast to support Marcks' corps.

Montgomery would have been appalled at Rommel's difficulties. It would have been cruel to have informed Rommel, on the other hand, of Montgomery's scope for action. Essentially Montgomery threw out the plans already prepared for the invasion. Using every bit of authority he had been given to plan, prepare, and conduct the invasion, he took even more and was supported because he manifestly knew what he was doing. He had already identified the essentials of the invasion concept. Now he devised the strategic plan that would underlie all else. The British 2nd Army would land with three divisions abreast on a two-corps (I and XXX Corps) front west of the Orne River. The Americans would land with two divisions as the lead elements of two corps (V and VII Corps) further west. The two lodgements would link up into a solid lodgement as quickly as possible. The British sector, being closer to open country and 150 miles closer to Paris than the Americans, would attract the strategic priority of the Germans and most of their armoured forces. The mission of 2nd Army was to hold this attention and the panzers while the American 1st Army built up sufficient forces for a major breakout of the lodgement which would in turn envelop the Germans concentrated against the British. There was a strategic elegance in the simplicity and practicality of the plan.[3]

Montgomery had another priceless advantage over Rommel. Although neither man had operational control over the naval and air forces in theatre, Montgomery had the fullest support and cooperation of those two arms in both the planning and conduct of operations. Rommel had to deal with national commanders of these services who were jealous of their authority to the point of obstruction of the war effort. But by the spring of 1944, the cooperation of the increasingly impotent Luftwaffe and Kriegsmarine were of questionable value anyway. Montgomery, on the other hand, had call on massive air and naval fleets of unsurpassed power and capability.

Without doubt the greatest advantage possessed by Montgomery over Rommel was the ability to read his enemy's thoughts. The British Goverment Code and Cipher School at Bletchley succeeded in breaking the coded messages from the seemingly unbreakable German Enigma coding machine. Enigma was in use throughout the Wehrmacht as the ultimate in secure radio communications. The exploitation of this ability was codenamed Ultra, and the Allies had taken priceless advantage of it in the Mediterranean Theatre where radio communications were vital. The Western European Theatre was more of a problem. Active operations had ceased in 1940, and four years of comfortable garrison conditions had allowed the Germans to install landline communications throughout the occupied countries. Prior to D-Day, Ultra was reading comparatively little from OB West. The destruction or disruption of the landline system in order to drive German communications into the vulnerable air, therefore, became a high priority for the few days just prior to the invasion.

In the advantages and disadvantages so far listed, Rommel had come off a poor second. In one arena, though, he retained a sharp and frustrating lead. The German soldier consistently demonstrated overall greater qualities of aggressive leadership, offensive-mindedness, and initiative at every level than his British and American counterparts. One senior British officer asked in exasperation how it was that they were reading the enemy's mail and still had not beaten him. The answer was in the mettle of the German soldier. General Harold Alexander noted of the Americans: 'They simply do not know their job as soldiers and this is the case from the general to the private soldier. Perphaps the weakest link of all is the junior leader, who just does not lead, with the result that their men don't really fight.'[4] If the Americans lacked a consistently good junior leader to follow, the British soldier, particularly the English, all too often lost heart and gave ground when his officers were killed and wounded. So noted was this characteristic that the Germans were making it a priority to kill junior

British officers in Italy. After D-Day one American battalion commander paid the Germans the ultimate compliment, although he was dealing with the elite Fallschirmjägers:

> You know, those Germans are the best soldiers I ever saw. They're smart and they don't know what the word 'fear' means. They come in and they keep coming until they get their job done or you kill 'em . . . If they had as many people as we have they could come right through us any time they made up their minds to do it.[5]

Traitor or Patriot?

In the list of Rommel's difficulties, none had become more ultimately dangerous to Germany than the continued leadership of Adolf Hitler himself. Rommel owed his very rise to Hitler's patronage. He had been an enthusiastic supporter of Hitler in the thirties, like so many German officers who saw in him a return to German pride and order. He had come to Hitler's attention with his brilliant account of small unit leadership in the First War, *Infantry Attacks*.[6] That had been the road that led to his command of the 7th Panzer Division, then the Africa Army, to a marshal's baton, and finally to an army group. But as the honours grew, so did the doubts about Hitler's leadership. Had not Hitler's 'Victory or death' order at El Alamein led to the defeat? Had not the 'Hold at all costs' order around Tunis led to the loss of an Axis army group and his beloved Afrika Korps? Now worse than doubts assailed him. He had forbidden the oppression of Jews in his area of operations in North Africa and left an unparalleled legacy of humanity and chivalry on the battlefield. But the general officer grapevine spoke of darker, hideous things. He forbade his son, Manfred, to join the Waffen SS as the young man had suggested. He did not want him associated with an organization that was committing mass murder on the Eastern Front.

All of these doubts found a receptive ear in his new chief of staff, General Major (Major General) Hans Speidel. Speidel was Rommel's conduit to the anti-Hitler opposition in the German military and political establishment. He was heartened by the existence of like-minded patriots who wanted to save Germany before she was ground down from east and west. The issue was not whether to remove Hitler but how. The conspirators in Berlin were determined to kill him, but their nerve and powers of conspiracy as well as Hitler's infernal luck had protected him. Rommel strongly objected to Hitler's murder and insisted that he be arrested and brought before a German court. Speidel strenuously tried to talk him around to the necessity of assassination. The very idea of putting the Antichrist on trial was ridiculous. Moreover, it was dangerous to leave him alive to rally his followers and sure to provoke civil war. But Rommel was obstinate on this point.

Whatever action they took, it had to be soon. The invasion was at hand. Every bright, clear day was dreaded now that the weather window was yawning wider and wider. Rommel and the conspirators met secretly in France to draft a memorandum to serve as the basis to end the war. If Hitler were arrested and removed from power, Rommel was convinced that Germany could have peace with the Western Allies. They were willing to pay the price of evacuating all of occupied Western Europe and pulling the Nazi system out by the roots. Danger lay if the invasion thrust itself ahead of the plot. A successful invasion would open Germany to inevitable defeat and occupation by the Western Allies and worst of all, the savage Russians. A sound defeat of the invasion, on the other hand, gave Germany a strong negotiating position with the Western Allies, but again only if Hitler were removed. To leave him in power after such a victory would only feed his megalomania, and the war would drag on for years to Germany's inevitable ruin.[7]

At the meeting, Speidel inquired out of Rommel's presence how the Berlin group planned to assassinate Hitler if it came to that. When told that it would be a bomb small enough to fit into a suitcase, he was worried. Only general staff officers and politicians in Berlin would think of such a small solution. Machiavelli's advice was uppermost in his mind then – if you strike at a king, you must be sure to kill him. The next morning he asked his staff to find him a skilled demolitions expert.

Countdown to Action

Friday, 2 June

Montgomery addressed the officers of his main and tactical headquarters staffs and his rear HQ in London in the afternoon. Eisenhower met him at a private dinner at his HQ before they both returned to Montgomery's HQ for a conference with the meteorological experts on the weather for the invasion. There was an ominous depression over Iceland. Nevertheless, Eisenhower decided to continue with the operation on 5 June with another meeting on the weather arranged for the following morning.

Under cover of darkness, the HQ of 12th SS Panzer Division and its 12th SS Panzer and 26th SS Panzergrenadier Regiments departed from their assembly areas around Lisieux to the area of Isigny-sur-Mer near the mouth of the Vire River and to the village of Balleroy on the road halfway between St. Lô and Bayeux. Hitlerjugend's 25th SS Panzergrenadier Regiment and other elements of the division under the 25th's commander, SS Standartenführer (Colonel) Kurt Meyer, were due to join the division on 6 June.

Saturday, 3 June

The weather conditions for the invasion on 5 June were deteriorating badly. Montgomery wrote in his diary:

My own view is that if the sea is calm enough for the Navy to take us there, then we must go; the air forces have had very good weather for all its preparatory operations and we must accept the fact that we may not be able to do so well on D-Day.[8]

Eisenhower postponed his decision until the next day.

Before dawn Sturmbannführer (Major) Jürgensen settled his forty-eight Panther Mark V tanks into the woods just north of the village of Balleroy northeast of St. Lô and barely ten miles from the sea. By morning the commander of the 1st Battalion, 12th SS Panzergrenadier Regiment, had his unit and tank commanders conducting personal reconnaissances of the roads to the sea.

Sunday, 4 June

Lieutenant General Kraiss introduced the commander of his 914th Infantry Regiment to Obersturmbannführer (Lieutenant Colonel) Max Wünsche, commander of 12th SS Panzer Regiment, over breakfast. Wünsche had expressed a willingness to begin joint training immediately with the Kraiss' 352nd Infantry Division, and now Kraiss offered him the opportunity to work with the 914th. They were scheduled to conduct a reinforcement exercise the next morning of the coastal defences manned by the 726th Regiment near St. Laurent. Wünsche jumped at the chance.

The weather had not improved as the Allied commanders met at four in the morning. It was a sombre meeting. For all the men in the room, decisiveness had been the ticket to success. Now they all stood in awe of the decision that lay with Eisenhower. Some of the convoys from the northern parts of Britain had already sailed to keep to the invasion schedule for 5 June. The meteorological experts predicted formidable wave action, low clouds, and high winds. They stated that naval gunfire would be inefficient, air support impossible, and the handling of small craft more difficult. Admiral Ramsey, who was to command the naval element of the invasion, stated that the naval end of the operation could still proceed but agreed that naval gunfire would be degraded. He took no strong position. Air Marshal Tedder, Eisenhower's deputy, was against going on 5 June. Montgomery, fearing the effects of delay, wanted to go regardless of the weather. As the rain beat against the windows, Eisenhower decided to postpone the invasion one more day to 6 June. It occurred to everyone that if bad weather persisted though 6 June, the next invasion window would be weeks away.

Rommel was preparing to leave the next morning for a quick trip home to Herrlingen for his wife Lucy's (he always called her Lu) birthday on 6 June to be followed by a meeting he had requested with Hitler at his Obersalzburg headquarters. He was reading the latest Luftwaffe weather report;

the front moving across the Channel and northwestern Europe would surely make an amphibious operation impossible. The Allies would probably miss their June opportunity with the moon and tides and that would give him another priceless month to strengthen the defences along the coast. His aide interrupted him. His son Manfred in Herrlingen, home on leave from his Luftwaffe flak battery, had just phoned him. It was highly unusual for Manfred to call; he was worried. But Manfred explained that his mother was sick with the flu, nothing serious, but she wanted him to come home after his visit with the Führer, when she was feeling better. After he had hung up, he called Speidel and informed him of a change of plans. He had an extra day now before he had to leave for Obersalzburg, time enough to get in another day with the troops. He would like to see how 12th SS Panzer was settling in and would spend the night in St. Lô with Marcks, and leave the next morning, on 6 June.

The thirty-seven huge Tiger tanks of the Heavy SS Panzer Battalion 101 began detraining at Le Mans under cover of night. General Bayerlein had his staff were at the train station to welcome the 'temporary' addition to Panzer Lehr's already great strength. Rommel had secured the attachment of the I SS Panzer Corps' heavy tank battalion for 'temporary' training with Panzer Lehr. He had wanted as much firepower as close to the front as he could get it, no matter the excuse. The officers of Panzer Lehr were simply there to see the famous Russian tank killer, Hauptsturmführer (Captain) Michael Wittmann. It wasn't every day that a celebrity showed up, especially one that had destroyed 117 enemy tanks.

Monday, 5 June

The Stonewallers had been aboard their transports since the night of 3 June. Now the storm was tossing them from one crashing wave to another off Weymouth. The entire regiment was in misery and felled by sea sickness. Not even the great Jackson himself could have roused them.

By 0330 that morning, the storm had reached near-hurricane proportions. Eisenhower watched the rain come down in almost horizontal sheets, shaking his head at the disaster that would have struck the convoys had he stuck with the original invasion date. The meteorological experts were again called upon. They described the storm that was pounding upon the shores of France at that moment but then announced that the next thirty-six hours of good weather would begin the next morning before the weather would again deteriorate. Eisenhower was not about to lose the opening. He looked at all the other great men in the room. There were enough to share the blame, but he did not ask their opinions again. 'This is the decision which I must take alone. After all, that is what I am here for. We sail tomorrow.'

Notes

1. Erwin Rommel, *The Rommel Papers*, tr., Paul Findlay; ed., B.H. Liddell Hart (London: Collins, 1953); (New York: Harcourt, Brace, 1953) p.453.
2. Bernard Law Montgomery, 1st Viscount Montgomery of Alamein, *The Memoirs of Field-Marshal The Viscount Montgomery of Alamein* (London: Collins, 1958); *The Memoirs of Field Marshal Montgomery* (New York: World, 1958) pp.218–219.
3. Bernard Law Montgomery, 1st Viscount Montgomery of Alamein, *Desert and Bocage: From Alamein to Normandy* (London: Hutchinson, 1947) p.238.
4. Nigel Nicolson, *ALEX*, p.211, cited in Max Hastings, *Overlord* (London: Collins, 1984); (New York: Simon and Schuster, 1984) p.25.
5. Joseph Balkoski, *Beyond the Beachhead: The 29th Infantry Division in Normandy* (Harrisburg: Stackpole Books, 1989) p.177.
6. Rommel, *Infantrie Greift An* (Potsdam: Ludwig Voggenreiter Verlag, 1937); *Infantry Attacks* (London: Greenhill Books, 1979, 1990). Rommel's book of aggressive, small unit leadershiip remains a classic.
7. Rommel, *Kriegstagesbuch*, Band III (Potsdam and Leipzig: Verlagshaus Hindrichs, 1963); *Rommel's War Diary*, Vol III (London: Greenhill Books, 1964) p.209. Rommel's wartime musings were published in 1953 as *The Rommel Papers*; the four volumes of *Rommel's War Diary*, (Volume III deals with the Normandy Campaign) were Rommel's exhaustive and definitive memoirs.
8. Montgomery, *Memoirs*, p.222.

CHAPTER 2

The Airborne Assaults
6 June

0010–0020. The Pathfinders were the first to land. Their task was to mark the landing and dropping zones with lights east of the Orne River. Between ten and twenty minutes past midnight, Captains Tate and Midwood and Lieutenant de Lautour leading the 22nd Independent Parachute Company, leading the way for the British 6th Parachute Division, were the first Allied soldiers to land on the soil of occupied France. The pathfinders for the American 101st Airborne fell softly to earth shortly thereafter and lit the way with their homing beacons. Their counterparts in the 82nd Airborne had fallen among the Germans and dared not.

Immediately after them 1,056 bombers of RAF Bomber Command struck the ten strongest coastal batteries covering the invasion beaches. They had to be out of the way in time for the vast air fleet of 850 transports carrying the American 82nd and 101st Airborne Divisions and 260 carrying the British 6th Airborne Division to their drop zones on the flanks of the lodgement area. They were joined by hundreds of other transports towing gliders filled with more troops and equipment for the three divisions.

The British Airdrops, 0015–0045

If the 6th Airborne was the spearhead of the British Army in this battle, the razor-sharp point was D company of the 2nd Battalion, Oxfordshire and Buckingham Light Infantry, commanded by Major John Howard. His mission was to seize two bridges crossing the parallel Orne River Canal and the Orne River south of Caen. Held by the British, they would allow the lodgement to be expanded northward; conversely, they barred the way to any German counterattack into the flank of the 2nd Army.

Major Howard's glider landed within fifty yards of the Caen Canal Bridge at 0015, its wings snapped off by the 'Rommel's Asparagus', tree trunks rammed into the earth and strung with wire, in the landing field. Howard remembered:

> . . . the skids seared through the ground and sent up sparks as the metal skids hit flints and it looked like tracer fire flashing past the door causing inevitable thoughts of surprise lost. Airborne again and suddenly there was what was to be the last searing God Almighty crash amidst smashing plywood, dust and noise

26

like hell let loose, followed by sudden silence as we came to a halt. The dazed silence did not seem to last long because we all came to our senses together on realizing that there was NO firing. There WAS NO FIRING, it seemed quite unbelievable, but where were we? . . . precisely where I had asked the GPs (Glider Pilots) to put it during briefing. To cap it all there was NO enemy firing. The sense of complete exhilaration was quite overwhelming! I automatically looked at my watch, it had stopped at 0016 hours.[1]

Howard was out the door and at the head of his men, shouting 'Up the Oxs and Bucks! Up the Oxs and Bucks!' as his first platoon swarmed over the bridge, silencing the pillbox with grenades thrown through the firing slits. He was quickly reinforced by two more platoons. The German defence was over-whelmed; the NCOs fought till they were killed while their men fled. The Oxs and Bucks had taken the bridge at a cost of two dead and fourteen wounded.

Apart from the firing going on a great deal of noise emanated from platoons shouting code-names to identify friends in the dark and there was an unholy babble of Able-Able-Able, Baker-Baker-Baker, Charlie-Charlie-Charlie, Sapper-Sapper-Sapper, coming from all directions; on top of automatic fire, tracer and the odd grenade it was hell let loose and most certainly would have helped any wavering enemy to make a quick decision about quitting.[2]

In ten minutes, one of the most spectacular actions of the invasion and of the war itself was over. The rest of Howard's force seized the Orne River Bridge with little opposition. At the canal bridge, Major Howard put his defence in order. The Germans were preparing one of their almost instinctive counter-attacks in Bénouville to the east of the bridge. He had to hold until reinforcements arrived from the 6th Division's 5th Parachute Brigade. While he waited, he noticed two distraught-looking Italian conscripts taken prisoner in the attack. They had been caught putting up the Rommel's Asparagus. 'I didn't have time to deal with prisoners so I let them go. Do you know what they did? Those silly sods went back to putting up the poles.' Despite the demonstration of Howard's technique in taking the bridge, the Italians evidently feared more the wrath of their German overseer if their work was not done when they surely recaptured the bridge.

While he waited, all three Allied airborne divisions were badly scattered over their drop zones. Inadequately trained Dakota pilots swerved wildly through the skies to avoid the enthusiastic German flak contributing to the navigation problems caused by low cloud cover. The glider pilots, on the other hand, were made of sterner stuff and coolly landed most of the time where they were supposed to. Major Howard remembered the coolness of his glider pilot when shown the photos of the Rommel's Asparagus that were sprouting in his landing area. It was a good thing, the pilot commented; the poles were spaced just right to shear off some of the wings upon landing and stop the glider from pitching over into the canal. Only seven of the British transports were lost as opposed to twenty-two of ninety-eight gliders which did not reach their landing zones. Seventy-one of the 196 members of the Glider Regiment involved in the landings were casualties. The British suffered least from the dispersion as the division dropped 4,800 paratroopers of its 3rd and 5th Brigades east of the Orne River. Three thousand of them would assemble with their battalions to fight as planned. They had had the safer and easier of the approach flights, straight from Littlehampton without crossing any heavily defended areas.

Nevertheless, the 6th Division could muster barely 60 percent of its strength after landing. The division commander had three missions: (1) secure the bridges the Oxs and Bucks had just taken: the Caen Canal Bridge controlled the most important road that would carry a German counterattack from Caen to Sword Beach as well as established communications between Sword Beach and the airborne division; (2) capture the powerful gun battery at Merville that could sweep the beach; and (3) destroy the four bridges over the Dives River to the east of the Orne to halt German reinforcements from counterattacking the beachhead.

The 5th Brigade's 7th Battalion of the Parachute Regiment rushed to rescue the Oxs and Bucks and were hurried along by the sound of terrific explosions from the Caen River Bridge. A strong wind had scattered them and some had been killed in the air on the way down. Their commander rallied them with his bugler sounding the regimental call at intervals. Howard's men had repulsed the first counterattack by destroying the lead German tank whose exploding ammunition had so worried 5th Brigade. Upon arrival, the 7th Battalion pitched into the Germans in Bénouville and cleared them out. General Richter, commander of the 716th Division, reacted decisively. He counterattacked again with tanks and infantry, but the mettle of his second-rate troops was not up to the withering fire of the paratroopers. The first attack broke up when the British cut down the supporting infantry. But Richter was nothing if not persistent. The counterattacks continued and nearly wiped out A Company which clung to the town after losing all of its officers.

Third Brigade's assault on the Merville Battery was to pass into legend. The Germans had built four large casements for 150mm guns that would be able to rake Sword Beach. The 9th Battalion of the Parachute Regiment was given the mission to seize the battery before the landing craft approached the beach. An elaborate plan had been devised in which the reinforced 600 men of the battalion would land behind the objective and seize it by breaking through its heavy defences of mines and barbed wire while an assault group of gliders landed on the battery itself. Nothing went right. The battalion was so badly scattered that barely 160 men, minus all the sappers and most of their equipment, could be assembled. The commander courageously decided to press on and attempt the mission whatever the situation. Luckily the preinvasion bombing had detonated many of the mines and chewed up the wire. Four ad hoc assault teams advanced through the holes, losing men to still-live mines and increasingly accurate machine gun fire. But they made it through to close with the defenders of each casemate in savage close-quarters fighting that collapsed the defence. The British had lost half their men dead and wounded, but the battery was theirs. To their chagrin they discovered that the fearsome 150mm guns were only antiquated 75s that would barely have reached Sword Beach.

The rest of 3rd Brigade's mission was easily accomplished as the 8th Parachute Battalion and the 1st Canadian Parachute Battalion destroyed the bridges over the Dives. At the Troarn bridge, the British encountered elements of the 5th Company, 2nd Battalion, of Colonel von Luck's 125th Panzergrenadier Regiment, 21st Panzer Division. The company had been out on a night exercise armed only with blank ammunition. Von Luck quickly concluded that such a large airborne operation could only be the van of the invasion itself. He ordered, 'All units are to be put on alert immediately and the division informed. No. II Battalion is to go into action wherever necessary. . . .'[3] The battalion came to the rescue of its 5th Company with a quick counterattack and captured a few prisoners but not in time to save the bridge. His regiment's first battalion with half-track armoured personnel carriers and an attached assault gun battalion were put on alert only a little to the south of its sister battalion. Every element of his training and considerable combat experience in Russia and North Africa screamed at him to attack, attack while the enemy is disorganized and dispersed. But von Luck had already exceeded his strict standing orders to take no offensive action without the permission that would proceed from Army Group B. He could go no further. As he paced his headquarters that night, the permission never came.

The American Airdrops, 0130

The indirect approach flight of the American airborne divisions carrying over 13,000 men begged for trouble. It was an indirect route wending first southwest from the English coast from Portland Bill and then turning eastward crossing the Cherbourg Peninsula to reach the dropping zones from the west. They then ran into low clouds and intense German flak that panicked many of the combat-inexperienced pilots. One transport blossomed into an orange ball as its ammunition store was hit. The others around it bolted in all directions, spilling their sixteen-man sticks of paratroopers. The loss of barely twenty transports in that great swarm was proof that the danger was more apparent than real, but that was little comfort to the American paratroopers who were falling wildly out of careening aircraft, dropped too soon or too late into the tracer-filled Norman night. For the 82nd Airborne, commanded by Major General Matthew Ridgway, there were not even the pathfinders' lights.

The two divisions were to interpose themselves between the Utah landing beaches and the German reserves inland. They were Utah's human shield, to blunt German counterattacks while the 4th Infantry Division struggled ashore and secured its lodgement. Ridgway's 82nd was to seize the communications hub of Ste.-Mère-Eglise which sat on the only high speed road linking Cherbourg and the rest of the defence complex to the east and through which ran the Atlantic Wall's major landline cable. His division was also to seize the bridges over the Merderet River to the west of the town to close them to counterattack from the German's 91st Division. The 101st, commanded by Major General Maxwell Taylor, was to drop between the 82nd and the coast to pry open the beach exits from the rear. It was also to block any German counterattacks from the south by taking Carentan three miles to the west of the Vire River.

Both divisions were badly scattered, the 82nd by far the worse. Two of its regiments that were to land west of the Merderet actually fell astride it and into the marshes that filled the shallow river valley flooded by the Germans. Hundreds drowned. A neutral observer might have decided that neither was operational after landing; so few men rallied to their regiments and battalions. By dawn only 1,100 paratroopers of Taylor's 6,600 reached their rendezvous points. The observer, however, would have failed to account for the innate pugnacity and aggressiveness of the American paratroopers. The 82nd and its sister division, the Screaming Eagles of the 101st, were elite units in every sense. They had been recruited from volunteers, the type of men that seek out danger and risk as iron filings rush to a magnet. Wherever they landed, they coalesced into ad hoc combat groups, built around battalion and company commanders or even sergeants and moved out to execute their missions. The very dispersion and disorganization was a left-handed boon for the paratroopers. The Germans had no idea what was going on. Paratroopers were reported landing everywhere in unknown strength.

Each division had one regiment that landed fairly intact. The 82nd's 505th Airborne Regiment was able to assemble its shrunken 2nd and 3rd Battalion in the vicinity of Ste.-Mère-Eglise. Already a stick from each battalion had fallen into the town in a tragic setting that not even Hollywood could have devised. The bombings had left a large building on fire in the town. A French bucket brigade guarded by Germans was attempting to douse the flames when the thirty American paratroopers began to descend. Two loaded with mortar rounds fell into the burning building itself to die as their ammunition exploded. Others were shot as they fell in wild vertical firefights, the Germans firing up while the Americans desperately freed their weapons to fire hopelessly down. One paratrooper was caught by his rigging on the church steeple and hung there wounded all through the night. The few survivors broke free of the town and escaped into the night. The Germans then went to bed, influenced more by routine than danger. Unknown to them, Lieutenant Colonel Krause's 3/505th had landed within a mile of the town, just where he had intended. Assembling ninety men and dragooning a drunken Frenchman as a guide, he marched on the town. Ordering his men to 'use grenades, knives, and bayonets', he slipped into Ste.-Mère-Eglise at dawn. After cutting the German landline cable, his men rousted thirty Germans from their beds, killed eleven, and drove more out of town. Ridgway's division was lodged like a bone in the throat of the German communications on the Cotentin Peninsula.

Ridgway's other two regiments, the 507th and 508th, had landed in the river marshes. Elements captured the bridges over the river but were dislodged by counterattacks of the of the 91st Division's 1057th Regiment. Isolated elements of the two American regiments formed strongpoints on the German side of the river that were able to disrupt German exploitation of their control of the bridges. By dawn Ridgway had assembled forty percent of his division and was keeping the enemy at bay.

To the south the 101st had landed in areas devoid of German reserves. Its 506th Regiment had landed more or less intact and two battalions quickly attacked the two southernmost exits from Utah Beach. The other two regiments, the 501st and 502nd, each had one battalion that dropped well but found their others badly scattered. In the southeast corner of the division's drop zone, the 101st fell into prepared German defences covering what the Germans rightly had suspected were ideal landing areas. The 2/501st's mission had been to take the bridge and lock at La Barquette north of Carentan on the Douve River. Control of the lock was necessary to reduce the flooding that would prove an obstacle to the eventual movement out of the beachhead. The mission of the 3/506th had been to take two bridges on the Douve just north of Carentan. Both battalions were to hold their objectives against all counterattacks. The Germans of the 91st Division had illuminated the drop zone by the light of a burning, petrol soaked building. The 3/506th was savaged in the descent and could barely muster one hundred men of the 800 that had dropped. All the senior officers were either killed, wounded, or captured, and command fell to a junior staff officer. To his credit he extricated the survivors and moved smartly to the Douve bridges, reaching them at 0430, and overran the western end of both. Heavy machine gun fire stopped every attempt to cross. The remnants of the 2/501st were just as dogged, though less successful. They reached their objective of the lock but were thrown back from its edge by the defenders of the 91st Division.

The Germans React

At 0111 in the morning, General Marcks was still up, working late on the last touches to tomorrow's wargame at Rennes. It was his birthday, and his staff had slipped a birthday party in their workaholic commander's schedule. He had just cut the cake when he received an urgent call from General Richter, commanding the 716th Division. He reported large paratrooper landings east of the Orne and around Bénouville. Marcks personally awakened Rommel and briefed him. In the next forty-five minutes, more reports came in of massive landings all over Normandy. Mixed in with the panicked reports of real paratroop landings were many that mistook the Allies' rubber and straw paratroop decoys, dropped throughout Normandy, for the real thing. The field marshal and Marcks saw the entire front ripple with reports of paratrooper sightings. The sightings seemed to mass east of the Orne River north of Caen, in a broad circle around Bayeux and wildly from Ste.-Mère-Eglise to Carentan. Rommel concluded that they were in the midst of the great invasion diversion that he had anticipated would fall in Normandy.

He made his decision. Despite the failing communication system, at 0200 he was able to phone Speidel at La Roche Guyon with an appraisal of the situation and an order to put the army group on its fullest alert. Speidel was to inform von Rundstedt at OB West. Marcks would move to Caen to sort out the situation there and was to employ the 21st Panzer to strike at any landings. Rommel would move to the north to do the same with 12th SS Panzer. Before leaving, he tried unsuccessfully to contact the commander of the 6th Parachute Regiment, Major Freiherr von der Heydte, at his headquarters north of Periers to immediately assemble his regiment at Carentan. Couriers were then sent with orders directly to his battalions which were closer, south of Carentan. By 0230 he was on the road to Isigny and the new headquarters of 12th SS Panzer. He was met by Hitlerjugend's commander, SS Brigadeführer Fritz Witt, who already had his two regiments on full alert ready to burst out onto the roads to hunt down the Allied paratroopers. The panzer and panzergrenadier battalions of the two regiments had already been cross-attached to form two combined arms battle groups to take part in the planned counterlanding exercise with the 352nd Division. At Isigny and at Balleroy were two forces each consisting of a panzer, a panzergrenadier, and an artillery battalion of twelve self-propelled 105mm guns. Max Wünsche commanded the force at Balleroy with the forty-eight Panther Mark V tanks of his 1st Battalion, 12th SS Panzer Regiment. The other battalion with its 91 Mark IV tanks was with Witt as was the reconnaissance battalion. Each panzergrenadier battalion added almost one hundred half-tracked armoured personnel carriers (Mittlerer Schützenpanzerwagen or m.SPW) to each battle group as well.

Rommel outlined his plan to Witt. Concentrate quickly at Carentan with the 6th Parachute Regiment attached to Hitlerjugend, then strike north along the two parallel roads running north and south behind the coast, Highway 13 between Carentan and Montebourg and the road that ran parallel to the coast just behind the inundated areas behind the beaches. As Witt gave the order, his division sprang to life. The reconnaissance battalion erupted onto the road heading for the bridges over the Vire to the west. Rommel turned to Witt. 'I shall be behind the recon and will meet you in Carentan.' With that he jumped into his staff car. A smile half touched his mouth as he looked to his aide, 'Well, Lange, just like old times. Let's go', and his car joined the cavalcade of armoured cars, halftracks, and motorcycles. Witt paused barely a second to wonder if a field marshal should be at the head of a reconnaissance. That wasn't even Witt's job, but he had more to worry about then. He wanted to be close behind Rommel with his battle group. Wherever Rommel went, there was sure to be excitement.

As Rommel sped off to Isigny, OB West headquarters was already being inundated with a surge of spot reports from the units along the coast of massive parachute landings. Speidel reported Rommel's initial appraisal of the situation directly to von Rundstedt at 0230 and added his own endorsement. The field marshal could barely contain his distress that Rommel had disappeared into the night on a tactical reconnaissance. He ordered Speidel to find him and get him back to his own headquarters. A few minutes later, Speidel was brought to the phone by a call from General Max Pemsel, Chief of Staff of 7th Army. He emphatically disagreed with Speidel. This was indeed the invasion. Speidel stood his ground. Strong character if not sound judgment was the hallmark of the General Staff officer. Pemsel was not convinced and ordered Speidel's words to be placed verbatim in the 7th Army log, 'the affair is still locally confined,' and the 'Chief of Staff of Army Group B believes that for the time being this is not to be considered as a large operation.'[4]

Von Rundstedt's judgment was better. At 0415 he stated that the airborne landings were 'definitely the opening phase of a landing to be expected at dawn.' He still considered this to be a diversion but one that would be followed up with a landing. While that landing would be secondary to the major landing to occur later, it was still dangerous. If successful, the Allies would not fail to exploit it whether or not another landing was in the offing. It had to be crushed quickly. He had to act quickly to get the panzer divisions on the road before dawn so that the morning mists would be a protective coat of invisibility as they closed on the landing beaches. At 0430 he ordered the nearest OKW Reserve division, Panzer Lehr, to move immediately to the Calvados coast. The 1st SS Panzer Division Belgium and the 17th SS Panzergrenadier Division just south of the Loire were also alerted and ordered to begin movement to Normandy. It had been understood that despite the designation of these divisions as OKW reserve, he as Commander of OB West would have the authority to commit them as the situation dictated. In Rommel's absence, he also ordered Army Group B's panzer reserves, 2nd and 116th Panzer Divisions, to Normandy as well. Then his judgment deserted him. He sent a message to OKW advising of his action as a proforma last thought, requesting approval of his action.

OB-West is fully aware that if this is actually a large-scale enemy operation it can only be met successfully if immediate action is taken. This involves the commitment on this day of the available strategic reserves . . . If they assemble quickly and get an early start they can enter the battle on the coast during the day.[5]

As the recon battalion sped into Carentan at about 0445, Rommel found the local commander and learned of the attacks on the lock and the Douve bridges. Elements of one battalion of the 6th Parachute Regiment had already straggled into the town. He knew that the Americans were attempting to seal the edge of their drop zone and he must break them quickly before the seal could harden. He assembled the commanders of the recon and parachute battalions and gave them orders for an immediate counterattack. They would cross the Douve to the east of the lock on the road to St. Côme-du-Mont but turn east and attack the Americans in turn at the lock and then at the Douve bridges. Witt was to follow through and strike with part of his force towards Ste.-Mère-Eglise and part to follow the recon and paras. The attack moved out immediately with Rommel close to the head of column. The combined column with the paras loaded into the recon vehicles crossed the Douve unopposed and swung east. By 0515 they had crashed into the Americans around the lock. Surprise was everything. There was a sharp fight as the recon vehicles attacked through them from the rear, and then the American positions caved in as the German paratroopers closed with them. Rommel was surprised at how few Americans there had been, thirty dead and as many prisoners with the rest scattered. One of the recon officers ran up to his car and brandished the Screaming Eagles shoulder patch. Rommel examined it briefly. He did not stop to worry about the enemy that fled but ordered the column to press on toward the Douve bridges.

He would not be with them. The key to the area was Ste.-Mère-Eglise. He ordered his car turned around and sped back toward St. Côme-du-Mont with a small escort to join Witt. Half way there a sheet of machine gun fire erupted out of the hedgerow along the road. The two motorcycles of his escort spun across the road, and bullets ripped through his staff car, killing the driver and plunging it into a ditch. The following armoured car burst apart from a bazooka round. The field marshal pulled his wounded aide out of car and into the bushes and the shadows of the pre-dawn. Americans jumped out the hedgerows to search the vehicles and dead. An officer pulled out his map case while a sergeant gave a shout of triumph as he waved the field marshal's silver-headed marshal's baton overhead. Pulling the badly wounded Captain Lange with him, Rommel crawled through a hole in the hedge and worked away from the Americans and the road.

Rommel's instructions to Witt had never reached him. Witt came barrelling through Carentan and crossed the river where he found a military police detail that told him the field marshal had gone east. Apprised of the enemy at the locks and bridges, he sent half of his force under the command of the panzer battalion's SS Sturmbannführer (Major) Prinz, to follow Rommel and attacked north up Highway 13 towards Ste.-Mère-Eglise. It was now about 0515 with dawn less than an hour away. His advance elements were still travelling in the dark, the cloak of surprise. As they passed through the village of St. Côme-du-Mont, they were ambushed. Bazookas knocked out two Mark IVs and several SPWs before his infantry were able to clear out the small band of American paratroopers. His teenage panzergrenadiers leaped into their first fight with an élan he had not seen in a long time. He was proud of them, but the Americans had also fought well before the survivors had slipped into the fading night. He was surprised to learn that he had prisoners from two American airborne divisions. Had he found the boundary between them? He did not have to push his men too hard; the Leibstandarte cadres knew their job and their boys were all eagerness. The battle group was on the road again in minutes, but within three miles they were again ambushed at the village of Blosville and again at les Forges the next mile on. By now the dawn was lighting up the battlefield no longer needing assistance from the clutch of burning German tanks and half-tracks, and the enemy was holding on and kicking back with a few antitank guns and bazookas. They held a hedgerow line running east and west along the road just south of les Forges. Witt began flanking the position, and realized as the fighting ran down the hedgerow line that he was up against more than platoon bands of dispersed paratroopers.

Ridgway had pulled together a few hundred men from the 507th and 508th to defend the approach to Ste.-Mère-Eglise from the south. His grip on the eastern edge of the two bridges over the Merderet had been pulled taut. Two miles to the east of les Forges was the bridge at Chef du Pont. There a few hundred more men were preventing the 1057th Regiment from crossing. As many were defending a similar bridge a few miles to the north at Fiere.

While Witt split his column, his reconnaissance battalion and the attached Fallschirmjägers surprised and scattered the Americans holding the ends of the Douve bridges. The column moved north to the village of Ste.-Marie-du-Mont to pick up the road that paralleled the coast. They sped through the village surprising the Americans there as well, shooting up everything in their path until they ran into a roadblock on the far side of the village. The Americans quickly recovered and began fighting back from the stone houses that lined the road. The Germans had quickly found that the Americans were in the area in strength. Company-sized counterattacks began isolating elements of the column strung up and down the main street. As the last of the night disappeared, both forces were locked in a close-quarters fight among the stone houses and gardens of the village and into the hedgerows of the neighbouring fields. The other half of Witt's column raced to the sound of the guns. With forty tanks, a dozen guns, and a panzergrenadier battalion, Prinz's men tipped the fighting. The Mark IVs began blasting each American strongpoint often at point-blank range. The few American bazookas destroyed a few tanks and halftracks, but could not stop the grinding progress of the Hitlerjugend. Yet the Germans seemed to have to take each house twice in the whipsaw of attack and counterattack. The Americans rarely surrendered. Bodies with their Screaming Eagle patches and silver runic double lightning bolts littered the rubble-strewn streets. It was the hardest sort of fight, elite against elite with neither side conditioned to come off second best. But numbers and heavy equipment eventually told. Slowly the Americans were pushed out of the village and back toward the coast and the small villages of Houdienville and Poupeville that covered the two southernmost exits from the beaches. Both villages were up against an inundated area and offered no flanks for the Germans to slip around.

By six that morning the situation north of the Vire was teetering on the edge of catastrophe for the two American airborne divisions. The 101st had been pushed out of its southern sector and thrown up against the villages that covered the exits from the beaches for the soon to land 4th Infantry Division. The Screaming Eagles could retreat no more. Several more battalions from the 101st had opened the beach exits to the north. To the west, the 82nd was barely holding a line a few miles south of Ste.-Mère-Eglise. Neither division could muster more than 1,500 men under direct control. Thousands more were dead or roamed in small groups such as the one that had ambushed the commander of Army Group B.

As the battle against the American airborne divisions roared and sputtered, Field Marshal Rommel was dodging several of those small groups through the fields and hedgerows. He would not leave his aide who begged him to save himself. Pistol in hand, Erwin Rommel broke open the door of a French cottage to the terror of its occupants. The farmer and his wife helped carry Lange to a bed where they did what they could for him. Then the Commander of Army Group B slipped away. The last time he had been so thoroughly alone on a battlefield had been on another French field in 1914. As a lieutenant then, his absence had not altered the scheme of battle. As a field marshal, his absence meant a great deal more.

As Rommel was playing hide-and-seek with American paratroopers, von Rundstedt's message seemed to be swallowed up in the lethargy of early morning. The message stirred no concern among Hitler's entourage, certainly not enough to wake the drugged Führer and subject themselves to one of his wild demonstrations. At OKW, no one thought it critical enough to wake its chief, General Alfred Jodl, either. All the while, the panzers were rapidly making their final preparations for getting on the road. By 0600 Jodl was awake and eating a Spartan breakfast when he finally read the message. Panzer Lehr was on the road. Chosen by Hitler for his rigid obedience, Jodl reacted furiously to von Rundstedt's defiance of Hitler's instructions. At his direction, the OKW chief of operations called von Rundstedt and Speidel at 0630 as thousands of landing craft were falling into practised landing formations off the Calvados coast of Normandy. He forbade the movement of not only the OKW Reserve but any panzer units. 'Nothing is to be done before the Führer makes his decision. You are to do what you are told!'[6]

It did not help that General Marcks was delayed at the same time Rommel was hiding in the hedgerows for his life. As he approached Bayeux in the early morning, the area was alive with German troops hunting paratroopers. He stopped long enough in Balleroy to brief the commanders of the 352nd Division and Wünsche's SS battle group on the situation. It was then at about 0700 that he spoke to Speidel who was frantically searching for Rommel. Marcks relayed his last information. He also attempted to convince the chief of staff that this was no diversion. It was too big. The Allies would not waste so many quality units on a diversion; this was the invasion. There were already reports of ship engine noises all up and down the coast. He had to have the 21st Panzer released to him immediately to counterattack the Allied airborne landings east of Caen. General Max Pemsel, Chief of Staff of 7th Army agreed. Speidel demurred. Then Marcks played his trump: Rommel had given him permission to use the 21st Panzer. Speidel had a better trump: Field Marshal Jodl had just refused permission for the employment of any panzer units, and evoking the Führer's authority, even those that had been previously released to Rommel. Von Rundstedt's chief of staff, General Günther von Blumentritt, had personally called the Führer's headquarters and spoken to Jodl. The panzer reserves would not be released without the Führer's permission, and the Führer was sleeping. Jodl had also forbidden the use of those elements of Hitlerjugend that had not departed Lisieux. Rommel's release was cancelled by higher authority. Speidel did, however, second Rommel's orders for Marcks to take up his post in Caen to deal with the airborne landings east of the Orne. With what, Marcks wondered, the old men of the coastal defence divisions?

As Speidel and Marcks spoke, a German patrol of the 91st Division found Rommel's shot-up staff car and escort vehicles. There was no trace of the field marshal. The officer on the spot immediately relayed the news that the field marshal was missing in action. Another patrol retrieved his baton from a dead American sergeant. So much depended on Rommel and not just the battle. With landline communications severed, Enigma-encoded traffic had begun humming and now carried the incredible story up the chain of command. Rommel was missing and almost certainly a prisoner.

Notes

1. Tonie and Valmai Holt, *The Visitor's Guide to Normandy Landing Beaches* (Ashbourne, Derbyshire: Moorland, 1989); (Edison, New Jersey: Hunter, 1989) p.196.
2. Holt, ibid., p.197.
3. Hans von Luck, *Panzer Commander: The Memoirs of Colonel Hans von Luck* (New York: Praeger, 1989) p.137.
4. Anthony Cave Brown, *Bodyguard of Lies* (New York: Harper & Row, 1975) p.652; (Toronto: Fitzhenry & Whiteside, 1975); (London: W.H. Allen, 1976).
5. Brown, ibid., p.659.
6. Bodo Zimmermann, *Command Decisions in the Invasion Battle* (London: William Kimber, 1949) p.223.

CHAPTER 3

The American Landings
6 June

'Bloody' Omaha Beach

0600. Captain Bill Scott gazed in awe out of the nose of his B-17. He was over the English Channel, and everywhere he looked, whether at the rough seas or the skies, was an incredible grandeur, and he was part of it. The sea was covered with a vast armada that stretched over the horizon, ships and craft of every description. In the air he was part of an endless bomber stream that also seemed to arch over the horizon. It was almost biblical in the way the Allies had filled the air and the sea. He had been on thirteen missions over Germany, this handsome 24-year-old pilot from Stiff Valley, Kentucky. He had ridden the flak over Frankfurt and Berlin and seen his comrades fall from the sky on too many occasions. His squadron commander's aircraft had disintegrated over Berlin, and part of it had come crashing through the nose, into the navigator's compartment. That had been bad, as bad as they said it could be today. 'Fly at twelve thousand feet', a terrifying altitude for men who have ridden the Berlin flak, were the orders. 'If an engine fails, you are forbidden to fall out of formation', were the orders. The clouds were at ten thousand feet, and they bombed by instrument. The bombs spilled out of the bomb bays and fell through the clouds on what they could not see. He shrugged. The Flying Fortress was a clumsy tactical weapon.[1]

For the men of the 16th and 116th Regiments, the first wave assault regiments of the Big Red One, the bluffs above Omaha Beach continued to grow as their landing craft approached. They had heard the waves of bombers dropping hundreds of tons of bombs directly on the beach defenders in their slit trenches and pillboxes. As at Gettysburg, a field familiar in memory to the Stonewallers, this preparatory bombardment had overshot the defences, falling harmlessly in the open country behind the bluffs, doing slaughter only on the dairy herds of Normandy. Low cloud cover had forced the bombers to drop their ordnance by instrument. In fear that the bombs would fall among the assault craft, a delay of several seconds had been added, a delay which caused them to miss the German defences entirely. They had also seen the naval gunfire rip the bluffs with their big rifles and the swarms of fighter bombers before and after swooping and diving to deliver more ordnance on the silent German defenders. That was more comforting. Men believe their sense of sight over that of hearing. They would

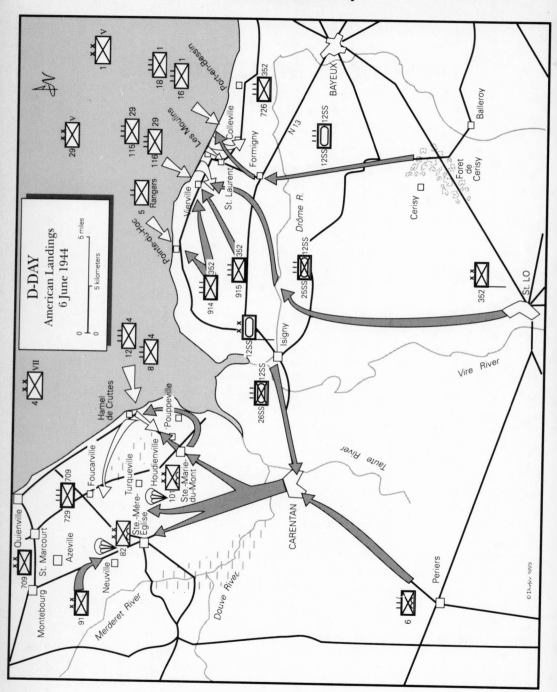

D-DAY
American Landings
6 June 1944

be deceived again. The German defences had been sighted not to fire directly out to sea, but to bring the beaches under fire. They were tucked into the bluffs and draws at angles that made them difficult to see much less hit from the sea. Still, those bluffs, some 200 feet high, grew in height faster in the imagination than in reality. The reality was bad enough. Omaha was the most formidable beach along the invasion front.

Those bluffs formed a greater defence than anything German artifice could devise, but they did have their flaws. Four draws broke the front of the natural rampart along the front of the two assaulting regiments, perfect passageways inland. Here the Germans concentrated their defences. And it was in these four places that the 1st Infantry Division planned to sunder the German hold on the beach. The assault waves were aimed directly at those four draws.

For the assault on Omaha, the Americans had combined elements of two divisions under the control of the Big Red One: the 29th Division's Stone-wallers of the 116th Infantry Regiment in the first wave and the Marylanders of the 115th in the second along with the 1st Division's 16th and 18th Infantry Regiments. Only on 7 June would the 29th resume its independence when its commander came ashore with the rest of the division. Until then, the two regiments of the 29th would be known as the 'Provisional Brigade' or unof-ficially as the 'Bastard Brigade' by men never comfortable except under their own commander. The brigade would be controlled by the 29th's Assistant Division Commander, Brigadier General Norman Cota. Cota had been an excellent choice. As Chief of Staff of the 1st Division, he had served with that unit from its first landings in North Africa to the desperate foothold on Sicily. 'Dutch' Cota was a natural leader, and the division hated to give him up.

Within the first wave of the combined division were eighteen sub-waves of different elements of the two regiments and their attached units. Four of these attached units had been prepared to play a special role in helping the infantry break through the formidable beach defences. Two of them consisted of the 741st and 743rd Tank Battalions each with sixty-four Sherman tanks, attached to the 16th and 116th Regiments. Half the tanks in each battalion were the Duplex Drive or D-D types, meant to swim ashore, the 741st with the 16th Regiment and the 743rd with the Stonewallers. The other half of each battalion would be landed directly on the beaches from their LCTs (Landing Craft Tank). The third unit was the specially trained and equipped engineers of the 149th and 299th Engineer Beach Battalions. The D-D tanks would waddle ashore ahead of the infantry to suppress defences; for example, as on the extreme right where they would take out the defenders in front of the Vierville Draw. The infantry would follow. Two minutes after, the engineers would land to destroy the obstacles that might hinder later waves and to support the infantry's breakthrough of the draws. Behind the tanks on the right were the 2nd and 5th Ranger Battalions. The objective of the 2nd was the heavy casemated battery at

Pointe-du-Hoc on the right flank of the landing beaches. Three companies of the 2nd Battalion would land on the beach beneath the battery and assault straight up the cliff. The 5th and two companies of the 2nd would land near the Stonewallers and strike inland to take the battery from the rear. Their fearsome objective housed four 150mm guns, termed by intelligence as 'the most dangerous battery in France', that could lethally range up and down the landing beaches.

The planned timetable for the landings was so precise and optimistic that it reminded more than a few of the older men of the 1914–1918 war. For Lieutenant General Leonard Gerow, the V Corps commander, it had an eerie resemblance to the St. Michel Offensive in which he had fought in 1918. The assault waves would hit the beaches, neatly divided into eight sectors, exactly at 0631 after the naval and air bombardments had ceased. By 0700 the wave would be ashore and the obstacles cleared by the engineers to allow for the next waves to come ashore every thirty minutes over the following two hours. By 0830 all enemy strongpoints would have been overcome when the artillery could begin landing. Within three hours the tanks and other vehicles of the 1st Division would be pouring off the beach into the interior. By nightfall, 40,000 men and 3,500 vehicles were to have been unloaded. The Russians had a common sense military proverb that seemed to belie the confidence of the plan, 'The plan was smooth on paper, but they forgot the ravines'.

The ravines so invisible to the planners were all too real to two general officers who would lead troops in the invasion. Cota had prepared a special study on how to assault a heavily defended beach. He had been sombrely impressed by the near defeat of the Big Red One in its Sicilian landing and concluded that the greatest chances of success demanded a night landing. 'The beach is going to be fouled up in any case. Darkness will not substantially alter the percentage of accuracy in beaching – not enough to offset the handicaps of a daylight assault.'[2] The major handicap was the deadliness of the aimed fire the Germans would be able to bring to bear on the fully exposed landing forces. The other officer was Major General Charles 'Pete' Corlett who had commanded the 7th Infantry Division in its amphibious assault on Kwajalein atoll in February. The Bayonet Division had overrun the atoll and wiped out its 9,000 defenders in a week in the most expert amphibious operation seen so far. Transferred to the European Theatre to assume command of XIX Corps, he was immediately apprehensive of the planning for the American landings. Why weren't the Americans using the LVT (Landing Vehicle Tracked) which had served the 7th so well in the Pacific? The Alligator, as it was known by the troops, swam ashore and then carried the troops forward on its tracks through the beaten zone along the beaches. Eisenhower and Bradley reacted badly to Corlett's blunt question.

I was pretty well squelched for my question. I soon got the feeling that American generals in England considered anything that happened in the Pacific strictly 'Bush League stuff,' which didn't merit any consideration. I felt like an expert according to Naval definition, 'A son-of-a-bitch from out of town.'[3]

The Allied planners had decided that the optimum time for the landing was low tide, exactly the opposite conclusion reached by Rommel. They had no intention of making things easy for Rommel by impaling the landing craft on submerged obstacles at high tide. At a rising low tide, the assault waves could be discharged without danger at the edge of the obstacle belt. The landing craft would then be refloated by the rising tide to return to sea to pick up additional waves. The obstacle belt would be neatly checked by this decision. Unfortunately, it left the infantry to cover 200 exposed yards to the dubious protection of the overhang of the bluffs. The American planners had also decided to load the assault waves aboard their landing craft eleven miles from the beaches, against the advice of the British who would transfer their assault waves less then half that distance. Because the assault would take place so early, the transfer at such a distance had to be made at night. The assault would be made with barely half an hour of naval bombardment as soon as dawn illuminated the shore targets. The British had recommended at least twice the time for the big naval guns to work over the German defences, extra time they would not begrudge their landing forces. The planners also turned down the British offer to share Hobart's funnies, the specialized armoured vehicles meant to break through the obstacles and minefields. These bizarre but effective vehicles were the brainchild of one of those dynamic British military eccentrics, Major General P.C.S. Hobart. In addition to the funnies he had created and trained the force that would employ them, 79th Armoured Division, whose elements would be attached to the British first wave divisions. The only specialized vehicle the Americans accepted was the D-D tank, leaving the entire 79th Division to support the British divisions. Finally, the Americans discarded British advice to land between the strongpoints that defended the four draws. They would aim directly for the strongest part of the German defences.

In perhaps the greatest miscalculation, one in which fortune tipped the scale, the planners assumed that the defenders of Omaha beach numbered only four battalions from the third-rate 716th Coastal Defence Division. In reality the 352nd had added four more high quality battalions to the defence of the shoreline. Behind them another regiment of the 352nd was in readiness to conduct an anti-landing exercise with the newly arrived battle group of the 12th SS Panzer.

The Beachhead
Things began to go awry for the Big Red One in the night before the invasion.

As a result of the re-embarkation of the assault waves in the dark, too many landing craft wandered out of position, especially those carrying the engineers. As dawn broke over the French shore, the naval gunfire preparation struck the defences, festooning the bluff with smoke and setting the grass on fire in many places. In an act of breathtaking misjudgment, the twenty-nine D-D tanks supporting the 16th Infantry were released 6,000 yards from shore where twenty-seven promptly sank in the rough seas, carrying their crews to their deaths. Only two were to trundle safely ashore to be joined by three more aboard a barge. Watching this catastrophe, the Naval lieutenant in charge of releasing the D-D tanks of the 743rd Tank Battalion disregarded his similar orders and continued straight for the beaches. The seas surging around Omaha were the heaviest faced by any of the five assault divisions. Ten of the infantry's landing craft (LCAs)[4] were swamped and sank. Many of the men loaded with seventy pounds of equipment followed the tank crews to the bottom. Many of the others were riding so low in the water that the waves just sloshed over them, drenching the men in the icy water. Frantic calls from sinking craft were being picked up on the radios, 'This is LCA 860! . . . LCA 860! . . . We're sinking! . . . We're sinking! . . . My God, we're sunk!'[5] The seasick listeners began bailing with their helmets. The wheeled amphibious vehicles (DUKWs) with the artillery proved to be grossly overloaded and capsized with a loss of twenty guns. Before they had even approached within rifle shot of the beach, the assaulting waves of invaders had been stripped of most of the tanks, engineers, and artillery. None had been lost by the hand of fortune, but by the conscious decisions of their own side. Few men in the assault craft were conscious of these errors. They were watching, when they weren't bailing, the effects of naval gunfire lashing the shore. Clouds of rockets whooshed off specially designed ships to crash onto the defenders. The effect was overwhelming. It seemed that nothing on the beaches could survive.

The tanks of the 743rd approached the beach still aboard their LCTs. One of the LCTs disintegrated in an orange fireball, spilling its four tanks into the water. The German guns in front of the Vierville and Les Moulins Draws could not miss their targets, nor could the 150mm guns on Pointe-du-Hoc nearby. A second LCT was struck and veered off as it filled with water and then sank. The tank crews and Navy crewmen barely had time to jump over the side. The Naval officer commanding rammed his craft onto the beaches. Steady, steady, the lieutenant guided his remaining LCTs, until each rammed into the beach. The ramps went down and the Shermans bolted ashore driving through and over the obstacles straight for the heart of the German defences clustered around the two draws. A dozen were hit in the first seconds from direct fire of antitank guns. More died from the accurate German artillery sighted in on the beaches from their positions inland. A direct assault was made on Vierville Draw but collapsed as they lost the slugging match with guns buried deep in concrete. In a few minutes half the battalion had been destroyed. The rest found shelter under the bluff to the right and left of the draws where antitank fire could not reach them. The five surviving D-D tanks of the neighbouring 741st waded ashore with their ungainly canvas surrounds. Three were promptly destroyed. The other two companies of the battalion landed over the beach and failed in similar assaults on the two draws in their sector. The Americans had thrown 128 tanks against Omaha, more tanks than most German panzer divisions possessed. In minutes this force had been wrecked, and the infantry had only begun to come ashore.

The assault waves of the Stonewallers were quickly dragged off target by the strong currents that ran along the shore. Two companies were to have landed to assault the Vierville Draw. G Company was pushed over a thousand yards to the east as was the entire 5th Rangers. A Company, which had already lost two of its four landing craft swamped, was right on target. So were the Germans. Their concentrated well-aimed fire massacred the two companies as the ramps fell into the water. The streams of bullets from the deadly MG-42s spewed into the packed open mouths of the landing craft. Death beckoned for those who scrambled into the back of the craft as well as those who took their chances in the water. All thirty-two men and the A Company commander, Captain Taylor Fellers, in LCA 1015 were killed. The craft was washed out in the rising tide carrying its load of corpses back among the next waves. Nineteen-year-old Second Lieutenant Edward Gearing's craft with thirty men aboard was blown to pieces 300 yards from the beach in front of the Vierville Draw. He eventually dragged himself ashore to find he was the only officer who had not been killed or wounded. For those who survived to get ashore, there was no hope of getting onto the beach itself. They clung to the small protection of the German obstacles and lay in the surf. It was suicide even to crawl out of the water and up the beach. The few remaining officers sacrificed themselves in vain to get their men out of the slaughter pen on the water's edge. Lieutenant Edward Tidrick had been hit in the neck as he jumped out of his craft. Rising to one elbow, he shouted to his men, 'Advance with the wire cutters!' only to be cut down a few seconds later as the bullet streams of two MG-42s intersected through his body. A Company had ceased to exist. Barely a third would survive the day.

Company F landed right in front of the Les Moulins Draw along with the errant Company G that should have been landing east at Vierville Draw. The smoke from burning grass on the bluff covered their landing, and they got ashore largely unscathed. A third company, E, drifted so far east that it landed in the zone of the 16th Infantry. The two companies in front of Les Moulins Draw went to earth behind a shingle embankment in front of the draw. Others tried to hide behind the beach obstacles. All along the beach, the surviving Stonewallers huddled in shock beneath the bluff or the shingle embankments. Those who tried to shelter behind tanks found that the metal hulks attracted German artillery. The engineers suffered as cruel an ordeal as Company A. The current had carried most of their landing craft too far to the east. Those that attempted to land found their stores of demolitions a curse. Several crafts were blown apart in fiery explosions when German fire found the explosives. The engineers found it impossible to clear the eight fifty-foot-wide lanes in the plan. The few that landed where they were supposed to, found the infantry hiding for dear life behind the obstacles in many cases. The engineers also made exceptional targets as they struggled to destroy what obstacles they could. German snipers were detonating the mines on top of the obstacles. Mortars were skillfully directed onto the engineers before they could clear the obstacles they had rigged for demolition. By the time the rising tide stopped them, they had barely cleared two small gaps. The survivors sought refuge from the fire with the stricken infantry to wait to try again when the tide went out.

Events on the beaches occupied by the 16th Infantry were brutally similar to those inflicted on the Stonewallers. Companies E and F of the 2nd Battalion of the 16th attacked straight against the Colleville Draw and suffered the same fate as the 1st Battalion of the 116th at Vierville Draw. Within a half hour, half of them were dead or wounded. Control of the 16th on the beach was crippled when the regimental executive officer arriving with the first headquarters element was killed along with thirty-five of his staff. The men of the Big Red One did not have even the tank support available to the Virginians of the 29th Division since half their supporting tank battalion was on the sea floor several miles offshore and much of the rest was burning on the beach. Their supporting engineers lost half their men and had cleared only three small lanes of obstacles. All along Omaha, the absence of the Hobart's funnies added to the catastrophe as men attempted to move through narrow gaps in the minefields single file, irresistible targets for German snipers and machine gunners that cut down whole files. There was a single bright spot, though. Four boat sections from the 2nd Battalion landed in a section of beach uncovered by German fire. The position that would have raked the boat sections had never been occupied. These Americans crossed the beach with only two casualties.

The three remaining companies of the 116th's 1st Battalion were to follow Company A beginning at 0700 in ten-minute intervals. C Company and the 5th Rangers were tugged east by the current and landed unscathed, but B and D Companies and two companies of the 2nd Rangers landed into the same sheet of well-aimed fire that had crushed A Company. They too left bodies to bob in the surf and piled around the obstacles as the survivors inched forward to join the paralyzed mass of men at the foot of the bluff on either side of the draw. All three company commanders had been killed. Up the coast the last company of 2nd Battalion and all of 3rd Battalion were supposed to land in front of Les Moulins Draw. Only one from each battalion, Companies H and I, made it; the others, Companies K, L and M, were pulled 600 yards up the coast by the obstinate current. Company H had the bad luck to land in front of a German strongpoint and took heavy casualties. One man remembered, 'Two of the men from my section got down behind a tetrahedron (hedgehog) to escape bullets. An artillery shell hit the tetrahedron and drove the steel back into their bodies. I tried to pry the steel loose from the men, but couldn't do it. Then I figured they were dead anyway.'[6]

The Guns of Pointe-du-Hoc

The attack on Pointe-du-Hoc had gone off forty minutes late. The three small assault companies of the 2nd Rangers, commanded by Lieutenant James E. Rudder, first had to struggle with the coastal current before they could come to grips with any Germans. The delay had already cost Rudder the heavy support that would flow to him under the plan. The rest of his 2nd Rangers and all of the 5th were to follow him to the beach when he fired flares signalling his men had scaled the cliffs. If the signals had not been received by 0700, the rest of the Rangers were to land with the 116th. When his 225 Rangers landed on the shingle beach below the cliffs of Pointe-du-Hoc, their supporting force had already gone ashore. Now they would have to do it alone.

The shock waves from the guns above them pulsed down the cliffs and over the Rangers as they rushed ashore onto the narrow beach. The gunfire support of the destroyers USS *Satterlee* and HMS *Talybont* swept most of the German defenders from the cliff top. Enough survived to throw potato masher grenades and fire their submachine guns down at the Rangers. Luckily there were few casualties. The Rangers were aggressively returning fire as they began an impetuous assault. Two amphibious DUKWs with tall extended ladders borrowed from the London fire department drove onto the beach. At the top of each ladder were Rangers with Browning Automatic Rifles or Thompson submachine guns who shot down any Germans that they could see on the cliff top. Resembling more the fury of a Crusader storm of the walls of a Muslim fortress than twentieth-century warfare, Ranger assault flowed up the nine-storey-high cliffs. Rocket-propelled grapnels shot up to anchor on the cliffside followed by swarming Rangers. Others, impatient to follow, climbed up with their hands, driving knives for handholds into the cliff. Here and there Germans tried to cut the grapnel ropes, sending Rangers hurtling to the beach. Others were cut down as they tried, sending gray-clad bodies down as well. One by one, Rangers clamoured over the top. The first few were killed, but others killed enough Germans to seize a foothold on the cliff top. Abruptly the remaining Germans fell back towards the emplacements around the guns themselves.

Rudder pushed forward his companies. So determined had been their attack that they had lost only twenty-five men so far. The cliff top was cratered like the face of the moon by the naval and air bombardments. The holes provided good cover for the Rangers to use as they rushed forward in small groups while others supported them with fire. The big guns had kept firing during the attack up the cliff and did not pause now that the Rangers were closing in on them. The cliff top quivered with each blast which luckily disconcerted the remaining defenders enough for the Rangers to be able to rush closer with few casualties. They reached the bunkers and tossed grenades and satchel charges through the firing slits. One final position with two MG-42s held them up for fifteen minutes. Rudder's men were crawling up around its sides when the Germans counterattacked. The volume of fire that swept through the Rangers from the flank told Rudder that a new German unit had joined the fight. It was now 0839, and the German gunners inside their casemates continued to serve their guns.

'Dutch' Cota Builds a Legend

In the dead space in the German defences on Omaha where Company C and the 5th Rangers had landed, the assault force command group landed with Brigadier General Cota and the 116th's commander, Colonel D.W. Canham. The beach reeked of disaster, littered with corpses, burning tanks, wrecked landing craft, and all the other debris of war. The Germans had exactly the same impression from their position atop the bluffs. The commander of the Les Moulins Draw defences called in his report to General Kraiss, commanding the 352nd Division.

> At the water's edge, the enemy is in search of cover behind the coastal-zone obstacles. A great many motor vehicles – among them ten tanks – stand burning on the beach. The obstacle demolition squads have given up their activities. Debarkation from the landing boasts has ceased . . . the boats keep farther out to sea. The fire of our battle positions and artillery is well placed and has inflicted considerable casualties on the enemy. A great many wounded and dead lie on the beach . . .[7]

Cota and Canham were determined that whatever the Germans thought at the moment would not be the final say on the matter. Canham was wounded shortly after landing but refused to fall out. They agreed to separate, Canham to rally the men further to the west of Les Moulins Draw and Cota those at hand. A few men had already tried to slip over the bluffs, and most had been shot down. The rest were still huddled in clumps sometimes of a hundred or more men. And the preregistered German artillery was causing horrific casualties, especially the 150mm guns on the Pointe-du-Hoc, as their shells landed amid the huddling troops. Cota walked among them with an assurance that had bled out of them since they hit the beach. His message was simple: you may die attacking but you will surely die if you stay here. He organized the first group of a hundred men to return fire up the bluffs to keep the Germans down.

He found a few engineers with bangalore torpedoes to blast a hole in a coil of barbed wire that ran along the base of the bluff. They blew a small hole in it and a brave man rushed through only to be felled almost instantly by a machine gun. He cried out, 'Medico, I'm hit! Help me!' He died crying, 'Mama.' The rest of the men were stuck fast where they crouched. Cota raced through the hole in the wire unharmed. He yelled for more to follow, and they did. No one was hit. For some strange reason, the machine gun that had killed the first young soldier was silent. Cota led the men through a field of reeds until they found an abandoned German trench. They followed it up the bluff single-file. Cota hurried them along. Unknown to everyone else, they had passed out of the hell on the beach. The German positions had been sighted to fire onto the beach and not to their rear behind the bluff where Cota was now leading his Stonewallers and their Ranger comrades. It was 0900. Something else had happened. By his very example, Cota had reignited the initiative and sense of purpose of men who had been stunned by their ordeal on the beach. Although they were mingled from many units, they were now a unit again.

They followed the German paths to within quarter of a mile of the outskirts of Vierville where they were taken under fire by a few machine guns. Cota organized a base of fire that drove off the Germans while an assault group attacked into the village. The Germans fled. Cota's force entered Vierville unopposed and were met by another group of Americans who had climbed over the bluff, Company C men who had escaped the slaughter on the beach. They were joined by more men from the 2nd Battalion and 5th Rangers led by Colonel Canham. Their arrival was a telling indictment of the decision to land directly in front of the heavily defended draws. The units that had inadvertently landed between the draws had come ashore with few casualties. More importantly, their nerve had not been broken by the Germans' firepower. Their eagerness had got them over the bluffs on their own. Cota's force was growing, and it was directly behind the still effective German defences of the draw. The Battleship USS *Texas* was now taking a hand and sending its fourteen-inch projectiles up the draw. Cota led his men to attack the defenders of the draw from behind. Smarting under the big guns of the *Texas*, the Germans were vulnerable to a determined attack from the rear. They surrendered quickly and Cota walked down to the beach to announce that it was now open for business. The beach covered by the draw was a sickening sight with thirty to fifty dead every hundred yards.

Cota moved to blow the antitank wall at the mouth of the draw and start the remaining tanks and men up the draw and through Vierville to the hedgerow country beyond. A runner arrived to tell him that the 2nd and 3rd Battalions had also climbed the bluff east of Les Moulins Draw and taken it from the rear. These again were units that had landed inadvertently between the draws. The Stonewallers had overcome not only the German defences but the suicidal elements of the plan they had had to execute, at a cost of over a thousand dead and wounded. Whole companies had been wiped out in the 1st and 2nd Battalions. Nothing had gone according to that plan, and it was the aggressiveness and initiative of individuals like 'Dutch' Cota and others that had seized this victory. One officer remembered:

> Everything that was done was done in small groups, led by the real heroes of the war. Most of them were killed . . . The minefields behind the beach were strewn with these guys; they were lying around the hedgerows on top of the bluffs and, of course, they were piled – literally – on the beach proper. . . . Very, very few were decorated, chiefly because no one was left to tell about what they did.[8]

The Presence of the Commander

To the east, the 16th Regiment had also moved off the beach, due to its commander, Colonel George Taylor, and the Big Red One's Assistant Division Commander, Brigadier General Willard G. Wyman, in a simultaneous reenactment of Cota and Canham's motivating force. As small units of the 16th started to move inland off the beach, Taylor and Wyman organized the reduction of the remaining German strongpoints. The regiment was responding to a single will again. One troublesome gun emplacement mounted one of the dreaded 88mm antitank guns that had shot up a number of the Shermans that had come ashore. It was the key to the Colleville gap and seemed immune to Taylor's and Wyman's efforts. A destroyer almost beached itself to get close enough to fire accurately. Normally immune to naval gunfire because of its thick concrete carapace, the emplacement was not immune to bad luck as the destroyer sent a five-inch shell directly through the firing port. The destroyed blockhouse became the Big Red One's first division command post, named Danger Forward. From there Major General Huebner, the Division Commander, directed the 16th to drive inland and take Colleville as Cota had taken Vierville.

The Germans had been lulled into confidence by the message from the Les Moulins Draw that described the collapse of the landings. That confidence grew the higher it went up the chain of command. General Marcks, however, was the man on the spot. Reports of paratroopers in the Bayeux area had drawn him to the area on the right flank of the Omaha landings. The messages he was receiving now told him that the Americans were getting off the beach. General Kraiss' initial optimism had quickly evaporated as he realized his coastal defences had failed in a number of places. He hurriedly recalled his 915th Regiment, which he had sent off to chase the dummy paratroopers, but they were hours away on foot. He was able to commit a battalion of the 914th Regiment to destroy the Americans at Pointe-du-Hoc. Initial reports indicated that the guns had been saved just in time. Everything else had been committed, and the British were also getting off the beach in their landings on his right flank.

Max Wünsche and the Art of Timing

Marcks had taken the precaution of ordering Wünsche's battle group of the 12th SS from Balleroy north to the Bayeux–Carentan highway that paralleled the coast as soon as he had learned that the Allies were landing in that sector. The highway was three miles inland, some nine miles from Balleroy. The battle group had been attacked several times from the air and lost half-a-dozen vehicles. The attacks had slowed him down: each time the column had to scatter and then reassemble. However, it arrived intact at Formigny by noon, directly between Vierville and Colleville. The sound of the guns drew his attention to Colleville on his right. Marcks had admonished him to attack as quickly as possible any movement off the beach. 'They will be most vulnerable then,' he had said. Wünsche assembled his commanders to issue his orders, and repeated Marcks' warning. He was joined by a battalion commander of Kraiss' artillery regiment whose guns were furiously firing on the beaches from around Formigny. The major was able to convey the latest intelligence he had. Most of the draws had fallen, he surmised, since he had lost contact with the defenders. The firing from Colleville meant the Americans were attacking off the beach. He was now only firing blindly at the preregistered beaches hoping to hit something. He would gladly support Wünsche's attack. Wünsche sent off the attached company of the reconnaissance battalion in that direction. The artilleryman laid out his map for the SS officers. It was familiar to them; they had planned for an exercise with the 352nd in this area for this very day. Marcks had taken one more precaution. He directed that the remaining elements of Hitlerjugend on their way from Lisieux be directed to this sector as well.

The battle group drove north to St. Laurent and turned east to Colleville, which they would be approaching from the west. German stragglers, over-age men from the 726th Regiment, told them that the Americans were swarming off the beaches and had taken Colleville. Already small parties of American infantrymen were being encountered. They were swept away as the SS sped down the road, their coming hidden by the hedgerows that lined the twisting roads. Wünsche called in the fire support from his own self-propelled battalion and that of Kraiss' battalion. The town was suddenly wreathed in explosions. Wünsche gave the signal, 'Achtung! . . . Panzer, maaarsch.' The SS burst into Colleville, Panther tanks in the lead followed by SPWs, and spread out through the orchards on either side of the town. The Americans had not had time to organize a defence, and in any case did not have the heavy infantry weapons to fight tanks. They had all been lost on the beach. Their only hope was the few remaining tanks from the 741st Tank Battalion that had accompanied them off the beach.

They had been surprised first by the artillery that struck down many of them as they moved through the town. Those that reemerged from cover were cut down by the tanks and machine guns on the speeding SPWs. Every time the Americans formed a nest of resistance, the Panthers would fire into it point blank until it was silenced. The few Shermans tried to block the Panthers only to see their shot bounce off the frontal armour. The German high velocity 75mm guns had no such problems. They sliced right through the thin hulls and turrets of the Shermans. In less than fifteen minutes the battle group had coursed through the town. The surviving enemy were fading away back toward the beach. Wünsche's losses had been light, and his boys, men now, had done well.

His intelligence officer had worked fast on a group of prisoners and reported that they were from the 16th Regiment of the 1st Division. The enemy appeared to be moving up from the Colleville draw. That was the key point. No time to lose. The battle group reversed its path through Colleville and took the road northwest that led to the draw. Again a high-speed approach produced the maximum shock among the columns of infantry that they literally ran over coming north out of the draw. The Panthers were crunching over men who could not run fast enough to jump into the hedgerows. The following panzergrenadiers shot them up from their armoured personnel carriers.

The 1st Division staff had moved into a burned out German bunker at the mouth of the draw and set up a sign that proclaimed it 'Danger Forward'. Major General Clarence Huebner was standing outside at 1450 when the SS attacked into Colleville. A frantic call from the 1/16th's radio in the town screamed, 'Tanks, tanks, all over the town!' then silence. The antitank guns of the 18th Infantry, which had landed in the second wave, were at the end of the column that was moving up the draw towards Colleville. He had to get them forward as fast as possible, but the draw and the hedgerow-bound road were packed tight with infantry and a few tanks and jeeps. All hell broke loose up the road. In a few minutes the sleek lines of a tank with a black cross careened down the draw scattering the Americans. Its tracks were red with blood and bits of flesh. Its machine guns sprayed the area with its crowds of targets. A bazooka hit it under the turret and left only a scorch mark. Another one struck it in the rear setting it on fire. The crew were cut down as they tried to clamber out. Huebner was getting an AT gun in place when two more monsters came slithering down the draw. One of them fired directly into Danger Forward killing most of the division staff inside. The machine gun of the other killed Huebner as he was helping to sight a 57mm AT gun toward the draw. More Panthers came out of the draw to clank up and down the beach spraying machine gun fire and shooting directly into landing craft approaching the beach at the range of only a few hundred yards. The tanks were followed by the panzergrenadiers who crushed any resistance left.

From the command ships ashore, observers saw the gray-painted tanks emerge from the draw and fan out up and down the beach. Men were fleeing to the landing craft only to die in them as they exploded. The sickened voice of one of the observers was relayed to General Bradley aboard the cruiser, USS *Augusta*. He looked as if he had been struck in the face. An officer began to sob as the voice narrated the havoc ashore. Rear Admiral Alan G. Kirk, commanding the naval task force, spoke first. 'I can get some of them off the beach if we hold off the enemy with naval gunfire, but we will lose a lot of men from our own guns.' 'No, don't kill any more of our boys. It's almost all over now.'[9] And it was. Everywhere men were surrendering as the Germans swarmed down onto the beach. A few made their way east and west away from the draw to link up with other units, but the bulk of the two infantry regiments and all the attached units had been lost. The proudest infantry division in the U.S. Army had been destroyed. It was almost 1600. Not even ten hours had passed since the Big Red One had landed.

All that remained on Omaha were the wounded Stonewallers around St. Laurent and Vierville and the 29th's second regiment to come ashore, the 115th Infantry from Baltimore. They were informed from the *Augusta*. The Germans' armour in the area had expended its supply of surprise at Colleville. The 29th was forewarned. Montgomery and Eisenhower learned of the disaster at the same time. Bradley recommended that the 29th be withdrawn and Omaha written off. It was doubtful that the decimated 116th already precariously positioned inland could resist the armoured force that had broken the 1st Division. They were a National Guard Division, for God's sake! How could they do better than the regular 1st Division? Could the British accept Omaha's second echelon divisions in their sector? Utah was in danger too. Montgomery encouraged him to 'fight it out, Brad. Don't Dunkirk on us.' Eisenhower supported his land forces commander. Fight it out, and prepare the 2nd Infantry Division to be put ashore immediately behind the 29th. Privately, Montgomery was more pessimistic. He immediately asked General Dempsey if his 2nd Army beachheads could accept V Corps' follow-on divisions. Yes, they could.

Wünsche had taken hours to get off the beach after resistance had collapsed. Thousands of prisoners had to be rounded up, and the draw was choked with bodies, debris and wrecked vehicles. It was not until early evening (1930) that his battle group was on the road again. He was proud of his men; they had conducted themselves like veterans and achieved an incredible victory in crushing this beachhead, a victory of the kind the Germans had not tasted since 1942. And the cost had been fewer than two hundred men out of his 2,500. His staff estimated that they had taken at least 5,000 prisoners. Their enthusiasm seemed boundless now. He would have to husband it carefully.

The night road-movement proved to be more difficult than the battle. Not all the Americans had been rounded up. Many small groups had melted into the countryside, and in the darkness clashed with his battle group. No firefight had been serious, only time-consuming. He was met by Kraiss at Formigny late that night (2213) when the battle group closed on the village and briefed on the situation to the west. The Americans had overwhelmed the coastal defence around the Les Moulins and Vierville Draws and were digging in further inland. Vierville was a strongpoint, it seemed. At least another infantry regiment had joined them as well as tanks and artillery had come ashore. Kraiss had attacked Vierville with his entire 915th Regiment but had been repulsed. Casualties had been heavy among his young Saxon soldiers. They had bounced off the Americans like a stonewall. At least the guns on Pointe-du-Hoc had been saved by a swift counterattack by the 914th. They had the remnants of an American commando battalion penned up on the tip of the cliff, and the guns continued to pound the landing beaches. The Americans had to be destroyed tomorrow at the latest or they would push so many troops through the beachhead that they could not be driven back into the sea. Available for the attack were Wünsche's battle group, a rocket launcher regiment being rushed forward by 7th Army, the 915th and most of the 914th Regiments, the 352nd Division's engineer battalion, and three artillery battalions. The rest of his division had either been overrun or pushed back by the British to the west where they were barely holding on outside of Bayeux. His division had one last effort left in it.

The Stonewallers and the Price of Tradition

While Kraiss and Wünsche were conferring, the 29th's commander, Major General Charles Gerhardt, came ashore. The plan had called for him to wait until the following day when enough of his men were to have been landed for Huebner to pass command to him. Now the plan and Huebner were gone, and it was a whole new game. Gerhardt was a tough, unrelenting man. He had worked his division hard in training and was not about to see it crushed on the beach. He and his staff came in behind the Marylanders of the 115th. The artillery regiment and the antitank battalion were just behind. Destroyers had laid enough smoke to obscure the aim of the guns at Pointe-du-Hoc and casualties had been acceptable. The battleships and cruisers of Admiral Kirk's task force were keeping up a constant drumbeat on the battery, hoping at least to neutralize its fire while the rest of the division got ashore. The Rangers had been evacuated in the night from their bitter toe-hold on the cliff. All through the night, scattered survivors from the Colleville disaster crossed through the 29th's lines. Many straggled down the beach, and the largest group, an entire battalion of the 18th Regiment that had been moving cross country when the Germans attacked down the draw, came in through the Marylanders outside St. Laurent. Gerhardt joined Cota outside of Vierville where the main line of resistance had been set up. Exhaustion had fallen over the remnants of the

Stonewallers. Men were sleeping were they could and could not be roused. The accumulated stress of the landings, the attacks over the bluffs, and finally the German infantry counterattack had emptied them of physical and mental reserves. Gerhardt was more concerned about getting the fresher 115th in defensible positions by morning and landing the division's third regiment, the 175th, just after midnight. The surviving regiment of the Big Red One, the 26th, had been attached to Gerhardt as well. They could start landing in the morning. The 29th had to be ready for a stronger counterattack that would hit them in the morning. The tanks that had crushed the 1st Division were still out there.

One of Marcks' couriers had found the commander of the 25th SS Panzergrenadier Regiment outside of St. Lô. Known as 'Panzermeyer', SS Standartenführer (Colonel) Kurt Meyer had an acute sense of hearing for the 'sound of the guns'. In his wake was not only his own powerful regiment but the rest of the 12th SS, over ten thousand men in all. The tanks were all with Wünsche and Witt, but the 12th Jagdpanzer Battalion had twelve of the new Jagdpanzer IVs. There were also plenty of dual purpose flak guns as well as most of the artillery regiment. He stopped long enough in St. Lô to find out from the LXXXIV Corps chief of staff where the enemy was. He was directed toward Vierville to counterattack immediately.

By nightfall, he was filtering his battle group into position for a break-in that would lead him straight to the draws through which the enemy was being reinforced. He peremptorily attached the 915th Regiment already in position. Kraiss swallowed his resentment and agreed. Panzermeyer was on the spot and ready. Kraiss would not be ready until tomorrow.

At 0200 on the morning of the 7 June, he attacked. Artillery fell into both the Vierville and Les Moulins draws, severing the troops inland from their lifeline to the beach. The Jagdpanzers fired their high velocity 75mms straight down the roads leading into the American positions and raced forward, the panzergrenadiers following in their armoured personnel carriers mixed with flak and self-propelled guns. As usual Meyer led the attack in his favourite command vehicle, a motorcycle. Both draws had been crowded with human and soft-skinned vehicle traffic moving up from the beach. Orange bursts of exploding shells lit the draw. Within minutes it was filled with shredded corpses, twisted equipment, and burning vehicles. The fire shifted then to the beaches which were equally packed. The Germans were through the American perimeter around Vierville in the first rush. Panzermeyer was behind the first company when the Americans began to react. Tanks emerged from the darkness firing into his still mounted grenadiers. The two lead Jagdpanzers were hit from the rear by a combination of antitank guns and tanks. They began to burn.

Meyer was not about to shrink back, nor were his young grenadiers. They had quickly dismounted and were attacking in the dark led by their veteran officers and NCOs. The battalions of the 915th Regiment were attacking around the perimeter as well. First Lieutenant Edward H. Lawson of Charlottesville remembered:

> The village caught fire and the moon was out so there was plenty of light. The Navy was firing illumination shells too. The Germans just kept coming. My platoon was down to seven men when they rushed us. Sergeant Collins' face disappeared. Then they were among us. I shot one, two, then felt a hammer hit my chest and blacked out. I woke later that night. The fighting had passed, and there were only dead men around me. All of my seven and other young faces in those cloth-covered German helmets. The German medics found me in the morning.[10]

Slowly the Stonewallers were pressed back through Vierville towards the draw. The hedgerows thinned out here along the bluff offering no protection to the short German rushes that had moved their attack forward so far. Naval gunfire lashed with high explosive and steel splinters the open ground that the Germans could not cross. It was cold comfort for Gerhardt. His division was bleeding to death. He doubted if the Stonewallers could muster a fit battalion now. They were played out and holding on by fingernails that could only slip. The 115th was fresher but had been pushed back to the Les Moulins draw as well. Reinforcements would only bunch up on the beach. The wounded now seemed to outnumber the unwounded. He reluctantly recommended the 29th be withdrawn.

General Gerow (5th Corps Commander) passed on the recommendation to Bradley aboard the *Augusta*. His great jaw set, then he said, 'Stop all reinforcement. Bring them off.' To the Navy's eternal credit, they did just that in the few remaining hours of darkness and the early morning. Naval gunfire kept the Germans at bay as first the wounded then the troops on the beach and finally the wasted infantry companies were one by one sent to the beach. The Germans did not cooperate. Panzermeyer's artillery and that of the 352nd continued to pound the draws and the beach adding to the butcher's bill paid by the 29th. Navy Lieutenant Jeffery Nelson was on one of the landing craft shuttling from the beach to the ships. By his third trip, the inch of water on the metal deck was pink. The wounded were being packed aboard as quickly as possible. Many of them were struck by shrapnel or high explosive as they filed down the beach and carried aboard bleeding. By the seventh trip in the early morning, the water on the deck was deep red. Everything except personal weapons was ordered to be abandoned. Corporal Peter Johnston, 2nd Battalion, 116th Regiment was one of those filing down the beach. His own Garand had been blown out of his hands in Vierville, but he saw his grim-faced division commander whose reputation as a razor-tongued martinet overwhelmed Johnston's fatigue. He snatched another rifle from the debris strewn about everywhere and passed the general with relief. Gerhardt was the last man off the beach.

Gerhardt stepped into the landing craft almost exactly twenty-three hours after the 1st and 29th Divisions had approached the shore of Normandy. It had been the bloodiest day for the U.S. Army since Antietam in 1862.

V Corps Losses at Omaha Beach
6 June 1944

Unwounded POWs	8,626
Wounded POWs	2,712
Evacuated Wounded	3,391
Killed	2,311
Missing	884
Total	17,924

Source: The Adjutant General, *Losses in the ETO, 1944*
(Washington, D.C.: Government Printing Office, 1948)
p.32.

Utah Beach, 0630

The first blow at the Germans defending Utah Beach, as at all the beaches, was struck from the air, here by 360 B-24 bombers of the U.S. IX Bomber Command. Flying at a lower altitude than at Omaha Beach, they had a better chance visually to identify their targets. However, about a third of their bombs still fell seaward of the beach high water mark, and many of their targets were not located at all. As at Omaha, the Army Air Force's contribution was negligible.

Shore Batteries vs the U.S. Navy

The noise of bombardment, however, awoke Leutnant Arthur Jahnke, commander of blockhouse W5 on Utah Beach. A week before, General Marcks had held a small parade in front of the blockhouse to pin the Iron Cross First Class on Jahnke for his service in Russia. Jahnke was also surprised to hear gunfire coming from the direction of Ste.-Marie-du-Mont and sent a patrol to find out what was happening. They returned with several American prisoners and the news that a battle was raging in the village. The Americans were being driven out of it and toward Houdienville, the village at the western end of a causeway that led over an area inundated with water, straight onto the beach and W5. He was immediately presented with a choice of crises as the invasion fleet opened fire, and his blockhouse started to crumble. It was 0550.

As the dawn began to illuminate the armada lying offshore, German coastal batteries began firing at 0535. Jahnke's battery had never been notified. Fifteen minutes later the U.S. Navy began the prearranged counterbattery fire that began to shake W5 apart. In less than half an hour W5 was inoperative, its 50mm, 75mm, and 88mm guns all disabled. Jahnke was wounded, and those of his men who had not been killed had been stunned by the ear-bursting violence of the bombardment. The naval guns kept pounding their targets until the first landing craft hit the beach.

Further up the coast, the casemated army battery at Azeville and the naval battery at St. Marcouf, were having much better luck. At 0500, the commander of the 210mm naval battery, Lieutenant Ohmsen, picked up the phone to call his superior, Admiral Henecke, the commander of naval forces in Cherbourg. 'Several hundred ships sighted in the Bay of the Seine. Question: Any German vessels at sea?' The admiral paused shortly for the message to sink in, 'No. None of our vessels at sea. Any vessels sighted bound to be enemy ships. Permission to open fire. Ammunition to be used sparingly. Message ends. Out.'[11]

The Germans and Americans opened fire simultaneously, and both with unerring accuracy. The U.S. Navy's gunnery dropped shells right on top of the battery. The German gunners had old-fashioned sights for their guns and needed to bracket their first target before getting a hit. But when they did, the 210mm shell, slightly bigger than an 8-inch, struck a destroyer between funnel and bridge. Thinking it was a cruiser, an understandable error at that range, the Germans cheered as smoke poured out of the ship and its bow and stern rose as it broke in two at the middle. 'That's the stuff! Keep it up,' shouted Ohmsen to his gunners. The Americans got the next good hit and wrecked one of the guns, but the Germans thought the trade acceptable, 'An American warship for one gun! That's not a bad swap.' They hit another destroyer and then a third was hit by another battery further up the coast. 'The destroyer tried to evade the shelling by zigzagging. But she suffered hit after hit. One shell apparently struck her rudder, for she kept going round in circles. Eventually she stopped. She listed to port. Her after-deck was slipping deeper and deeper into the water.'[12]

In their fury, the Americans concentrated the fire of their three battleships, USS *Nevada*, *Arkansas*, and *Texas* against the battery. At 0990 one of the *Nevada*'s fourteen-inch shells struck right through the embrasure of No. 2 gun. The twenty by twenty-six foot armoured door for the casemate had been shipped from the depot in Bad Segeberg but had never arrived and was probably lost in some bombed out French railway station or waiting on some siding with countless other vital parts. With both guns destroyed that could fire out to sea, Ohmsen directed the fire of his third gun onto the beaches that were alive with landing craft and troops.

'Teddy' Roosevelt in the First Wave

The U.S. 4th Infantry Division was coming ashore in a column of regiments, led by the 8th, to be followed by the 22nd and 12th. A fourth regiment, the 359th attached from the 90th Infantry Division, would land last on D-Day. The 4th hoped to quickly overwhelm the beach defences and to rush across the northern three of four beach exits, the western ends of which all should be held by the 101st Airborne Division. The 8th Infantry Regiment was to seize the third exit and push down the road from Ste.-Marie-du-Mont to les Forges and then cross the Merderet to link up with the 82nd Airborne Division. The 22nd would push north and seize the fourth exit at les Dunes de Varreville and continue north to take Quienville and its high ground. The 12th Infantry Regiment would follow them over the exits and move to the high ground northeast of Ste.-Mère-Eglise held by the 82nd Airborne. By the end of D-Day a large triangular beachhead was to have its base running from Quienville to the mouth of the Vire and its point stretching across the Merderet River. The plan all depended on the two airborne divisions to seize crossings over the Douve River running through Carentan, the beach exits, the communications hub of Ste.-Mère-Eglise, and the bridgeheads over the Merderet.

Unknown to the invasion force speeding to the beach, both airborne divisions were in serious trouble. The 82nd had failed to take the Merderet bridgeheads and was barely holding on to Ste.-Mère-Eglise against elements of an SS panzer battle group and two infantry regiments. The 101st had failed to take the Douve crossings and had secured only the third and fourth beach exits. The paratroopers of three understrength battalions were at this moment being driven out of Ste.-Marie-du-Mont and into the second and first beach exits by another SS panzer battle group. As they withdrew eastward toward the beach exits, they could hear the rumble of heavy artillery hitting the coastal defences. At the same time most of the German 6th Fallschirmjäger Regiment was passing through Carentan to reinforce the two German battle groups.

As at the other beaches the infantry was to be preceded in the first wave by D-D tanks launched two instead of four miles from shore as originally planned. Someone showed enough common sense and initiative to change the order when rough seas made it manifestly suicidal to launch that far out. The Germans threw this part of the landing plan out of sequence when the tanks' control craft struck a mine and leaped out of the water like a breaching whale and exploded. The loss of the control craft put back the launching of the D-Ds by fifteen minutes. Disaster clung to them as the first craft to let down its ramp dropped it onto another submerged mine. On another LCT, Sergeant Orris Johnson watched as the front of the LCT shot upwards and watched as a tank 'soared more than a hundred feet into the air, tumbled slowly end over end, plunged back into the water and disappeared.'[13] The other LCTs launched their D-Ds into relatively calm sea sheltered by the Cotentin Peninsula. All surviving twenty-eight made it ashore, right after the infantry.

Luckily, the coastal current that was playing havoc with the Omaha landings at the same time set the two-battalion assault wave of the 8th Infantry Regiment down 2,000 yards south of the intended Utah Beach. They rushed ashore through sparse beach obstacles against weak German resistance. Had they landed where they had planned, they would have found a much stronger defence. As it was, the infantry had little need for the tanks to precede them over the beach. Engineers blew holes through the sea wall, and the tanks and infantry poured through to mop up the demoralized defenders. Jahnke had tried to crank up his mini-tanks called Goliaths, small tracked vehicles carrying explosives meant to be sent into the crowded assault waves as they struggled ashore. None would start. By then it didn't matter anymore. The Americans were all around W5 ready to blow it open. Jahnke surrendered his position.

Moving among the American troops was the feisty and arthritic assistant division commander, Brigadier General Theodore Roosevelt, Jr., able son of a beloved president, a man of singular determination and good judgment. He was the only Allied general officer to come over the beaches with the first wave that day. Cota of the 29th had come in shortly after the first wave. His presence there was no part of the plan. Unable to bear not sharing the dangers of his men, he wheedled a reluctant permission out of his division commander. He leaned on his cane, map in hand, by one of the few tetrahedrons on the beach with members of his staff around him. A fast map study revealed that they had landed on the wrong beach, some 2,000 yards south of where they had planned. With the rest of the division about to arrive in quick succession on 'some' beach, Roosevelt jabbed his cane into the sand and decided that they would follow onto this beach, where the battle had been joined. They would seize whatever opportunities now presented themselves. To do so they had to get inland. He dispatched his two leading battalions with tank companies from the 746th to the third and first beach exits. The 3/8th and the 70th Tank Battalion, which were just landing, he directed to exit two. The 3/22 was also landing and would be sent north to begin the drive on Quienville. The 4th Division had been lucky so far. The coastal defence had been broken with fewer than 200 casualties.

Houdienville and the Battle for the Causeway

Both the luck and the opportunities were about to desert them. Roosevelt ordered the battalion commanders to seize and cross the three nearby causeway exits over the inundated areas behind the beaches and dunes and make contact with the 101st Airborne. The Screaming Eagles, however, were bringing the contact to them. Fewer than three hundred had escaped the German attack on Ste.-Marie-du-Mont to barricade themselves in villages of Houdienville and Poupeville covering the access to the causeways on western side of the inundated areas. The panzergrenadiers of Hitlerjugend had harried them all the way, but the hedgerows made every few yards a good delaying or ambush point. They broke up into two groups. The smaller moved off to the southeast

towards Poupeville and exit one. The larger group entered Houdienville to
cover exit two. Many of the less than 200 paratroopers who reached the villages
were wounded. Few had much ammunition left. If they lost this village the
landings behind them would be smashed on the beach. Following them was the
mixed battle group of SS and Fallschirmjägers sent by Hitlerjugend's commander. Sturmbann führer Prinz sent one tank company, under Ober-
sturmführer Ernst Kiesch, with the Fallschirmjäger battalion riding on the
tanks after the smaller group of Americans. He pursued the larger group with
his remaining tank company and his panzergrenadiers. The reconnaissance
battalion, he put in reserve.

The American paratroopers had barely set up a hasty defence in Houdienville
to repel the following Germans when from across the causeway a crowd of
Germans came running towards them from the beach. Waiting until the
Germans were close, they opened fire. About seventy were cut down before the
survivors threw down their weapons and surrendered. Prisoners explained they
were fleeing the invasion. A patrol got halfway across the causeway when it ran
into the advance elements of the 3rd Battalion, 8th Infantry. They were hurried
along to the beach as the infantry mounted the Shermans of the 70th Tank
Battalion in their column and raced into the village. The panzergrenadiers had
crashed into the village about the same time with a company of the battle
group's Mark IVs in support. The Germans and Americans collided in a
meeting engagement like two locomotives.

As the German and American tanks raced into the little village square at the
same time, the reaction time of the lead German tank was faster. It fired the
critical first shot through the turret of a Sherman which burst into flames. The
following Sherman was faster still and killed the Mark IV and the one behind it.
The 25-ton Mark IV and the 32-ton Sherman were evenly matched in relia-
bility and killing power, especially at close range. There was no advantage in
equipment, only in training and courage. The battle now engulfed the village
and spilled into the nearby fields as each side tried to get around the other's
flank. The Shermans and Mark IVs were firing at point blank range in the
narrow village streets. Little stone houses collapsed as long-barrelled German
75mms or short-barrelled American 75mms fired into doorways chasing squads
of infantry. Against each other, the tanks were equal in armour and guns. There
were no Panthers or Tigers here today whose armour was proof against U.S. and
British shot. If there was any advantage, it was in the faster turret traverse of
the Sherman. Sturmbannführer Prinz was a Russian Front veteran, faster on his
feet to use all his resources than his less experienced American opponent. He
called in artillery from his accompanying self-propelled battery. The fire fell on
the end of the causeway across the Americans' rear, causing heavy casualties in
the reserve company that had been stopped there. His American opposite also
had fire support, in the form of a naval fire control party. With the village

splintering around them, the fire controllers called in their fire missions. The battleship USS *Nevada* and the cruisers USS *Tuscaloosa* and *Quincy* and HMS *Black Prince* responded. Sheets of steel began raining down on outskirts of the village and among the houses themselves. The Germans were stopped cold by the barrage that reminded the veterans of the fury of massed Russian artillery. Tanks were tossed on their backs and halftracks disintegrated by the naval rifles that pounded the ruined village, pounding its broken stone into finer and finer fragments. Prinz died as his command tank was bracketed by a salvo from *Black Prince*'s guns. His operations officer kept his head and got the survivors back into the cover of the hedgerows to their rear.

The Battle on the Beach

The paratroopers heading for Poupeville had longer to go over country not so restricted by hedgerows. There had been fewer than one hundred left in the group, and it was just too far to the village. The panzers were faster and ran them down half way there. A few dispersed into the hedgerows. The remaining eighty-three surrendered. Sturmbannführer Kiesch was impatient to move on; he was only twenty-two and a child of the Russian Front. What he did next was easy. He lined them up on the road and machine-gunned them down, to the horror of the Fallschirmjägers who had climbed back on the tanks. The tanks roared to life and sped down the road toward the first beach exit.

The tanks of C/746th Tank Battalion were in the lead of the 2/8th task force that had just passed through Poupeville when they heard the machine guns from the southwest. The task force commander ordered them to speed to the sound of the guns. Again the Germans reacted faster. Inadequate reconnaissance led the Americans right into the tank ambush hastily set up by the panzer company which had sent out adequate reconnaissance. In a few minutes ten Shermans were burning, and the Mark IVs moved out to attack the infantry before they could dig in. A battery of 57mm antitank guns shot up two of the Mark IVs before they were blown away. Another two Mark IVs fell victim to the remaining five Shermans. These were trying to back up over hedgerows and getting hung up. Each was hit and burned, catching fifty yards of hedgerow on fire. The German tanks kept moving with the Fallschirmjägers following to drive the Americans back down the road. The Germans shouldered the 2/8th off the road and drove through the village to the causeway. Leaving one company of Fallschirmjägers to guard the entrance, fifteen Mark IVs with the rest of the German paratroopers riding atop advanced over the causeway.

Roosevelt's attention had been focused on the battle at Houdienville. It was suddenly torn to the south as shells started screaming laterally down the beach from that direction. Advancing down the coast road and across the beach were a wave of German tanks with infantry in the rear. They overran engineers and rear elements of the 8th Regiment, shooting directly into the landing craft lining the beach emptying the following battalions of the 22nd Infantry. An anti-aircraft battery near Roosevelt turned its quad fifty calibre machine guns towards the Germans, cutting down many of the following Fallschirmjägers. A destroyer, the USS *Butler* ran inshore parallel to the attack flinging its five-inch shells at the tanks and infantry moving down the beach until its guns grew red, picking off one tank after another at 800 yards. Getting closer and closer to the shore, the *Butler* ran aground with a force that threw its crew to the deck. They were on their feet again as the ship resumed firing. More destroyers raced towards the shore to add to the growing enfilade fire. The bigger ships were now joining the fight with cruisers USS *Hawkins* and HMS *Enterprise* dropping their heavier projectiles into the centre of mass of the Germans. Like a piece of paper thrown into the fire, the German attack flared, burned, and collapsed into ashes. The few survivors were running towards the dunes.

The attack had been broken but had badly disrupted landing operations and caused severe casualties on the beach. Not the least had been Brigadier General Theodore Roosevelt, Jr. who had fallen at the side of the quad fifty battery of a heart attack.

The Siege of Ste.-Mère-Eglise

When SS Brigadeführer Fritz Witt sent half of his battle group towards the coast, he had continued pressing north against the American paratroopers with the other half. As Prinz began his attack on Houdienville, Witt began his attack on the Americans holding a line on the edge of les Forges about two miles south of Ste.-Mère-Eglise. The guns of Witt's two Mark IV companies began firing directly into the American positions along the hedgerows. The few American antitank weapons were quickly outclassed. His two companies of panzergrenadiers pressed forward under the cover of the tanks as the Americans withdrew from the hedgerow line.

Matthew Ridgway's 82nd Airborne Division was in the centre of a vice. His division had been badly scattered in the drop, and he had been able to assemble only 1,400 men, and not all of them from his division; he must have had at least a hundred from the 101st. This was less than the strength of one of his regi-ments that had jumped the night before. In the early morning hours, his 3/505th Parachute Infantry had seized the key objective of Ste.-Mère-Eglise with fewer than two hundred men. The 2/503rd with about 400 men was just north of the town, and the 1/503rd was at the eastern end of the crossing of the Merderet River at la Fiere with about five hundred men. Several hundred more were roaming lost in the two mile-diameter circle with Ste.-Mère-Eglise on one side and les Forges on the other. Pressing up against the circle from the south was a strong panzer force that had fought its way up from Carentan in the predawn hours past small groups of scattered paratroopers. As he gathered more and more men, he had sent them to block this force at les Forges. Other men who came in from the east reported a German infantry force between them and the coast. He had little word so far from his other two regiments dropped west of the Merderet River and no word of the landings at all. The immediate threat would be from the German tanks attacking les Forges, and his only recourse was to concentrate his strength for the defence of Ste.-Mère-Eglise. His dilemma was that other than the small battalion already there, the Germans were closer to the town than his other two battalions. And the Germans were driving while his men were on foot. He could hear the firing to the south coming closer, and he knew that his ragtag force would not be able to hold the Germans for very long. It was about 0830 when the RAF fighter bombers arrived over the town and circled. So his prayers had been answered after all! He quickly directed them to the fighting in the south.

Witt's men had pushed to almost to Fauville, a mile from Ste.-Mère-Eglise when the RAF Jabos (Jagdbombers – fighter-bombers) attacked. Firing rockets and strafing with 20mm cannons, the Typhoons made pass after pass. They circled for fifteen minutes, swooping in pairs to chase one vehicle after another to its death. The section of 20mm flak halftracks commanded by Oberscharführer (Sergeant) Willi Stempel put up a brave defence. He brought one of the planes down to crash next to a burning tank and sent another one trailing smoke off into the distance. When they left, fifteen armoured vehicles had been destroyed or disabled and over 120 men killed and wounded.

All over the Cotentin Peninsula that morning, orders, both German and American, were going astray in the confusion. American paratroopers were still roaming in small groups all over the drop zones, clashing with German patrols. The rash of small contacts was overwhelming the ability of German tactical intelligence to find patterns, except one. The main road between Cherbourg and Carentan had been cut and the Americans held Ste.-Mère-Eglise. The units that Rommel had sent into the Carentan in the dark of the morning had known about as much and had developed the situation by finding the enemy and engaging him. Witt's battle group had dispersed into the hedgerows, hamlets, and woods after the morning's air and naval gunfire attacks. The SS made contact east of the town with the 795th Georgian Battalion, a reserve unit of the 709th Division defending the coast. Witt immediately placed them under his command and put them on the high ground west of the town, able to attack east or defend west. He also began gathering the various flak and artillery units scattered within his reach. By 1100 he had gained a sketchy but fairly accurate picture of what was going on in the Cotentin. A simple climb into a village church bell tower eloquently explained the massive landings underway. The Georgian battalion had reported not only American paratroopers to the east but tanks and infantry as well. To the north of the Georgians, the German inland fortifications were heavily engaged with the tanks and infantry. To the south, the other half of his battle group was digging in around Houdienville after some nasty fighting that kept the Americans from breaking out across the inundated areas behind the beaches. He had contact with both regiments of the 91st Division, though the division headquarters seemed confused and sluggish. Their commander had not returned from the wargame at Rennes. At least, the 91st's two regiments were pressing on Ste.-Mère-Eglise from the north and west. He was on the south and the Georgians were on the east.

By noon he had reestablished contact with Marcks at LXXXIV Corps, and by 1300 with Pemsel at 7th Army. As senior officer in the Cotentin, Pemsel placed him in command of all forces around the lodgement to include the 91st and 709th Divisions. Pemsel ordered him first to stabilize the situation by preventing the Americans from expanding their lodgement and linking up with their paratroopers in Ste.-Mère-Eglise, and then to counterattack to take the town and smash the Americans on the beach. Reinforcements were on the way. Seventh Army's Sturm Battalion, the 100th Panzer Battalion, a flak regiment, and a regiment-sized battle group from the 243rd Division on the west coast of the Cotentin had been given orders to move out immediately. Unfortunately, there would be no panzer reserves. OKW had not released any, and they would be likely to go to the crisis around Caen first.

Witt's own 12th SS Panzer Division Headquarters was arriving in the area, badly harassed by the Jabos. They would have suffered more had not a strong element of the division flak battalion been along as escort. At last, he had a proper division staff and communications about him to run a proper battle. At about 1330 the main body of the strong 3,500 man 6th Parachute Regiment, minus its 1st battalion already committed and destroyed behind the tanks on the beach, was passing over the causeway north out of Carentan. The 6th was as elite as the 12th SS; recruited from teenage volunteers and cadre with veterans. Average age of the enlisted ranks was seventeen-and-a-half. It was much better equipped than the standard German infantry regiment. Each company had twice as many light machine guns as its army counterpart, and the heavy weapons companies with twelve heavy machine guns and six mortars each were much superior as well. Witt immediately sent them to reinforce the defence around Houdienville and Poupeville with orders to relieve the other half of his battle group and reconnaissance battalion which was to join him. His repeated attempts to contact the rest of his division around Lisieux got him nowhere. He desperately needed the extra panzergrenadier regiment, and the assault gun battalion and engineer battalions. Just as much he needed the support units without which he could not fight much longer. Another call to Pemsel. They had been detached as 7th Army reserve. Witt would have to make do with what local reserves 7th Army had already designated. That was the dilemma. He would have to crush the Americans in Ste.-Mère-Eglise before he could mass enough forces to strike the beachhead which was every minute straining to expand. But he couldn't take too long or the beachhead would be too strong to break. The town had to fall quickly, and it would have to be down under the cloak of night. Getting a grip on the German units in the area and coordinating a night attack presented even greater problems. If he had had his complete division with him, it would not be a problem. Hitlerjugend responded to his command like a well-trained team of spirited horses. He had only a small part of it under his direct command. The rest of the team were assorted nags and plough horses.

Major General Raymond Barton had come ashore soon after Roosevelt's death. There had been no loss of control, but the situation was developing badly as he saw it. The 8th Infantry had been badly handled trying to get through the two southern exits over the flooded areas. The Germans still held Poupeville and the end of the causeway. They had fallen back to good defensive positions in the hedgerows around Houdienville; two attacks out of the town had been shot up by the German tanks and 88s. The 1/8th with one tank company had managed to cross the Varreville exit but had run into a strong German force within two miles. The 22nd Infantry had attacked with one battalion to the right of the 1/8th and been stopped by strong German inland fortifications around Foucarville, and another battalion along the coast was also stalled at a German resistance point at Hamel de Cruttes. There were also several small battalions of the 101st Airborne fighting with his battalions. Most of his tanks were bottled up around Houdienville. The 12th Infantry could not get ashore until late that day and the 359th not until the next morning. He was completely committed, with only one battalion of the 22nd in reserve, and completely stopped, and nowhere near his D-Day objective line.

The bone rammed into the throat of German communications before dawn at Ste.-Mère-Eglise was about to be reinforced by Colonel Vandervoort's 2/505th. By dawn he had collected 575 of his 630 men, by far the best assembly record of any battalion that day. He led his battalion from a farmer's wheelbarrow due to a broken leg suffered in the jump. Initially he had moved to block a German counterattack from the north of Ste.-Mère-Eglise down Highway 13. In a confusion of contradicting orders, he moved on Ste.-Mère-Eglise, leaving a platoon, commanded by Lieutenant Turner Turnbull, a half-Cherokee paratrooper, at Neuville to the north of the town. It was not long before an infantry company from the German 1058th Regiment showed up marching and singing down the road. A burst of machine gun fire sent them to earth. With the relentless aggressiveness of the German Army, the company began working its way around the platoon. Turnbull conducted a masterful defence, keeping them at bay for hours. At one point, Colonel Vandervoort arrived in a jeep he had pulled out of glider, towing a 57mm antitank gun which he turned over to Turnbull who told him, 'OK, everything under control, don't worry about me.' The colonel unhooked the gun and left. Just in time. The Germans brought up a self-propelled gun and a Mark IV tank to lead the attack. Turnbull's men destroyed them both with two well-aimed shots from the antitank gun. Now that it was infantry against infantry, Turnbull extracted every ounce of advantage from the defence and his considerable store of ammunition until late afternoon when the Germans had just about surrounded them. With more than half his men dead and wounded, Turnbull seized the last advantage and led the survivors of his platoon through the narrow gap in the closing German ring. Turnbull had held the German counterattack north of Ste.-Mère-Eglise long enough for the town to be thoroughly secured. Ridgway was to have more than enough to deal with from the south of the town along the Carentan road.

By dusk, the 82nd's commander had a strong and tight perimeter around the town. He had a little over 1,500 men, mostly from the 505th with stragglers from the other two regiments and the 101st. Ammunition was going to be a problem soon if they and the 4th Division did not link up quickly. An airborne division did not carry much in the way of logistics into battle but depended upon a rapid closure by advancing ground forces. The paratroopers had improvised the lack of transportation by requisitioning horses and running mounted patrols through the town and outlying countryside. Unknown to each other, both Witt and Ridgway were developing similar and complementing pictures of the battle. Ridgway concluded that he would have to hold until relieved, and that as long as he held onto this communications windpipe, the Germans could never get a deep enough breath to power a serious push against the 4th Division. And that was his mission, to support the expansion of the lodgement by Barton's division. The longer he could hold, the weaker would be Barton's opposition. But he had only a fraction of his division under his command. He had one big ace up his sleeve, though. Supplies and equipment were to arrive by glider this evening. His fourth regiment, the 325th Glider Infantry, was due to land next morning in the vicinity of the town. The additional 1,500 men and the supplies brought in by glider could just see them through.

Witt's plan was to attack about an hour after dusk fell on the long June day, about 2030. He was to be joined by the other half of his battle group as soon as they had been relieved in place by 6th Fallschirmjäger. His SS would be reinforced by a battalion of 1058th Regiment ordered up from Carentan so that the attack could go in from south as well as southwest of the town. The other half of his nutcracker would be the 1057th Infantry Regiment attacking from the north. They had edged closer to the town after the lengthy delay caused by Lieutenant Turnbull and his gallant platoon. The Georgians just by holding in to the east would do enough. The minutes to the attack fell away, and still no sign of the rest of his battle group. Most of the 1058th's battalion was in place. 2045 . . . 2050 . . . 2100 . . . the sound of machine engines carried through the night. But not quite the right pitch. They were aircraft engines. The moonlit sky quickly showed up a glider stream approaching the area between les Forges and Fauville. The tracers reached up across the terrain. Every German weapon that could serve as anti-aircraft was searching for targets. Stempel's battery now had more company, with 88s and quad-barrelled 20mms. Dozens of gliders were released right over them. Some splintered and flew apart, others flamed as the flak found fuel or ammunition. Others that survived the flak snapped apart among the Rommel's Asparagus that dotted the landing fields. Fire swept the downed aircraft, setting more alight. The Germans would count thirty wrecks the next day. Now their infantry rushed out to hunt down those lucky enough to have escaped alive. The men that had ridden in on the gliders had not been combat units, but were the support for the beleaguered men in Ste.-Mère-Eglise. A few hid in the woods and hedgerows, but the rest were killed or captured. The gliders that had not been destroyed gave up a treasure for the Germans in fuel, medical supplies, and food. The teenage SS were agog at such things as canned peaches, chocolate bars, and condensed milk in such quantity. Witt was more pleased with the ammunition and antitank guns that would not help the Americans.

Unknown to Witt, another serial of gliders landed north of the town at the same time. These landed close enough to the town for the paratroopers to rescue most of the crews and their cargos. The 57mm antitank guns and their crews were the real prizes that night. Each found a place in the defences as they were driven into down behind jeeps that had accompanied them. Small arms and machine gun ammunition was also thankfully replenished. Though the fate of the first serial was being decided only a few miles away, the Americans in Ste.-Mère-Eglise didn't notice it at all. By this time, the accumulated stress of the last thirty-six hours was taking its toll. Men were simply winding down. It had been Ridgway's special brand of leadership that had been their mainspring so far. His 'perpetual drive, his habitual boring forward to the zone of personally aimed fire, his inquiring mind and his persistent question to any subordinate: "Do you know anything that will help me right now?"' had wrung out of elite troops even more than could be expected.[14] They were in place and ready around the town, but now even they ran down.

German bodies, even elite ones, also ran down, as Witt was discovering about the same time. The destruction of the glider landing had used up and disorganized his battle group. Only about midnight did the other half of his force arrive from Houdienville. Putting the infantry of the 1058th in the line, he pulled back his battered battle group for a rest.

While his men found the sleep that soldiers can snatch at will out of any time and place, Witt stayed awake fretting. Twice he had tried to move on the town, and twice had been prevented, first by the air strike and second by the unexpected glider landing. He worried about time. Would there be enough to break the American paratroopers in the town tomorrow before the forces moving inland could relieve them? Would those forces be too strong to dislodge by then even if he took the town? His reinforcements were meagre. Where were the panzer reserves? A battle group like his could only stretch so far. He wasn't fully aware of the extent of the American lodgement on the Carentan, but what he knew was faintly encouraging. They were bottled up on the southern half of their beachhead and had only pushed inland four or five miles on a rather narrow front pointing toward Ste.-Mère-Eglise. The triangle formed by the town, his position to the south and southeast, and the point of the American penetration inland was obviously the battle's geographic centre of gravity. It was there he would have to strike for the situation to fall their way.

Another general was fretting about the same time over the same situation. Major General J. Lawton Collins, commanding the U.S. VII Corps, had just come ashore at Utah with his staff. His appraisal of the situation would have brightened Witt's pessimism considerably. He was under no illusions. Seventh Corps had been grimly sobered by the collapse of the 1st Division on Omaha; Collins didn't think the 29th would survive the next day. Utah was now the only American beachhead and had failed to meet any of its D-Day objectives. There was a nasty SS panzer unit out there and paratroopers as well, both of them big surprises. Worst of all at the moment was the silence from the 82nd at Ste.-Mère-Eglise. Except for the first signal announcing the fall of the town, no one had heard a thing from Ridgway's men. What was going on there?

Witt had one worry that didn't afflict Collins. Collins hadn't lost Montgomery, after all. Rommel was still missing. The radio traffic from higher headquarters was becoming progressively more hysterical. The German command's peace of mind would not have been improved had it known that as D-Day was coming to a close, Hitler's star commander was a prisoner of war. That afternoon as he worked his way in the direction of Carentan, a huge form shot out of the bushes at him and carried him to the ground. He was looking up at the warpainted face of an American paratrooper who pressed a knife to his throat. His pistol was torn out of his holster by another paratrooper. Together they hauled him to his feet and pushed him through a hole in the hedge to a small barn. Inside were about a dozen more. He was been recognized immediately. What Allied soldier had not seen Rommel's picture countless times? If Sergeant O'Connell had dragged Betty Grable through the barn door, there would have been more surprise, but not much. They had not so much a prisoner as a celebrity on their hands. Second Lieutenant Charles Eberly called the whole band of fifteen men to attention as he saluted. Rommel, every inch a field marshal despite the torn and bloody uniform, returned the courtesy, and then offered his hand. The hardness of the older man's handshake broke through Eberly's rapt attention. The other men pushed forward to shake hands with the great man. Cigarettes, canned fruit, and candy bars were pressed on him. Private Heintzelmann was translating as fast as his boyhood German could handle it. They even asked for autographs. Eventually, Eberley remembered his

official duties and asked for some identification and was duly impressed with
Rommel's paybook. Then he cleared his throat, and asked Heintzelmann, 'Ask
him where the hell we are.'[15]

Witt was trying to pull the battle group back together when Stempel's
section started firing at a new target, small observation aircraft which quickly
moved out of range. A few minutes later, the ground heaved with incoming
artillery of huge calibre. He watched as vehicles were flung about or dissolved in
the enormous spouts of earth and flame. Any dismounted man who hadn't
thrown himself into a ditch or hole was dead. After a ten-minute workover, the
guns stopped. Huge craters dotted the area. Vehicles that the aircraft had left
burning were now overturned twisted piles of metal. Tracks and roadwheels
were the only evidence that some armoured personnel carriers had been there
moments before.

Notes

1. William F. Scott and Harriet Fast Scott, *Two Air Force Lives* (Novato, CA: Presidio Press, 1983) p.248.
2. Joseph Balkoski, *Beyond the Beachhead: The 29th Division in Normandy* (Harrisburg, PA: Stackpole Books, 1989) p.124.
3. Balkoski, ibid.
4. Landing Craft Assault (LCA) was a small wooden craft for ship-to-shore movement of assault infantry. In 1938, the British gave up the idea of one all-purpose landing craft and recognized the need for specialization of landing craft types. The LCA prototype was developed in 1938, and the first large orders for LCAs were placed in September 1939 and subcontracted to small boat and yacht firms. The engines came from the United States.
5. Cornelius Ryan, *The Longest Day* (New York: Simon and Schuster, 1959) p.203; (London: Gollancz, 1960).
6. Balkoski, *Beyond the Beachhead*, p.132.
7. Ryan, *The Longest Day*, p.259.
8. Balkoski, *Beyond the Beachhead*, p.140.
9. Alan G. Kirk, *Witness to Normandy* (New York: Dodd, Mead, 1947) p.188.
10. George C. Jackson, *Virginians in Battle* (Lexington, VA: Virginia Military Institute Press, 1954) p.165.
11. Paul Carrell, *Invasion: They're Coming* (London: Harrap, 1962); (New York: Bantam, 1964) pp.127–128.
12. Carrell, ibid., p.128.
13. Cornelius Ryan, *The Longest Day* (New York: Simon and Schuster, 1959) p.204; (London: Gollancz, 1960).
14. S.L.A. Marshal, *Night Drop* (Boston: Little, Brown, 1962).
15. Eberly, Charles H., *We Captured Rommel* (New York: *Harper's Weekly*, 2 Nov 1944) p.43.

CHAPTER 4

The British Landings
6 June

Sword Beach, 0725

The Germans took the first honours in the struggle for Sword Beach. The British invasion fleet arrived off the coast in the night. Just before daybreak aircraft laid a heavy smoke screen between the ships and the German 11-inch guns in the coastal batteries at Le Havre. Out of the morning's halflight, thickened with smoke, four German E-Boats emerged, launched torpedoes and disappeared back into the haze. The battleships HMSS *Warspite* and *Ramillies* were able to turn barely in time. Like bullets fired in a crowded room, the torpedoes were going to hit something: the Norwegian destroyer *Svenner* was struck in the boiler and sank by the stern.

The German attack failed to affect the timing for the landings. The British, more patient than the Americans, had insisted on a full two hours of preliminary naval bombardment. The big guns of the two battleships, four cruisers and thirteen destroyers provided the heaviest concentration of firepower against any of the invasion beaches that day, on a strip three miles long and one-and-a-half deep. All this was preparing the way for the 3rd Division's assault which would be on a single brigade (8th Brigade) front of two battalions, followed by the 9th Brigade, 27th Armoured Brigade, and 185th Brigade. Coming in on the right of the 3rd Division forty minutes later would be the 1st Special Service Brigade, three Army and one Royal Marine Commandos and two Free French Commando troops, commanded by Brigadier the Lord Lovat. (The 1st SS Brigade's patch showing a double letter S was to arouse such hostility from the French population that it was quickly changed.)

As the flotillas of landing craft began forming for the assault, the misty weather punctuated with occasional showers 'lent a rather chilly and sinister atmosphere'. An officer of C Squadron, 13/18th Royal Hussars was watching:

. . . the infantry assault troops were being loaded into their assault craft, which were alongside ready to take them to the enemy shore. We had often seen the infantry do this before, but this was to be the last time – this was the real thing. I certainly felt sorry for them. Many looked very sick and knew they would be wet before long. But, as always, they were trying to be cheerful. One could not help wondering how many would be alive by evening, and how many would see

71

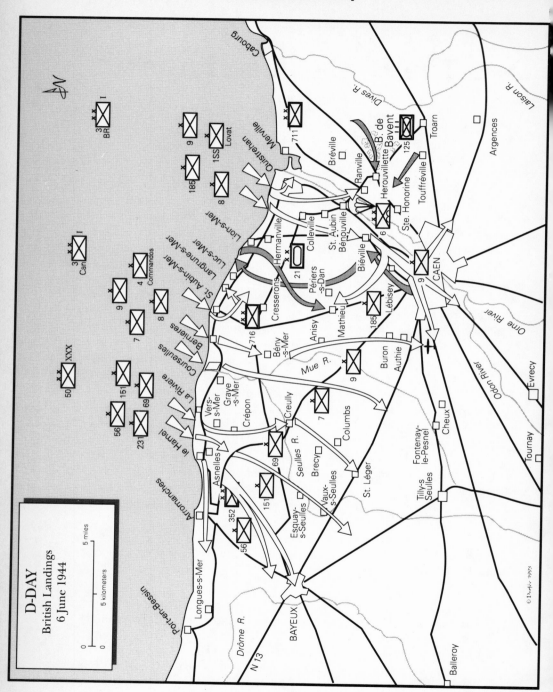

D-DAY
British Landings
6 June 1944

5 miles
5 kilometers

England again. I think at this moment we were all glad to be in a tank. We could at least keep dry, and it gave one a feeling of security as distinct from nakedness, even though, later, we found this feeling to be often a false one.[1]

The assault hit the beach right on schedule at 0745. Forty D-D tanks of 13/18th Royal Hussars, 27th Tank Brigade, were released into the rough sea, 5,000 yards from shore. They were the lancehead of the attack, meant to break open the crust for the following infantry. It was a tradition, as recalled by Sergeant Howard Clewlow:

> D-D tanks were compulsory. The one I was in did the charge of the Light Brigade and that was it, the charge of the Light Brigade came all again - officers with big moustaches and they all thought they were charging at Balaclava. . . .
>
> The real panic came when the other stuff started to back up on us. We were supposed to be ahead of it but we were going that slow that the other stuff was catching up on us. If we got too close the landing craft just ploughed into you and sunk you. They didn't worry. Their idea was to get to the shore and if you were in the way that was just your hard luck. Being outside the tank instead of inside we could see these landing craft coming closer and the stuff was going over from the battleships, the fifteen inch shells, sixteen inch shells. The air force was flying around at about five hundred feet. You didn't know what to do and you were sick and you'd got all this gear on. People say, 'Were you panicky?' There was that much confusion you hadn't got time to feel frightened.[2]

Sergeant Clewlow's fears were realized when landing craft hit two of the D-D tanks and sank them like stones. Two more sank in the rough water, but twenty-one survived to clank up onto the beach. In one of them was Lance Corporal P.L.M. Hennessey:

> On the beach we dropped our canvas screen and opened fire. The tide was coming in and the water where we stood was getting deeper. We could not move further inland because the mines had not yet been cleared. A large wave swamped the engine, the tank was immobilized and was becoming flooded. We took to the rubber dinghy, but hit by machine gun fire we were sunk and obliged to swim for the shore, now some 300 yards away. Halfway there I clung to a post sticking up out of the water and glancing up I saw a large black Teller mine attached to the top of it — I swam on.[3]

As the D-D tanks swam ashore, four LCTs landed another sixteen. Right behind them were another four LCTs carrying Hobart's funnies of the 22nd Dragoons and the Westminster Dragoons with sapper groups to begin destroying the beach obstacles. The sappers who ran ashore to precede the specialized vehicles were magnets for the enemy's fire. Lieutenant Charles Mundy of C Squadron, 22nd Dragoons watched from his flail tank.

They were flung about as German machine-gun fire hit them, clutching various parts of their bodies, jolting like rag dolls, then sinking out of sight into the water . . . Even slightly wounded, the weight of their equipment dragged them under.[4]

Mundy's CO, Major Tim Wheway MC, was also in the thick of the fight:

We land at 0725 and the impact nearly shoots the tanks through the doors. The flails stream out in 3 feet of water, followed by the AVREs. We are met by terrific shell, mortar and 88 and 75 AP and small arms fire at 300 yards range. The CT with our CO, Colonel Cox ARE, is hit. Leading flail on the ship manages to get off but Corporal Brotherton is killed and crew wounded of the second and also Colonel is killed. Several tanks are hit as the landing craft doors go down. Mines are sighted on top of the wooden beach obstacles. We go as far as possible in the water to be able to use our guns effectively and then open fire on concrete gun emplacements, houses and dug-in infantry. Tanks are brewing up right and left. We then proceed flailing our gaps, but no mines are encountered so we speed up and get within fifty yards of our gapping places and open fire right into the slots of gun emplacements.[5]

The German gunners did not give an inch. They blew the flail arms off Lieutenant Robertson's tank; pumped three armour piercing 88mm rounds through the turret of Lieutenant Allen's tank and three through the engine of Corporal Agnew's, brewing it up; and punched a hole through the frontal armour of Sergeant Cochran's tank, killing the driver and wounding two more. But the British were relentless. Their flails braved the fire to sweep lanes for the East Yorks and South Lancs behind them. The bridging AVREs moved up to bridge the antitank ditches. The bridges were dropped, but the crews were wiped out dismounting to secure them, and their tanks were left burning. A wild German counterattack rushed out of the houses behind the beach and was thrown back, leaving German dead to mingle with the British. But the British were stopped for the moment. Finally more flails were found up the beach and were thrown into the breach. Snipers took their toll of commanders, but the Germans were spent. The British would not let go, and the German resistance snapped.

Behind the D-D tanks and funnies landed the first infantry, two companies each of the 1st South Lancashires and the 2nd East Yorks. Machine gun fire felled them in windrows as they moved over the beach, but they kept moving to pitch into the fight, carried by the tanks into the teeth of the German defences around the La Breche strongpoint. Most of the 200 East Yorks dead and wounded fell in those few minutes as did most of the South Lancs' casualties. Major Wheway would count forty-two casualties and five destroyed tanks. Twenty-five men and five tanks were also missing. But Wheway's tanks had destroyed ten 75mm and 88mm and two 50mm guns. After three intense hours, the German grip on the beach was broken. By 0930 the tanks and infantry had broken through the dune defences and captured the village of Hermanville a mile inland. About this time General Richter committed his last reserve into a counterattack. The 3rd Battalion, 736th Regiment, attacked supported by the four 150mm SP guns of the 1716th Artillery Battery. The middle-aged infantrymen and gunners moved down the gentle slope to the beach strafed by British aircraft and ran straight into strong small arms and tank gun fire. Incredibly they reached the western end of the landing beach at Lion-sur-Mer only to be overwhelmed by British firepower. The SP guns retreated to their original position with barely twenty surviving infantrymen of the battalion behind them.

The Piper of Sword Beach

At 0820, while the fighting for the La Breche strongpoint was still raging, Lord Lovat's commando brigade landed, having lost three landing craft to enemy fire, just to the east of the tanks and 8th Brigade. Piper Bill Millin was at Lord Lovat's side.

> Lovat got into the water first . . . I followed closely behind him . . . he's a man about six feet tall and, of course, the water came up to his knees . . . I thought it would be alright for me so I jumped into the water and it came up to my waist . . . anyway I managed to struggle forward and then I started to play the bagpipes. I played *Highland Laddie* towards the beach which was very much under fire. At that time there were . . . three . . . burning tanks, . . . bodies laying at the water's edge, face down floating back and forward. Some [men] were frantically digging in . . . others crouched behind a low sea wall. No one could get off the beach. I made for cover at an exit . . . I just got there behind a group of soldiers and they were all cut down . . . about nine or twelve of them . . . they're shouting and seeing me with the kilt and the bagpipes they shouted, 'Jock! Get the medics.'. . . Then I looked around and to my horror I saw this tank coming off a landing craft with the flails going and making straight for this road. I tried to catch the commander's attention . . . his head was sticking out of the turret . . . but he paid no attention and went straight in and churned all the bodies up.[6]

Amid the carnage, Millin saw Lovat and the Brigade Major standing up in full view. He joined them, and Lovat asked him to play. Overcoming his sense of the ridiculous, Millin marched up and down the beach adding the screech of the pipes to the sound of the battle. He was interrupted by a sergeant who dashed across the beach to yell at him, 'Get down you mad bastard. You're attracting attention to us.' But Piper Millin was by now into the grand spirit of the moment and continued to serenade both sides until the commandos moved off the beach. You had to be there.[7]

The commandos raced across the beaches past the heaps of dead left by the East Yorks from the water's edge to the end of the beach. No. 4 Commando and the Free French troops under Major Kieffer peeled off and attacked into the town of Ouistreham on the eastern edge of Sword Beach. Their objective was the battery of guns dug in around the casino which were shooting up the British forces fighting off the beach. On the road to the town, a French gendarme ran out to meet them with detailed information on the German positions. The French led the attack that overwhelmed the Germans with heavy casualties on both sides. The silencing of the German guns at Ouistreham considerably assisted the 3rd Division's fight to break the Germans at La Breche.

As Kieffer was attacking the casino, Lord Lovat had moved his brigade quickly inland with No. 6 Commando in the lead, outflanking the German defences to seize the village of Colleville-Montgomery. He was marching to a more urgent tune than any played by Piper Millin. His mission was to reinforce the 6th Airborne Division holding the Caen Canal Bridge at Bénouville. Lovat had promised the 6th Airborne's commander, Major General Gale, that he would be there 'sharp at noon'. The recognition signal was to be the sound of a piper playing *Blue Bonnets Over the Border*. Lovat was to lose his bet as his men crossed the bridge at 1203 with Piper Millin playing beside him. The Airborne had been relieved, and no one was complaining of the bet.

The commandos filed across the bridge under small arms and mortar fire to add to the strength of the bridgehead to the east of the Orne. They were in time to reinforce the 6th Airborne when the Germans threw in their first serious counterattack. Colonel von Luck was ordered to strike through to Ranville and the two Orne bridges via the route from Escoville to Herouvillette. That was a tall order for such a small command. Von Luck's 125th Panzer Grenadier Regiment had been reduced to one motorized battalion which was already engaged in heavy fighting with the British paratroopers. Von Luck could disengage only limited elements of his battalion for the attack, reinforced only by the division reconnaissance battalion. Nevertheless, the attack got off to a good start around 1600 when the reconnaissance battalion went into the assault directly from the march.

Then all hell broke loose. The heaviest naval guns, up to 38cm in calibre, artillery and fighter bombers plastered us without pause. Radio contacts were lost, wounded came back, and the men of the reconnaissance battalion were forced to take cover.

I had gone up with the attack and saw the disaster. I managed to run forward to the commander of the battalion and gave him fresh orders.

'To avoid further heavy losses, break off the attack at once and take up defensive positions on the southern edge of Escoville. Set up a line of defense there and prevent any further enemy advance . . . See that your men, and also the rest of the armored cars, dig in themselves.'[8]

21st Panzer Division Stirs

General Edgar Feuchtinger, Commander of the 21st Panzer Division, was in that drowsy half-sleep after sex, in the early morning hours before dawn. The scent from the French girl's long black hair on the pillow next to him was a dreamy delight. He was jarred awake from his reverie when the phone rang. It was his adjutant, the only one he had entrusted with his actual 'whereabouts'. Officially, he had been inspecting the conversion of more old French equipment as assault guns for his division. 'Herr General, Listug here. You must return to headquarters immediately. Something serious is up.' In Feuchtinger's absence, the senior officer present ordered the division headquarters to displace forward from St. Pierre-sur-Dives, 18 miles southeast of Caen, to its operational location closer to the city. Feuchtinger arrived there shortly after 0600 and soon had a good idea of the situation of the 6th Airborne Division's positions in Ranville and on the Bois de Bavent Ridge. He immediately called Army Group B for permission to attack. He was informed that what they had seen was merely a diversionary manoeuvre, straw parachute dummies. Barely controlling his voice, he informed them that von Luck's 125th Panzer Regiment had captured a medical officer who had landed astray from his unit. Under polite questioning he had revealed much of the mission the 6th Airborne Division. The 716th Division had reported strong attacks by airborne forces all along the lower Orne. Feuchtinger also added his own observations. 'General, I have just come back from Paris and I've seen a gigantic armada off the west coast of Cabourg, warships, supply ships, and landing craft. I want to attack at once with the entire division east of the Orne in order to push through to the coast.' It was refused.[9]

Every few minutes he would walk to the door and stare out into the growing light past the red, black and white headquarters sign, almost as if he could hear the fighting that was reported to the northwest. The 716th, a static defence division, 'a static division, by God', had been fighting all night while his panzer division stood still, its feet nailed to the ground by lack of orders. For that matter, he wasn't even sure who was in a position to issue him orders. For such an orderly army, his chain of command was a staff officer's dream, a compromise that satisfied everything but this present banging emergency. He was technically subordinated to the 716th Infantry Division now in battle. Its commander had ordered him to immediately attack the airlandings, but his standing orders were not to move until ordered by Army Group B.

Enough was enough. It was 0630. 'Bergsdorf!' he shouted. His chief of staff rushed up to him. 'We move. The panzer regiment attacks the British bridgeheads on the Orne. Pass the order, and let's move out.' The headquarters began to come apart as men flew to their vehicles with the last few pieces of equipment that had not already been packed. By 0800 they were already half way to Caen when two things happened. The Royal Air Force strafed the column, destroying his headquarters communications van and three trucks. Everyone drove off the road or dived out of their vehicles. When it was all clear, they reassembled and started off again, and he was handed a message by his operations officer. 'I received my first intimation that a higher command did still exist. I was told by Army Group B that I was now under command of 7th Army.'

Feuchtinger had problems enough without the chain of command. He was rushing into the counterattack with a green division against an elite enemy force. Twenty-First Panzer Division had been one of Rommel's rapiers in the Western Desert, but the men had all been surrendered in Tunis. The only original members of the division were those who had been recuperating from wounds in Germany at the time. Starting with 3,000 cadre in 1943, the division was rebuilt. Most of its men had never seen action. Its equipment, Mark IV tanks and a few remodelled captured French tanks, were inferior to the Cromwells and Shermans of the Allies. Even so, the men knew that the scrap heaps of the Reich had been picked over for these out-of-date tanks.

This would be 21st Panzer's first action as a new division, and Feuchtinger didn't even have control of the full division. Everything but the two battalions of 22nd Panzer Regiment and the 200th Assault Gun Battalion were under the operational control of LXXXIV Corps. The four battalions of his 125th and 192nd Panzer Grenadier Regiments, 155th Armored Artillery Regiment, the 200th Antitank Battalion, and most of his flak units had been detached to flesh out the understrength defenses around Caen. He would not be attacking as a combined team.

By 0900 both battalions of Colonel Hermann von Oppeln-Bronikowski's 22nd Panzer Regiment were on the road to Caen along with the division headquarters. Also at 0900, Feuchtinger was informed that he was now subordinate to LXXXIV Corps. An hour later, just when he was about to commit the panzer regiment, he was ordered to break off the attack and retrace his steps, cross the Orne at Caen, to meet the enemy coming south. He turned the attack over to von Luck but stripped him of his I Panzergrenadier Battalion mounted in SPWs and ordered one panzer company to stay behind and assist the counterattacks on the British Airborne. Harried all the way back to Caen by the RAF, Feuchtinger lost another half dozen vehicles. He thought better of leaving the company behind and ordered it to rejoin the regiment. As it was, 21st Panzer took hours to pass through the rubble-choked streets.

3rd Division Strikes Inland

As 21st Panzer was heading back toward Caen, the three battalions of Brigadier

K. Pearce Smith's 185th Brigade had come safely ashore and assembled near the village of Hermanville ready to embark on its primary mission: the seizure of Caen, the final and critical 3rd Division objective. They were awaiting the tanks of the Staffordshire Yeomanry, one of three regiments of 27th Armoured Brigade, which would give them the punch and speed to shoot through to Caen with the 2nd King's Own Shropshire Light Infantry mounted aboard. The 2nd Royal Warwickshire and the 1st Royal Norfolk would follow in their wake to mop up any resistance on either flank. But the tanks were nowhere to be seen. They were stuck on jammed Sword Beach, along with all the rest of the incoming traffic. It took an hour for them just to reach the road behind the beach and then inch along it unable to go off-road because of the German minefield on either side. Lieutenant Colonel F.J. Maurice, the Shropshire's commander, bicycled to the beach to find out what was wrong and then reported back to Smith who then ordered the brigade forward tanks or no tanks.

Ahead of the 185th, 8th Brigade had been busy reducing a German strongpoint codenamed 'Morris'. The 1st Suffolks took it after a short but intense bombardment which convinced its 65-man garrison to surrender. The next strongpoint, 'Hillman' was even easier and was taken by the Suffolks on the bounce. It was practically empty except for the staff of the sector headquarters and a few machine-gunners. Its strength and size caught the Suffolks up short when they searched it. For once Allied intelligence had failed to accurately gauge the strength of a position. 'Had it been properly defended,' remembers 8th Brigade's commander, Brigadier 'Copper' Cass, 'it would have held up the entire operation, and 3rd Division would never have got as far as it did that day.' As 185th Brigade marched past Hillman, the tanks of the lead squadron of the Staffs caught up with them. Maurice waved to the captain in the lead tank, 'I never thought you'd make it this fast.' 'Yes, sir, and neither did we. The new GOC [General Officer Commanding] himself, MacDonald, came by and ordered us to push everything else off the road ahead of us. The rest of our lot should follow soon.' The man's enthusiasm lifted a load from Maurice's mind. He had worried over how the division would be handled ever since Tom Rennie had broken his hip in that air crash ten days before. Rennie had been bulldog tough and his last minute replacement had been something of a question to his subordinate commanders. Not any more. Now married up to at least part of their tanks, the Shropshires moved quickly off down the rode toward Caen as planned.

Shortly after midday, 9th Brigade had been successfully landed with its three battalions of the 2nd Lincolnshire, 1st King's Own Scottish Borderers, and 2nd Royal Ulster Rifles. Brigadier J.C. Cunningham quickly found the next two links in his chain of command, 3rd Division Commander Major General Ian MacDonald and I Corps Commander Lieutenant General John Crocker in

Hermanville. Cunningham exclaimed, 'I've never seen anything like this. I've been in half a dozen campaigns but never before have I been beaten onto the battlefield, not only by my Division but my Corps Commander!'[10] They both laughed; then Crocker explained the situation on a map resting on a broken wall. 'You see how 185th Brigade has moved out smartly toward Caen. You will follow as planned and strike west of the city to seize the Carpiquet Airfield. No change in plans. You had a close call, you know. A tank attack was forming up on 6th Airborne Division holding on to the bridge over the Orne, and we planned to divert you that way. But the tanks seem to have withdrawn. Now it appears that you and Smith have a clear shot at Caen. There are no heavy forces in the way.' General MacDonald added, 'Yes, I'm also giving you a squadron of 13/18th Hussars to speed you onto your objective. They should be available soon. They are all that's left of their regiment. Resistance on the beach was about what we expected.'

Brigadier Smith was to write after the War, 'I did not expect on my race to Caen, to confront 21st Panzer Division or any other Armoured Division . . . Information concerning the strength and dispositions of 716th Division was somewhat nebulous and what with the speed of my advance and with the expected support of the Staffordshire Yeomanry tanks, 7th Field Regiment, Royal Artillery, I did not anticipate much opposition.'[11] The mobile group first began proving him wrong when it ran into strong resistance on Periers Ridge from three 88mm antitank guns of the 21st Panzer and a few infantry. They broke through at a cost of nine Shermans left blazing and moved on the village of Biéville almost three miles south of Hillman. Luckily, the other twenty-one 88s of 21st Panzer's antitank battalion had been scattered throughout the sector. The mobile group's first attack on Biéville was thrown back with a vengeance. The village was strongly held by a company of 2/192nd Panzer-grenadiers. Maurice was surprised to find out from prisoners that they were the intended garrison of Hillman that had arrived too late to take their positions.

Supported by the Staffs, the Shropshires fought through the village, taking a number of unnecessary casualties rather than destroy houses where the French population was cowering. Captain Robert Rylands learned there one of the horrible necessities of war, 'The civilians refused to evacuate themselves, and at that early stage we were too soft-hearted to shell their homes – a proceeding which might have facilitated our advance considerably.'[12] The fight took until late afternoon when the last of the Germans surrendered. Maurice had lost 113 men and three more Shermans, and it was almost 1600 in the afternoon. By then the Norfolks came charging down the road mounted on the backs of the rest of the Staffords. Brigadier Smith jumped off the lead tank and shook Maurice's hand, 'Well done, the Shropshires!' 'I've lost over 100 good men, Sir.' 'Yes, of course, Maurice . . . since the Norfolks are fresh and mounted, I want them to lead the way into Caen now.' 'I suggest you take a look at Lébisey from here.' They climbed a half-ruined bell tower. Maurice pointed south, 'Brigadier, you can even see the activity and hear the noise of tanks between the woods and Caen. There's more there than we expected.'

The German Counterstroke

General Marcks, LXXXIV Corps Commander, joined Feuchtinger's command group as it emerged from Caen's northern suburbs. 'Feuchtinger, throw in everything. Now is not the time to hold back. Your tanks will need infantry support. I'm giving you the two battalions of your panzergrenadiers that are in defence of Caen.' Marcks then turned to the commander of the panzer regiment, Colonel Hermann von Oppeln-Bronikowski, 'Oppeln, if you don't succeed in throwing the British into the sea, we shall have lost the war.'[13] With that, the former German Olympic equestrian saluted and leaped into his command vehicle. The regiment and the assault gun battalion, a force of almost 170 armoured vehicles, drove north through Lébisey Woods where the Panzergrenadiers left their positions and joined the column. It was 1630 in the afternoon as the first German armoured counterattack of the battle began.

Von Oppeln-Bronikowski attacked north in two balanced columns. The right-hand column drove toward Biéville and Ouistreham while the other toward Lion-sur-Mer. Each column had one of his tank battalions and one panzergrenadier battalion. The assault gun battalion brought up the rear as his reserve. The British now could not have missed the approach of the panzer division and were waiting for them, after Maurice's warning. The right-hand column's Mark IVs began exploding, struck by the long-range 17-pounders of Lieutenant Colonel J.A. Eadie's Staffordshires' Sherman Fireflys. This was something Eddy had clearly thought out long before the invasion. 'I know what the German armour will do. They will drive their command tanks onto an eminence effectively out of range of my six pounders (about 1,000 yards), make a quick plan, get back into their tanks before any effective field artillery concentration can be brought to bear, and withdraw behind the ridge. They will form up their squadrons, give out their orders, then drive straight for their objectives. What they do not know is that I have three troops of 'Fireflies' . . . which I will station at Hermanville ridge and leave as a backstop.'[14] It worked perfectly. He was wrong in only one particular. He had fifty-seven Shermans on line instead of just his three troops of Fireflies. In a few minutes twenty-seven Mark IVs and a number of personnel carriers were burning, including the command tank of 2nd Battalion commander, Major Vierzig. Oppeln turned the regiment west away from the deadly fire toward the gap every panzer leader lusts for, the enemy's open flank. He led the way as 21st Panzer's forces charged towards the sea. In a few minutes they reached the coast near Lion-sur-Mer where some of the 716th Infantry Regiment had held out. Most of 21st

Panzer's offensive power was now poised to strike down the beaches jammed with men and vehicles.

As he prepared to attack, a mass of enemy gliders of the 6th Airlanding Brigade appeared in the sky over them on their way to reinforce the Orne River bridgeheads. The Germans could only conclude in dismay that the mass of gliders were meant to land behind them and spring a great trap. How could they not? It was an awesome sight: 250 gliders in tow by 250 transports protected by swarms of Spitfires and Hurricanes. The gliders carried two battalions of the 6th Airlanding Brigade, the 6th Airborne Division's artillery, light tanks, and reconnaissance regiments. 'We looked up,' said panzergrenadier lieutenant, 'and there they were just above us. Noiselessly, those giant wooden boxes sailed in over out heads. We lay on our backs and fired, and fired into those gliders, until we could not work the bolts of our rifles anymore. But with such masses, it seemed to make little difference.'[15] Feuchtinger pushed through the mass of stalled vehicles and found Oppeln and his staff transfixed by the spectacle. It was then that the big guns of the Royal Navy concentrated on the panzers. A broadside lashed at the concentrations of armoured vehicles, tossing Mark IV and assault guns into the fields and disintegrating the SPW armoured personnel carriers. A salvo from *Warspite* struck the regiment's command group just as Feuchtinger reached them. Captain von Gottberg watched in horror from his command vehicle of the 1st Battalion, as the clutch of vehicles disappeared in an eruption of earth and high explosive. One command 'Shoot' aboard a British ship had now made him commander of a trapped panzer division. He ordered a withdrawal.

When 21st Panzer careened off the Staffs on the 3rd Division's right, General Crocker, I Corps Commander, had just moved up to Biéville and joined Smith and his battalion commanders. 'Oh, my God, they'll get to the beach', muttered one of the Shropshire officers. Crocker turned to the officers around him. 'This is what we will do. Smith, attack with the Staffords and Norfolks immediately into the rear of that German herd. The Shropshires can follow. I want to slam the door shut on them and press them into the sea. Quickly, Gentlemen. This is the key to Caen.'[16] He then ordered the 9th Brigade to detour east, move up quickly, seize Lébisey Woods and strike for the city.

As 21st Panzer streamed back toward the city in the late afternoon, they were struck by fire from their right by the Canadians at Anisy and from their front by the whole of the Staffs which had been flung behind the 21st when it raced towards the sea. The Staffs and Norfolks had barely time to hunt out firing positions in the village of Mathieu and folds in the ground on either flank before the German stampede ran into them. The Staffordshires' fire crushed the head of each column. The Germans attempted to counterattack, but it was a disorganized movement that got even worse as one Mark IV after another brewed up. The Germans surged up to the Staffs, burned, and recoiled, then

came again. A few tanks and two companies from 1/192 Panzergrenadiers
struck towards Lébisey Woods, breaking through the Staffs on their right. They
ran into the slower Shropshires coming to the aid of the British tanks.

It was a meeting engagement of the worst sort. The German tanks and
SPWs had an advantage in open ground. Sergeant Harry Miles of B Company
wrote later, 'They were on us as we were force-marching behind the Staffs. The
tanks cut right through us. Their infantry firing from those personnel carriers as
they drove through us. Every man in my section was down. I even saw the
Colonel go down. If it hadn't been for the few AT guns, they would have killed
us all.'[17] It was suicide for infantry to stand against tanks and APCs in the high
wheat, so they went to ground leaping up to return fire before diving into the
wheat again. The Germans rode through the field, spraying their automatic
weapons, crushing living, wounded, and dead under them. The adjutant stood
guard over his wounded CO and was cut down in bloody rags over him. Three
company commanders were down in the first few minutes. But the antitank
gun platoon coolly unlimbered its 6-pounders and shot back, knocking out a
tank and few APCs. The grenadiers unlimbered one of their own Pak-75
antitank guns to duel with the British gunners. Both sides stood their guns
without flinching. The Pak was silenced first. Lance Corporal Harold Williams
of X Company raced alongside one APC, shot a German off the side, crawled up
the side to kill the other grenadiers in the rear before dropping a grenade
through the driver's hatch. Nevertheless, a complete slaughter was prevented
by the arrival of a troop of the 13/18th Hussars of 27th Armoured Brigade.
They struck the Germans from the left rear, making torches of a half dozen
armoured personnel carriers and two of the tanks. The Germans panicked,
pulled back and disappeared into the fighting with the Staffs and Norfolks
leaving 286 of the Shropshires dead and wounded and the carcasses of a dozen
burning vehicles on the field.

The Dash to Caen

Meanwhile, 9th Brigade moved up past Biéville and attacked in the dusk
toward Lébisey leading with the Lincolnshires and Scottish Borderers supported
by 13/18th Hussars. As night fell and the battle in the wheat fields west of
Biéville died down, 9th Brigade had fought its way through the remaining
Germans in Lébisey Woods. Brigadier Cunningham was barely over a mile
from Caen but with his brigade engulfed in a strange wood in the night. Many
men would have stopped. 'I'm all teed up to capture Caen and know exactly
what to do,' he told his battalion commanders. 'I must stick to my objective.
Push out immediately towards the city. Don't let anyone dawdle.'

Flames lit up the city from dozens of buildings set afire by the bombing and
provided illumination for 9th Brigade's night attack into Caen. The defenders
were a few flak units and the rear service personnel of 21st Panzer. A few flak

guns held them up here and there, but the tanks of 13/18th Hussars brushed them aside. The Germans were streaming out of Caen east across the Orne River bridge or south down Route 26. Cunningham and his staff had set up a command post in the town square by 2000. He was anxious about securing the bridge over the Orne. He stepped into the rubbled street to hurry the 2nd Royal Ulster Rifles toward the bridge when an enemy officer was led up to him by three of the Scottish Borderers. General Marcks limped forward on his cane. The leg he had lost in Russia had not made him any less a soldier as he saluted. 'Allow me to introduce myself, Colonel; I am General Erich Marcks, Commander, LXXXIV Corps.' Cunningham was getting used to running into corps commanders this day. He returned the salute, and extended his hand. 'Congratulations on a spirited defence, General.' 'No, Colonel, it is I who must congratulate you. You have just won the war.' 'Not bloody yet', Cunningham said to himself, 'if I don't get that bridge.' Turning Marcks over to his adjutant with instructions to notify Crocker and see to Marcks' proper treatment, he pushed on to join the battalion fighting toward the bridge.[18]

German survivors of the clash with the Staffords and Shropshires pushed through to Caen in the dark hoping to find a refuge but ran into more 27th Armoured Brigade's 1st East Riding Yeomanry moving into the city as well as the Warwicks, held in reserve on the outskirts. Firefights flared through the night as platoons and individual tanks fired and disappeared. The survivors of 21st Panzer milled around in the dark, stopped by fire from Caen when they tried to enter the town and trapped by the British columns moving south. As first light broke, they began surrendering. Over 1,800 Germans gave themselves up the next day. Third Division later counted 143 destroyed or abandoned tanks and assault guns between Caen and Lion-sur-Mer. A few units and individuals had swung further east and skirted Caen, but 21st Panzer was finished.

By midnight the Ulsters and Hussars had overwhelmed the flak platoon guarding the bridge and pushed two companies and a tank squadron over the Orne River bridge, the same bridge that 21st Panzer had crossed earlier in the day. By 0200 3rd Division was digging in along the southern and eastern edges of the city. The Warwicks supported by the tanks of the East Riding Yoemanry moved onto Carpiquet Airfield southwest of Caen without resistance. Ninth Brigade had rounded up another 800 prisoners in the fight for the city. Two hundred more quietly surrendered at the Airfield. The 3rd Division had secured its objective but was spread out over nine miles from the beachhead to the southern outskirts of the ruins of Caen and west to the Airfield just south of the Bayeux to Caen highway. Eighth Brigade had moved up in reserve to Biéville where it could reinforce either Caen or the 6th Airborne. Firefights flared in their rear from fugitive elements of 21st Panzer just enough to keep people awake. They had lived on adrenalin all through the night and by early morning were spent. In particular, 185th Brigade was burnt out. The Shropshires had been gutted, losing over two thirds of their men. The Norfolks had lost half, and only twenty tanks remained of the Staffs.

As the division took its first fitful rest, its commander worried for them all. The 21st Panzer had been an unexpected complication, MacDonald thought to himself. Luckily, they had bested it neatly, but where was the real threat? Where was the SS?

Gold Beach, 0725

The naval gunfire began just before sunrise. The four German 155mm guns in the Longues (le Chaos) Battery in heavy concrete casemates to the west of Gold Beach had just survived 1,500 tons of bombs dropped by the Allied air forces. Their crews still had plenty of fight and immediately returned fire. Their first salvo straddled the HMS *Bulolo*, which was carrying the headquarters of the British XXX Corps. One of the guardian cruisers, HMS *Ajax*, rushed to the rescue pumping 114 rounds from her six-inch turrets at the German battery at a distance of seven-and-a-half miles. For *Ajax* it was a matter of precision gunnery. Two projectiles slammed through the German casement apertures. Within twenty minutes three of the big German guns were destroyed and the fourth disabled. The Royal Navy was doing its all to make sure the men of 50th Division would have no more difficulty than they could help.

The 50th Northumbrian Division was as dependable as they came on the 6th of June. Without doubt, the 50th was the single most combat experienced division among the five landing, having fought in France, North Africa, and Sicily. Reinforced for D-Day, the independent 56th and 231st Brigades joining the 69th and 151st, with the attached 8th Armoured Brigade, the 50th would land on the right flank of the British 2nd Army. Theirs would be the task of linking up with the Americans coming out of Omaha Beach. A striking force of the attached 47th Royal Marine Commando was to push inland seven miles and move west behind the coastal defences to seize the German strongpoint at Port-en-Bessin, separating Gold and Omaha Beaches. The rest of the division would strike inland to seize the ancient Norman city of Bayeux and drive south to cross the N13 highway linking Bayeux to Caen, some eight miles.

The infantrymen in the heaving landing craft approaching the shore were coming in on a two-brigade (69th and 231st) front, meaning that two of three battalions were in the first wave with the third following. Each battalion's front was two companies in the first wave and two following, so that the brigade's initial attack would be delivered by only four infantry companies, one of the details of warfare overlooked by armchair generals. The 231st Brigade was to land on the right and the 69th on the left. After overcoming the German beach defences, they were to peel left and right to allow the follow-on two brigades to land. Thereafter, the division would advance inland on a four brigade front.

The Germans had studded the area with powerful concrete fortifications and gun positions. The strongest resistance nest on the beach was at le Hamel where the 231st would land, consisting of a number of strongpoints equipped with infantry guns. In addition to the coastal minefield five rows deep, another one eight rows deep surrounded le Hamel. Here the mines were reinforced by an antitank ditch. The defenders had been judged to be second rate *Ostruppen* of the 726th Regiment. Unknown to the 50th, this regiment had been attached to the first rate 352nd Division which had elements in the area.

For the men of the 50th vomiting in their tossing landing craft, the enemy had ceased to be an immediate priority. The 'Bags, Vomit' were full as they lurched amid the worst seas tormenting any of the landing divisions that morning. They would gladly have faced the enemy so long as it was on dry land. So rough were the Force Five wind-whipped seas that there was no question of swimming the D-D tanks from their LCTs. The tanks were supposed to arrive ahead of the infantry, but now they were to be landed directly onto the beaches from their landing craft. They might not get there just ahead of the infantry as scheduled, but they would get there.

The first men ashore were the Royal Marine frogmen attempting to blow lanes through the maze of steel and concrete obstacles. The density of the German efforts made it impossible, but they tried. As the first obstacles exploded the infantry landing craft were coming in. Frogman Jones turned to see a landing craft heaved to the side by a sudden wave land right on top of three mined steel triangles. He saw the 'the men, standing to attention, shot up into the air as though lifted by a water spout . . . at the top of the spout bodies and parts of bodies spread like drops of water.'[19]

The first wave infantry was coming ashore almost exactly on time at 0730. The tanks and Hobart's funnies were among them giving cover and supporting fire. Opposite le Hamel, the 1st Hampshire Regiment came ashore with 1st Dorsetshire Regiment on its left. A and B Companies landing directly in front of the Germans were unable to break into the defences against the heavy machine gun fire and the fire of 88mm guns sited further inland. The minefields which should have been detonated by the air bombardments were too strong to be penetrated under the heavy German fire. Many of the flail tanks were destroyed on the beach. The attack on le Hamel had been stopped cold. C and D Companies landed at 0740 and tried to break into the town from the east as did tanks from the Sherwood Rangers Yeomanry. First they had to get through the mines. They gave covering fire to a sapper officer and his small party who manually removed them. By then Major Peter Selerie had only five of his original nineteen Sherman tanks, but he pushed on down the lane into the town. The lead tank was struck in the mantelet by an antitank gun in a concrete position but survived. The others concentrated their fire and destroyed the gun. Outside the town they were overtaken by an AVRE (Armoured Vehicle Royal Engineers) Churchill tank, the sole survivor of his troop, which eagerly joined the column. As they fought their way into the town, Selerie identified a tall multistoryed house as the centre of resistance. He ordered the AVRE forward. Its stubby spigot mortar resembling a 'short and very wicked piece of drainpipe sticking out of the turret,' fired one of its Petard fortification-busting projectiles into the building. 'It collapsed like a pack of cards, spilling defenders with their machine-guns, antitank weapons and an avalanche of bricks into the courtyard.' At the same time C and D Companies found a gap to the east of the town and captured Asnelles behind it. The Germans were not finished in le Hamel, though. The *Ostruppen* fought stubbornly here, at least until their German officers and NCOs were dead. Resistance was finally snuffed out by 1730.

The 1st Dorsetshire landed with the mission of seizing the high ground dominating Arromanches. The battalion fought its way ashore far more easily than the Hampshires, but found more opposition than expected on the high-ground. Supported by another squadron of the Sherwood Rangers and a self-propelled artillery battalion, they overwhelmed the defenders who abandoned their guns and equipment and fled.

To the east the 5th East Yorkshires and 6th Green Howards led the landing of the 69th Brigade. The Green Howards were landed several hundred yards west of their assigned beach. A Company stormed the German resistance nest in front of them that guarded a beach exit. Captain F.H. Honeyman aided by Sergeant H. Prenty and Lance Corporal A. Joyce leaped over the seawall and cleared the beach of Germans in a rapid sten gun and grenade melee. Up the beach D Company was taken under fire by two pillboxes it had bypassed. The company commander, Major R. Lofthouse, barked out, 'There's a pillbox there, sergeant-major!' Sergeant-Major Stan Hollis ran towards the enemy firing his sten gun from the hip until he reached the pillbox. He threw a grenade through the door and then sprayed the inside with his sten killing two Germans. Hollis didn't pause but continued along the communications trench toward the main pillbox. Its garrison of twenty-five men quickly surrendered.

To the left of the 6th Green Howards, the 5th East Yorkshires were heavily engaged by the German defences in the village of la Riviere. One company braved the fire to drive inland a thousand yards to overrun a German battery smashed by the air bombardment. The left hand company was in trouble in front of la Riviere where the air bombardment had missed a fifty-yard swath along the front of the village. The company was now huddled behind the sea wall as the German machine guns and a casemated 88mm gun swept their position and down the beach. The Germans were pouring well-aimed fire into the landing craft that were lurching between the obstacles trying to drop their ramps and among the men trying to rush ashore. Two AVREs trying to trundle ashore were destroyed. Stuffed with their demolition ammunition, they exploded with special destructiveness, killing many of the infantry around them. The Germans sensed they had the upper hand and pressed it, adding mortar fire to the fire that beat the beach and tossing potato-masher grenades over the seawall. The Yorks were not beaten yet. A platoon followed a D-D tank over the seawall and began clearing the houses that faced the sea. At the same time, another platoon supported by AVREs and D-D tanks had pushed inland and now attacked la Riviere from the rear. The German defence collapsed, and the village was cleared by 0900.

By 1000 6th Green Howards had captured the Mauvaines Ridge over a mile inland. Once more, Sergeant-Major Hollis was in the van.

> . . . the Company encountered a field gun and crew, armed with Spandaus, at a hundred yards range. CSM Hollis was put in command of a party to cover an attack on the gun, but the movement was held up. Seeing this, CSM Hollis pushed right forward to engage the gun with a PIAT [Projector Infantry Anti-tank] from a house at fifty yards range. He was observed by a sniper who fired and grazed his right cheek, and at the same moment the gun swung round and fired at point blank range into the house. To avoid the falling masonry, CSM Hollis moved his party to an alternative position. Two of the enemy gun crew had by this time been killed, and the gun was destroyed shortly afterwards.[20]

When he found that two of his men had been left behind, he went after them in full view of the Germans who energetically did their best to kill him. Firing a Bren gun, he distracted them long enough for his men to slip away and followed completely unscathed. For this exploit and the one earlier, Hollis would be awarded the Victoria Cross, the only one to be awarded for D-Day.

The reserve battalion, 7th Green Howards had landed and moved inland to seize the little crossroads village of Crepon more than two miles inland by 1230. Sixty-Ninth Brigade had broken through. Its three battalions pushed aggressively inland. By 1500 they had seized the crossing of the Seulles River three-and-a-half miles inland. German resistance flared south of the river, but the Howards and Yorks pitched into them and drove them back everywhere. Files of German prisoners began to impede traffic moving inland. By 1800 the 7th Green Howards and tanks of 4/7th Royal Dragoon Guards had fought through Creully and were pushing onto the Coulumbs. The fight at Creully had been the first for the Dragoons since landing, but not for its A Squadron Commander, Major Jackie D'Avigdor-Goldsmid. He had fought in France in 1940, and the experience had ensured that his command would be trained to a fine edge the next time around. Today he was careful to study the ground to find the hiding places in the folds and woods to use for tactical bounds. 'Shake out into two-up formation – 1st Troop left, 2nd Troop right, 3rd and 4th behind 1st and 2nd respectively. Now let's go!' It was a glorious summer day and Goldsmid exulted in the beautiful tank country. He knew enough to realize that it was beautiful antitank country as well and was scanning for any movement or giveaway that the enemy was waiting. Then two of his lead tanks exploded. 'Speed up. Make for cover – the line of trees 400 yards ahead on the left of the road.' A third tank was hit, and 'Immediately a near solid column of dense black smoke spiralled vertically upwards for about 100 feet.' Lieutenant Alistair Morrison, all of twenty years and following with 4th Troop, was surprised.

> Throughout their training he had formed a mental picture of a tank 'brewing up'. He had expected to see a few sparse flames lick from the stricken tank followed by the hurried disembarkation of the crew, possibly wounded or burned, and after a short interval the thud of ammunition exploding inside. But reality was quite different. The tank had without warning become an instant inferno. And to his right he could see the turret of one of 2nd Troop's also glowing red. Above both tanks a black pillar of smoke hung as if suspended from some invisible beam.[21]

Morrison joined 1st Troop, commanded by Lieutenant Peter Aizelwood and 'saw a spark as if someone had struck a match against the side of Aizelwood's tank. Then *"woomph"* from inside the tank, and immediately the tell-tale column of black smoke began to erupt from the stricken tank.' But Morrison had seen, by sheer luck, a flash at the foot of a telephone pole in the distance and a thread of smoke drift away. He had found the killer. To advance against it courted the same fate as the pillars of smoke around him. Direct fire was prevented by the bow of the ground. Indirect fire was another method, although one in which Morrison had not shone in training which had 'entailed a lot of mumbo-jumbo about "bracketing"'. To his amazement, the second shot landed in front of the target. He adjusted, and the third shot resulted in flame and smoke in a direct hit. He had had little time to savour his first kill when a heavy bombardment of large calibre shells fell on them. It passed quickly but not before killing one officer and wounding another. The 7th Green Howards whom A Squadron had been supporting were caught out in the open and badly hurt. Goldsmid was puzzled. The shelling seemed to be coming from behind them. HMS *Orion* recorded in its log that day, 'Enemy Tanks destroyed – well done'.[22]

To the southwest of Creully, the other two battalions were engaged in a set piece fight for the village of Brécey which seemed to have sucked the German defenders in that direction. Seventh Green Howards saw its chance and pushed on to St. Léger on the Bayeux–Caen highway, the division D-Day objective line. As the fighting died down around Brécey around 2130, the 7th Green Howards with a few tanks were in control of the town. Their night was enlivened by shooting up unsuspecting German traffic driving into the town from either direction.

Following 231st Brigade, 47th Royal Marine Commando landed at 1000. Three landing craft were lost with seventy men from the still active German defenders of le Hamel. Many of the seventy eventually showed up and rearmed themselves with captured German weapons. Their first assembly area south of le Hamel was already occupied by a German company. The Commando immediately attacked. Unfortunately, the German company's fields of fire were excellent and their machine gunners expert. The Commando staggered back with sixty casualties. Another attack wilted leaving as many more dead and wounded. Finally the weight of rocket firing Typhoons and the six-inch guns of HMS *Emerald* beat down the defenders long enough for the Royal Marines to break into their position and clean them out. But it was late in the afternoon, and the Commando still had seven miles to march before reaching its objective of Port-en-Bessin.

The two reserve brigades were ashore by 1100, and moving inland by 1500 organized into all arms mobile columns. They brushed aside occasional German resistance and headed southwest towards the division's objective line. Major G.L. Wood of 151st Brigade's 6th Durham Light Infantry described the advance.

> The mobile column under Major Thomlinson moved off at 1500 hrs., two hours behind the time planned. Movement was slow because of the congestion of troops and material on and near main roads, and the difficulties of driving Shermans through narrow village streets. Some enemy pockets were met near Villiers-le-Sec by the mobile column, but quick action by Lieutenant Kirk, in command of the vanguard, drove the enemy from their position.
>
> During the whole of the move of the mobile column we encountered no enemy artillery fire and were held up only by small pockets of enemy, which were beaten up. The battalion reached its first objective at Esquay-sur-Seulles by 2000 hrs.[23]

Dusk was falling as Major General D.A.H. Graham, commanding the 50th, realized just how much luck had fallen his way. Once his two leading brigades had broken through the crust of the beach defences, German resistance seemed to have crumbled. The 7th Green Howards had actually cut the Bayeux to Caen Highway at St. Léger. From every unit he was hearing the same story as related by Major Wood of the 151st Brigade's mobile column. The surprise of finding elements of the German 352nd Division in the sector had been a shock that quickly wore off. This division was nowhere in serious strength. He knew nothing of the catastrophe on his right at Omaha Beach where the 352nd had been concentrated in strength. Kraiss, for better or worse, had gambled everything on crushing Omaha. If Graham had known, it might have stayed his hand. But now he could only see opportunity and was determined to gather as much of it in his arms as he could. Push on. The division objective line was within grasp. Push on.

The extra exhortation from above pushed the tanks of the Sherwood Rangers with the 2nd Essex of 56th Brigade into the city of Bayeux by 2300. The city, the first to be liberated in France, was empty of Germans. The 151st Brigade was roused from its position at Esquay-sur-Seulles to continue south till it crossed the Bayeux to Caen highway and cut the railroad a mile further on. By midnight, 50th Division had everywhere reached and in some cases exceeded its D-Day objective lines. Only 47th Royal Marine Commando was behind schedule in approaching its target of Port-en-Bessin. The 50th Division had torn a lodgement eight miles deep and seven miles wide in Hitler's Atlantic Wall. The enemy had receded before them.

Juno Beach, 0745

Of all the divisions to be landed on the 6th of June, none was more an object of apprehension that the 3rd Canadian. The massacre of the 2nd Canadian Division at Dieppe two years before left a nagging fear among the senior commanders and political leadership of the Alliance that perhaps a second national catastrophe awaited the gallant Canadians. The Canadian troops themselves, like their British and American counterparts, felt mostly seasick as they were heaved about the four-foot waves of the retreating Channel storm. Underneath the seasickness, which in any case would be quickly cured by enemy fire, was the hard-edged determination to avenge Dieppe. It burned deeper, hotter, and more recent than the British memory of Dunkirk. The British had had their lucky exit from the Continent; the Canadians had left the French beaches soaked with blood.

The Canadians would not be making the same mistakes again. This time there would be no landing directly into a fortress port. This time there would be massive preparatory air bombardments and naval gunfire support. This time there would be every possible device to overwhelm the obstacles erected by German skill, energy, and cunning. D-D tanks and the rest of Hobart's funnies, AVRE bunker-busting tanks with their stubby petard-firing mortars, the Royal Marines' 95mm howitzer mounted on Centaur tanks for fire support, and several regiments of self-propelled artillery firing from their landing craft were all gladly worked into the landing plan for Juno Beach. Two brigades would make the landing and push inland. Hopefully the situation would develop so that the reserve third brigade would be able to shoot ahead and capture the high ground around the Carpiquet Airfield outside of Caen and just south of the Bayeux to Caen road, Highway 13.

This time the odds were much more in the Canadians' favour. Against twelve fit and honed Canadian battalions, the Germans would have only four coastal defence battalions of the 716th Division. Barely 400 men, the equivalent of only one weak battalion, were manning the coastal defences. The rest were stationed two to four miles inland, unable to contest the landings. The defence of the beach was in the hands of the 5th, 6th, and 7th Companies of the 2nd Battalion, 736th Infantry Regiment. They occupied four resistance nests built around concrete emplacements surrounded by mines and barbed wire at Vaux, Courseulles, Bernières, and St. Aubin, armed with assorted captured artillery and machine guns. Each of them was garrisoned only in platoon strength. The remaining Germans occupied the fortified villages and buildings along the coast. These 400 Germans were to be struck by 2,400 Canadians in the first wave alone.

Because of low cloud cover, the British air bombardment of the night before and the American of early that morning were the least successful of any delivered in support of landing forces that day. The British effort yielded poor results, and the Americans missed entirely, dropping their bombs in the unoccupied fields behind the beaches. The only slaughter was again among the omnipresent Norman dairy cattle. Naval gunfire was more successful. The cruisers HMSS *Diadem* and *Belfast* added their power from 0500, joined an hour later by seventeen destroyers, concentrating on the concrete battery positions at Ver-sur-Mer and Beny-sur-Mer. While the naval guns only destroyed fourteen percent of German bunkers, they demolished the German positions among the French vacation villages and houses along the beach.

The Canadians were coming in on a two-brigade front, like the 50th Division to their right. They would have one brigade, the 9th, in reserve. The 7th and 8th Brigades would each land with two infantry battalions supported by a D-D tank battalion in the first wave. Each infantry battalion would attack with two companies in the first wave and two following in fifteen minutes. The tanks were to emerge from the water just ahead of the infantry to provide a firing moving shield to shoot them across the beach. The 3rd Canadian Division would be the last Allied division to hit the beach that day for the tide to carry the landing craft over the Bernières reefs. Rough seas added another ten minutes.

The same seas made it too dangerous to launch the D-D tanks, and it was decided to land them directly over the beach. A mile-and-a-half from the beach, the commander of 7th Brigade decided to launch them. They arrived as planned just ahead of the infantry. Eighth Brigade's tanks came clanking off their craft barely after the infantry. German fire was negligible against the incoming landing craft. More deadly was the lost ten minutes. The incoming tide was now flushing through and submerging the beach obstacles that Allied landing had hoped to avoid by landing at low tide. Royal Marine frogmen had landed first and cleared a few lanes of obstacles and mines. The landing craft had to force their way ashore, threading the mine-tipped obstacles amid the heaving tide that threw craft aside or onto them. Surprisingly, there were few losses among the troops on the numerous holed or destroyed landing craft. Most struggled ashore following the assorted tanks that were blowing and flailing their way through minefields and defences.

The 7th Brigade landed with the Little Black Devils of the Royal Winnipeg Rifles and the Regina Rifle Regiment from right to left each supported by a squadron of the 6th Armoured Regiment (1st Hussars) on either side of the defences of Courseulles, the strongest German position on Juno. B Company of the Reginas found almost no resistance and cleared its assigned sectors. A Company landed directly into the teeth of the undiminished German defences, and the men raced across the beach to the safety of the seawall. Luckily the tanks of the 1st Hussars had landed just ahead of them and were engaging the German guns from 200 yards as the infantry raced to safety. The tanks moved through the obstacles to support the infantry attack into the town, duelling with the German guns which were bravely and energetically though not accurately served. The last gun emplacement was passed by Sergeant Leo Gariepy's tank. He stopped the tank, broke open a bottle of rum and shared it with his crew, then reversed, and pumped seven rounds through the gun port. All the while the Reginas had been fighting through the trenches and dugouts of the resistance nest killing and capturing Germans.

The Little Black Devils fought a surprisingly similar action. C Company encountered little resistance and pushed inland behind Courseulles to capture the village of Graye-sur-Mer. B Company ran into a buzz saw: 'the bombardment had failed to kill a single German or silence one weapon'. The killing started as the Winnipegs waded through chest-deep water to the beach. The tanks had not arrived as the infantry huddled on sand under accurate fire for an eternity of six minutes. When they did arrive, the Winnipegs followed them in a rush, leaving bodies in windrows behind them. As they smashed into the town with the tanks, there were only twenty-six men left in the company. Of the 128 Winnipegs killed that day, most had fallen on the beach. Supporting the attack were two troops of the 26th Assault Squadron, Royal Engineers, who were clearing exits off the beach with their AVREs. Faced with an antitank ditch with a flooded culvert behind, the AVREs of one troop dropped their fascine bundles to create a passage over the antitank ditch. The second troop crossed to fill the culvert, but the lead AVRE slipped down the cratered edge and disappeared under water, leaving only the fascines showing.

Within two hours Courseulles had fallen, and 7th Brigade was moving inland. By noon they had linked up with 50th Division on their right. The only remaining enemy resistance was still being offered by a group of Russian *Ostruppen* holed up in a sanitorium west of Graye-sur-Mer, too desperate or too afraid to surrender. For them, the end came at 1800. There was a hard edge to the Canadian victory, though. Able Seaman Edward Ashworth had come ashore off his LCT to pick up a German helmet as a souvenir. He saw Canadian soldiers march six German prisoners behind a sand dune and later emerge alone. Thinking to find his helmet, he went behind the dune and found the Germans lying on the ground. He looked at one, 'the man's throat was cut – every one of them had his throat cut'.[24]

To the east, 8th Brigade's landing had put the Queen's Own Rifles of Canada and the North Shore Regiment ashore ahead of their tanks of the 10th Armoured Regiment (Fort Garry Horse). B Company of the Queen's Own Rifles had drifted two hundred yards east of their assigned sector and directly into the fire of the guns and machine guns of the Bernières resistance nest. Like the Americans at Omaha they could not advance across that beaten zone and had to huddle under the little protection offered by the beach obstacles. In a few minutes sixty-five men were dead and wounded. Lieutenant W.G. Herbert led Lance-Corporal Réné Tessier and Riflemen William Chicoski in a dash for the ten-foot high seawall. They worked their way along it using Sten guns and grenades through the gun ports and wiped out one German position after another. Elsewhere a flak ship almost grounded itself to fire into the town and silence its defenders so thoroughly that sniper fire was the only obstacle to further Canadian advance. The North Shore Regiment's landing sector at St. Aubin was bravely defended by the crew of a 50mm antitank gun which destroyed two D-D tanks as they drove ashore from their landing craft. The little gun was finally smothered by the combined efforts of the 95mm gun of a Royal Marine Centaur, the petard of an AVRE, and the 75mm guns of two Shermans of the Fort Garry Horse. The fighting would go on into the night as the North Shore men struggled to reduce the headquarters complex of the 2nd Battalion, 736th Regiment, long after its subordinate companies had been overwhelmed down the coast.

Behind 8th Brigade had landed the 48th Royal Marine Commando with the mission to strike inland and head east to link up with the 41st Commando coming from Sword Beach seven miles away. The Commandos had a rough start at the hands of the still active German machine gunners and artillerymen. The German gunners were still frantically pumping shells down the beach which forced a tank to button up and race wildly up the beach to escape the German fire. With the limited sight imposed by narrow glass vision blocks, the crew could not see that they were driving over the dead and wounded littering the beach. A Marine officer, Captain Daniel Flounder raced through the German fire screaming, 'They're my men!' Climbing aboard a moving tank, no easy task, he hammered on the commander's hatch with his swagger stick but to no avail. He leapt off and threw a grenade into the tank's track and blew it off. As the heavy track flopped off the rollers and into the sand, the tank stopped. The crew emerged only then to discover what they had done.

Despite this last pocket of resistance, the fighting for Juno Beach was over within two hours, and most of the companies of the 7th and 8th Brigades' first-

wave battalions were pushing inland with whatever tanks they could find. Eighth Brigade's reserve battalion, the French Canadian Le Régiment de la Chaudière, had already joined it for the push inland. A few 88mm guns and machine guns around Beny-sur-Mer threatened to hold up the advance but were overwhelmed by a combination of air support and naval gunfire. The few Frenchmen that emerged from Bernières were surprised to hear that the Tommies marching through the town spoke French. Except for a few snipers, the advance resembled a training road march more than an attack into enemy territory. A sense of triumph and relief surged through the Canadians as they pushed on deeper into the quiet Norman countryside. For the Commandos who were pressing east to link up with their counterparts from Sword, the rest of the day would be more frustrating. About a mile east of Juno, the Commandos approached the village of Langrune which the Germans had turned into a fortress by bricking up every door and window facing outward and blocking the streets with concrete walls. Two Royal Marine Centaur tanks advanced with the Commandos. The first exhausted its ammunition and was replaced by the second which promptly hit a mine and blew up. The Commandos were stopped. Without artillery, tanks, or even scaling ladders, the Commandos had no way to break into the village.

On the beach, the efforts of the beachmaster, Captain Colin Maud, Royal Navy, were keeping the flood of men, equipment, and supplies from clogging the beach. The Royal Engineers were busy blasting open holes in the seawall and clearing mines from the dunes. Exit after exit was quickly cleared and prepared for follow-on units. One German bunker that continued to defy its attackers was finally dealt with by an engineer who was annoyed that it continued to hold up his work. Driving a bulldozer, the engineer filled up the bunker with sand through its rear entrance. When the reserve 9th Brigade landed at noon, it was efficiently guided through the mass of men and equipment on the beach, through the exits, and pointed on its way inland. With bagpipes skirling, the three Canadian Scots regiments of the brigade, the Highland Light Infantry of Canada; the Stormont, Dundas, and Glengarry Highlanders; and the North Nova Scotia Highlanders moved quickly inland. With them like the steel point of the spear were the Shermans of the Sherbrooke Fusiliers Regiment. Their objective: Carpiquet.

By early evening the advance of the Brigade had reached Anisy on the division's left boundary. From the village church steeple, a tank battle was visible in the sector of the British 3rd Division, but the brigade continued to push south. Within two miles, the brigade was in action against a company of the 716th Division's reserves. Darkness had finally driven out the long summer's day about 2330, when the advance guard of the Shermans of the Sherbrooke Fusiliers and North Nova Scotia Highlanders drew heavy fire as they attempted to enter the crossroads village of Buron. Two tanks blazed up quickly and illuminated the night. An 88mm gun had a perfect field of fire down the road and quickly cleared it. Fire from 20mm flak guns and machine guns scythed the edges of the road where the infantry columns had thrown themselves. Rifleman Robert Duncan had entered the village behind the tanks, walking along the buildings. He plastered himself into a doorway and watched as the hatch flew open on the lead tank. 'I watched a human torch struggle halfway out of the commander's hatch and then collapse over the turret. The fire roared out of the hatch and just fed on him. He was the first man I had seen killed. Despite all that came later, the scene still haunts me.'[25]

The Highlanders were fighting their first action and at night. It was not surprising that their reaction was a bit stiff, but their companies finally worked west around the town and broke in. The Highland Light Infantry worked around from the east and cut off the Germans. House by house the Canadian Scots fought until Captain David McLeod and three of his men of A Company rushed the 88mm gun with grenades from the rear. With the gun crew dead, the surviving Germans surrendered. At the cost of 85 dead and wounded, the Brigade had captured 133 Germans and killed 79. It was 0113 before the Brigade was on the move again.

At Authie just outside of Caen to the west, they ran into Germans rushing south even more eagerly. This time it was the Canadians' turn to fire first and several German SPWs and tanks were destroyed. The Germans either scattered or went to earth and surrendered. There was no fight left in these men from the 21st Panzer Division, which had suffered some sort of hair-raising defeat at the hands of the British. By 0235 a nervous patrol of the Sherbrookes commanded by Second Lieutenant John P. Avery, rolled through the hangars and support buildings of Carpiquet Airfield. Expecting more Germans, Avery was surprised to find the high silhouettes of other Shermans of the East Riding Yeomanry. The Canadian 3rd Division had linked up with the British 3rd Division. 'We knew it was momentous, but we were just too tired to do more than shake hands and radio battalion.' Lieutenant Avery could not have known about the collective sigh of relief from the great men commanding the Allied armies and governments. For barely a thousand casualties, the Canadians had won a signal victory and advanced farther than any other division that day. For Lieutenant Avery sleep beckoned, and the darkness seemed safely empty of Germans.

1.   Field Marshal Erwin Rommel inspects the defences of the Atlantic Wall with General Karl Schlieben, Commander of the 709th Coastal Defence Division, southeast of Cherbourg. *U.S. National Archives*

2.   German Navy E-Boats laying smoke in the Channel after a raid on Allied shipping. Torpedo boats like these caught a U.S. convoy unawares off Slapton Sands in April 1944 and sent many of the transports to the bottom. *U.S. Army Center for Military History*

21 ARMY GROUP

PERSONAL MESSAGE
FROM THE C-IN-C

(To be read out to all Troops)

1. The time has come to deal the enemy a terrific blow in Western Europe.
   The blow will be struck by the combined sea, land, and air forces of the Allies —
   together constituting one great Allied team, under the supreme command of General
   Eisenhower.

2. On the eve of this great adventure I send my best wishes to every soldier in the Allied
   team.
   To us is given the honour of striking a blow for freedom which will live in history;
   and in the better days that lie ahead men will speak with pride in our doings. We
   have a great and a righteous cause.
   Let us pray that 'The Lord Mighty in Battle' will go forth with our armies, and that
   His special providence will aid us in the struggle.

3. I want every soldier to know that I have complete confidence in the successful outcome of the operations that we are now about to begin.
   With stout Hearts, and with enthusiasm for the contest, let us go forward to victory.

4. And, as we enter the battle, let us recall the words of a famous soldier spoken many
   years ago: —

   > "He either fears his fate too much,
   >   Or his deserts are small,
   > Who dare not put it to the touch,
   >   To win or lose it all."

B. L. Montgomery

General
C.-in-C.,
21 Army Group.

6 June 1944.

3.   Montgomery's personal message to the invasion force under his command on
the eve of the assault.

4.   'The Deadly Guns of Pointe-du-Hoc' - A German painting of the 150mm guns duelling with the U.S. Navy before turning on Omaha Beach, packed with the U.S. 1st and 29th Infantry struggling ashore. *U.S. Army Center for Military History*

5.   The successful British landings smashed through the German coastal defences and surged inland to meet all that day's objectives and more. *U.S. Department of the Army*

Daily Mirror

JUNE 7

No. 12,627
ONE PENNY
Registered
at the G.P.O.
as
a Newspaper.

Midnight news: Landings are successful • **Naval losses "regarded as very light"**

INVADERS THRUSTING INLAND

What the Germans are saying

GERMAN radio last night reported new Allied landings at Calais and Boulogne.

Powerful paratroop formations dropped behind Boulogne and north of Rouen were said to be engaged in "vicious" fighting. Other paratroops had a firm grip on a nineteen mile stretch of the Cherbourg-Caen road.

Seriorius, military commentator, said the offensive had extended to the entire Normandy peninsula.

Paris claimed a German counter-attack in the Cher-

MIDNIGHT COMMUNIQUE FROM SUPREME ALLIED H.Q. ANNOUNCED: "REPORTS OF OPERATIONS SO FAR SHOW THAT OUR FORCES SUCCEEDED IN THEIR INITIAL LANDINGS. FIGHTING CONTINUES.

"Our aircraft met with little enemy fighter opposition or AA gunfire. Naval casualties are regarded as being very light, especially when the magnitude of the operation is taken into account."

In Washington, Mr. Henry Stimson, U.S. War Secretary, said the invasion was "going very nicely." President Roosevelt said it was "running to schedule." Up to noon, U.S. naval losses were two destroyers and a landing vessel. Air losses were about one per cent.

6.   In the first press reports of the landings, no mention is made of the American disaster at Omaha Beach.

7.   Infantry from the first wave of landing craft at Omaha Beach. The high bluff overlooking them contains a deadly surprise: the tough young Saxons of the 352nd Infantry Division instead of the old men of the 716th Coastal Defence Division. *U.S. National Archives*

8.   An American glider wrecked in a field of 'Rommel's Asparagus': logs rammed in open fields and strung with wire. *U.S. National Archives*

9.   Men of the U.S. 1st Infantry Division stumble ashore on Omaha Beach after their landing craft has been sunk. Their tank and artillery support lost at sea, they were at the mercy of the strong German defences. *U.S. National Archives*

10. Looking straight down the cliff from the German defences on the Pointe-du-Hoc, at the vertical path that the 5th Rangers would take in their assault. Their drive towards the guns was stopped only yards from the casemates. *Frank Shirer*

11. German prisoners taken on D-Day by the 4th Infantry Division on Utah Beach. *U.S. National Archives*

12. Stonewallers of the 116th Infantry holding off the counterattacks of the 12th SS Panzer and 352nd Infantry Divisions at the perimeter around Vierville. *U.S. National Archives*

13. An SS machine gun team in action against the American landing at Omaha Beach. These fanatical teenage warriors shattered the 1st Division's hold on the beach and forced the 29th to evacuate. *U.S. National Archives*

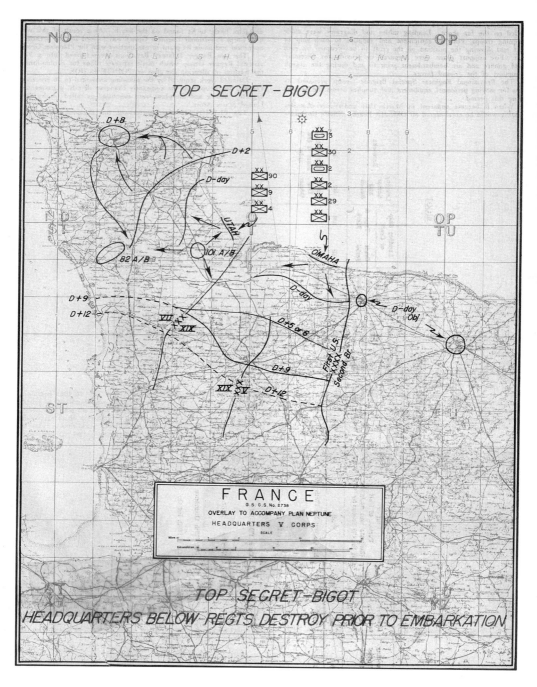

14. A map from the V Corps operations order captured by the Germans. The VII Corps version was found by Russian Ostruppen on the body of a dead officer. These orders and the landing of the British 1st Airborne Division wrecked the Allies' carefully woven deceptions and convinced Hitler that the main invasion was at Normandy. *U.S. Department of the Army*

Notes to chapter 4

1. Charles E. Miller, *History of the 13th/18th Royal Hussars (Queen Mary's Own) 1922–1947* (London: Chisman, Bradshaw, 1949) pp.92–93.

2. Tonie and Valmai Holt, *The Visitor's Guide to Normandy Landing Beaches* (Ashbourne, Derbyshire: Moorland, 1989; Edison, NJ: Hunter) pp.168–169.

3. Holt and Holt, ibid., p.176.

4. Max Hastings, *Overlord* (New York: Simon and Schuster, 1984) p.102; (London: Michael Joseph, 1984).

5. Philip Warner, *The D Day Landings* (London: William Kimber, 1980) pp.147–148.

6. Holt and Holt, *The Visitor's Guide to the Normandy Landing Beaches* (Ashbourne, Derbyshire: Moorland, 1989); (Edison, New Jersey: Hunter, 1989) p.181.

7. Holt and Holt, ibid.

8. Hans von Luck, *Panzer Commander: The Memoirs of Colonel Hans von Luck* (New York: Praeger, 1989) p.142.

9. Von Luck, ibid., p.138.

10. Unpublished account by Brigadier J.C. Cunningham, IWM, quoted in Carlo D'Este, *Decision in Normandy* (London: Collins, 1983); (New York: E.P. Dutton) pp.141–142.

11. Brigadier K. Pearce Smith, letter to Carlo D'Este, ibid., p.129.

12. Hastings, *Overlord* (London, New York: Simon and Schuster, 1984) p.115.

13. Lieutenant General Sir Giffard Martel, unpublished interview with Lieutenant General Erich Marcks, 20 July 1944.

14. Major General Sir Nigel Tapp, letter to Carlo D'Este, *Decision in Normandy* (London: Collins, 1983); (New York: E.P. Dutton, 1983) pp.139–140.

15. Douglas Botting, *The Second Front* (Chicago: Time-Life Books, Inc., 1978) p.161.

16. J.T. Crocker, *Objective Caen* (London: Ivor Nicholson and Watson, 1948) p.97.

17. John W. Baxter, *The History of the 3rd Division* (London: Hutchinson, 1947) p.211.

18. J.C. Cunningham, *Race to Caen* (Aldershot: Gale and Polden, 1951) p.69.

19. Cornelius Ryan, *The Longest Day* (New York: Simon and Schuster, 1959) p.243; (London: Gollancz, 1960).

20. Holt and Holt, *The Visitor's Guide to Normandy Landing Beaches* (Ashbourne, Derbyshire: Moorland, 1989); (Edison, New Jersey: Hunter) p.142.

21. Garry Johnson and Christopher Dunphie, *Brightly Shone the Dawn: Some Experiences of the Invasion of Normandy* (London: Warne, 1980) pp.73–75.

22. Johnson and Dunphie, ibid., pp.76–77.

23. Ewart W. Clay, *The Path of the 50th* (Aldershot: Gale & Polden, 1950) p.247.

24. Ryan, *The Longest Day* (New York: Simon & Schuster, 1959) pp.246–247; (London: Gollancz, 1960).

25. Gerald A. McKenzie, *With the Canadian Scots in Normandy* (Toronto: Dundas Press, 1955) p.89.

CHAPTER 5

Operation ROYAL OAK
7 June

At 0500 the Panzer Lehr (130th Panzer) Regiment had stopped for a breather to refuel and let the tank engines cool. It still had thirty miles to go to reach its attack sector midway between Bayeux and Caen. The entire Panzer Lehr Division was moving along five separate routes into Normandy. General Bayerlein's orders were to attack the centre of the British lodgement. His right would rest on the 21st Panzer around Caen and his left on the 12th SS Panzer somewhere north of Bayeux. The rest of the situation was obscure. Colonel Rudolf Gerhard's Panzer Lehr Regiment had already been reinforced with a battalion each of the 901st and 902nd Panzergrenadier Regiments so that they would enter the battle area ready for combat. Panzer Lehr was one of the few German tank divisions in the West to be at full strength with eighty-six Panthers and ninety-seven Mark IVs in the 1st and 2nd Battalions of its panzer regiment. An attached company had fourteen of the new Royal Tigers and nine assault guns. The panzerjäger (antitank) battalion had 31 assault guns including a company of the new Jagdpanzer IVs. As division reserve was SS Heavy Battalion 101 with its 42 Tigers and its renowned tank killer, Michael Wittmann. Bayerlein had traced the regiment's route of advance to place it in the centre of the lodgement: Aunay-sur-Odon to Villers-Bocage to Tilly-sur-Seulles. The panzergrenadier regiments would be taking parallel routes on either side.

Also at 0500 the men of the British 1st Airborne Division were making their final checks before loading their Dakota transports and gliders in southern England. The forces available to Major General Robert E. 'Roy' Urquart, a tough veteran, were the 1st Airlanding Brigade, and the 1st and 4th Parachute Brigades. With supporting arms and services he had 9,000 men and an additional 1,100 glider pilots. Attached for this operation was the Major General Stanislaw Sosabowski's 1st Polish Parachute Brigade of 1,500 men. The air transport units that had dropped three airborne divisions the day before with small loss in aircraft would be supporting the single drop of Urquart's complete division at 1030. The aircrews were tired, but their ground crews had worked miracles in turning their aircraft around. Urquart had not been happy about the last minute change of targets. Initially the division had prepared for brigade drops clustered around Evrecy. Now that had all been changed. Brigades would be dropped in a wide arc from Villers-Bocage to Aunay-sur-Odon to Thury-Harcourt on the Orne. Their mission was to hold these crossroads towns for only a few hours until relieved by 7th Armoured and 3rd Canadian Divisions. There wasn't much else he could do. It would be impossible to fight as a division along a fifteen mile front.

Seizing Opportunities

Montgomery arrived at his newly established headquarters in the Château de Creullet, on the northern bank of the Seulles across from Creully, early in the morning. His appraisal of the situation to his staff that morning emphasized the opportunities presented by the landings. The linchpin of his grand strategic plan, the success of the American landings, had fallen out with the disaster at Omaha and the tenuous foothold at Utah. Under these conditions, to draw the German panzer reserves upon the British forces without the great American right hook building up as a counterweight seemed to court disaster. Not so. Contingency planning had already thought this through. The British divisions had met all their objectives and in a few cases gone beyond. In the process, the only German panzer reserve within striking range had been destroyed. Although strong German forces remained in the Omaha sector, the British had torn open the front in their sector. Opportunity beckoned for a rapid exploitation that could strike deep to the south and then wheel west to trap the Germans up against the very beach at Omaha.

Now was also the time to reap the rewards of confusion in the German chain of command. Without revealing its Ultra source, he announced that according to the Germans, Rommel was missing in action or possibly a prisoner. 'Will someone check the prisoner pens? If we have him, I would like to have him to dinner.' They did, however, have a very live German corps commander in their possession. He would have been even more pleased had he known that the middle link in the German chain of command in Normandy was about to be snipped as well. General Dollmann, 7th Army Commander, was rushing to LXXXIV Corps headquarters at St. Lô by car to take personal control of the situation, when a pair of Typhoons strafed his car, leaving him dead in the burning back seat.

Montgomery now pointed to the area southwest of Caen, the arc of crossroads towns that the Red Devils would seize. The 1st Airborne Division was even now airborne and should be hitting its drop zones by 1030. The Red Devils, strung like gems on a strand would be the shield that would hold approaching panzer reserves as far forward as possible. At one stroke, they would double the depth of the lodgement area and open up opportunities for 2nd Army to manoeuvre west to recoup the loss of Omaha and salvage the grand plan. Again Ultra had informed him that Panzer Lehr was making a forced march to attack somewhere between Bayeux and Caen.

It was late in the morning before 2nd Army could work out the planning and disseminate the instructions necessary for the drive inland to support the 1st Airborne, now codenamed Operation ROYAL OAK. Hours before the British were ready to move, eyes lifted skyward all along the coast to see the second great airstream of transports and gliders to cross into France in two days. The truth was that 2nd Army's divisions were not neatly arrayed along the forward edge of the lodgement everywhere. The beaches had been organized to push new troops and supplies inland and were working well, but the press of traffic meant that new divisions were being unloaded over several days and were not immediately available. The divisions already ashore had been spread across their sectors by the fighting. The 50th and 3rd British were still in combat on the flanks and in reducing isolated strong points. Only the 3rd Canadian Division was in a position to put more than one brigade into the push. In all, six brigades including two weak tank brigades would be making this push. Behind them, the elements of 49th Division, which was also landing on 7 June, would be committed as reserve as its elements came ashore.

Case Three Revisited

Within minutes of the passage of the airborne stream over the coast, von Rundstedt was informed. This Junker of the old school swallowed his contempt of the man he scorned as the Bohemian Corporal. He called OKW and demanded to speak immediately to the Führer. Jodl again tried to be a buffer for his master who had worked into the morning as usual and was now sleeping late. But von Rundstedt was in an angry mood and exercised his right as a field marshal to demand immediate access to the Supreme War Lord.

Hitler's voice was vague when he answered. Von Rundstedt cut through the man's attempt at small talk:

> The Allies are, as we speak, conducting another massive airborne drop south of Caen, perhaps in the direction of Falaise, Lisieux, and Argentan. We can expect a landing in strength equal to that of the invasion. Such a landing will sever our communications with Normandy from the north and west. While we defeated the Americans at one landing, I must make it clear again that the British have ripped open the front in their sector and are pouring inland. Both Rommel and General Marcks, commanding LXXXIV Corps are missing and presumed captured. General Dollmann was killed only an hour before. Panzer Lehr is the only reinforcement approaching the front and cannot hope to stop the British advance. I believe that the Allies have now expended the last of their airborne divisions. They would not do so for only a diversion. Normandy is the main landing. Mein Führer, I must have Case Three. I need your decision at once.

Von Rundstedt heard nothing for a moment. Then Hitler's strangely weary voice said flatly, 'Yes, Field Marshal, execute Case Three'.[1]

The Race to Reinforce

Whether the residue of drugs in Hitler's body had overridden his normal assertiveness or whether he had indeed thrown the dice with the ruthless certainty of earlier victories didn't really matter. Case Three kicked into action as fast as the orders could be relayed down the German chain of command. Almost every panzer and good quality division in OB West as well any needed coastal division near the fighting began to move toward the new front in Normandy. As a calculated risk, Hitler declared that the remaining coastal defence divisions would have to hold whatever further landings might come. The Allies through Ultra learned of the gamble as soon as von Rundstedt. Now

German Divisions in Action in Normandy 6–7 June

21st Pz	6 June	711th CD	6 June
91st Inf	6 June	716th CD	6 June
352nd Inf	6 June	Pz Lehr	7 June
709th CD	6 June		

German Divisions Ordered to the Normandy Front Under Case Three, 7 June

DIVISION	EXPECTED ARRIVAL	DIVISION	EXPECTED ARRIVAL
2nd Pz	8 June	19th LF	14 June
116th Pz	8 June	1st SS Pz	18 June
346th Inf	8 June	2nd SS Pz	19 June
17th LF	8 June	9th SS Pz	24 June
77th Inf	9 June	10th SS Pz	24 June
84th Inf	9 June	11th Pz	25 June
3rd FJ	10 June	265th CD	26 June
17th SS PzG	11 June	266th CD	26 June
5th FJ	12 June	275th Inf	26 June
331st Inf	13 June	276th Inf	26 June
85th Inf	14 June	277th Inf	26 June
353rd Inf	14 June		

Pz	Panzer	LF	Luftwaffe Field
PzG	Panzergrenadier	CD	Coastal Defence
FJ	Fallschirmjäger		

Allied Divisions in Action in Normandy 6 June

1st Inf (U.S.)	49th Inf (Br) (elements)
3rd Inf (Br)	50th Inf (Br)
3rd Inf (CA)	51st Inf (Br) (elements)
4th Inf (U.S.)	79th AR (Br)
6th AB (Br)	82nd AB (U.S.)
29th Inf (U.S.)	101st AB (U.S.)

Allied Reinforcement Schedule for 7–30 June

DIVISION	EXPECTED ARRIVAL	DIVISION	EXPECTED ARRIVAL
7th Ar (Br)	7 June	9th Inf (U.S.)	14 June
1st AB (Br)	7 June	79th Inf (U.S.)	19 June
90th Inf (U.S.)	7 June	43rd Inf (Br)	24 June
2nd Inf (U.S.)	8 June	53rd Inf (Br)	27 June
30th Inf (U.S.)	10 June	59th Inf (Br)	27 June
2nd Ar (U.S.)	10 June	83rd Inf (U.S.)	27 June
3rd Ar (U.S.)	12 June	Gds Ar (Br)	28 June
11th Ar (Br)	13 June	2nd Inf (CA)	30 June
15th Inf (Br)	14 June		

AR   Armour   AB   Airborne   Inf   Infantry

the battle would be a race between the ability of the German divisions to enter the battle rapidly and the ability of the Allies to land follow-on divisions into the lodgement.

At dawn on 7 June, the Allies had ten divisions ashore, eight that had made and survived the initial landings on D-Day and the follow-on 51st Highland and 49th Divisions that began landing later that first day. The Germans had four divisions in action and parts of several others. Both sides had already written off divisions from their orders-of-battle. The Americans were still in shock over the loss of their incomparable 1st Infantry Division, and the Germans had lost almost all of the middling 21st Panzer Division save for Colonel von Luck's tenacious 125th Panzergrenadier Regiment. The 716th Coastal Defence Division had just disappeared. If simple logistics were everything, the Germans would win the race to reinforce their forces in Normandy and achieve an overwhelmingly favourable correlation of forces against the Allies. The overland movement of German forces was far simpler than the transportation by ship of forces across the Channel and their landing and resupply over the beaches.

Running the Gauntlet

Allied foresight had planned for a few complications to disrupt this German advantage. The preinvasion air campaign had already tangled into junk much of the railway system, upon which much of the reinforcement depended. It was essential that the long distance movement of armoured forces be by rail. Tracked armoured vehicles require much more care and maintenance than wheeled vehicles and will break down with distressing frequency when forced to make long road marches. To the ruin of the railroads was now added a relentless attack on the roadbound German columns by the Allied air forces and by the French resistance forces. The latter had been activated for just such a contingency. Among them, the recalcitrant and proud Bretons and Gascons were the most determined and ferocious. Only the 15th Army's 84th and 346th Divisions were able to slip into the battle without hindrance, announcing their presence with strong attacks on the British 51st Highland and 6th Airborne Divisions east of the Orne on 8 June.

The rest passed through a gauntlet of air attack and ground ambush that slowed their advance and inflicted heavy losses before anyone had seen a single Briton or American. Of them all, the 2nd SS Panzer Division 'Das Reich', stationed in Perigord near Montauban, had the most horrific journey. Das Reich had been one of Hitler's favourite divisions, and he had personally chosen Montauban in the golden south of France for the division to recover from its huge losses in Russia. In April Das Reich received nine thousand replacements, a collection of twelve nationalities including *Volkdeutscher* from Hungary and Romania, and Alsatians, human material the Waffen SS would not even have considered a few years ago. The officers and NCOs were all veterans of the fighting in Russia and quickly instilled an esprit de corps among their questionably Aryan replacements that would lead to an incredibly low desertion rate. No officer but the division commander was older than thirty-four. They had been drawn from lower and middle class backgrounds that would have disqualified them from the Army, but they were men of natural talent that made the Waffen SS at the regimental and lower levels without peer as warriors. The opposite obtained at the division and corps level, where the lack of higher training and political preference told. SS Brigadeführer Heinz Lammerding, Das Reich's commander, was a good example. Cold and colourless, his rise had been due to Himmler's favour. He showed little flair as a commander and had made his mark hunting partisans with that mercilessness that seemed to excite Himmler so much. By D-Day, the division had been rebuilt to a strength of 17,000 men. Its replacement equipment was slower in coming. Its armoured strength did not exceed 44 Mark IVs, 25 Panthers, and 33 assault guns when the table of organization called for 231 such vehicles. Despite this, Das Reich's intact appearance in Normandy was considered with dread by the Allies. For that reason, Das Reich would be the object of very special preparations.

Lammerding quickly found every alternative slammed in his face as he tried to prepare his division for movement to Normandy. On D-Day, one of the best agents of the Special Operations Executive (SOE) in France led his team to destroy most of Das Reich's fuel dumps. The Allied air forces destroyed all bridges over the Loire River between Orleans and the Atlantic on 7 June. That night the 'Dambusters' of RAF 617 Squadron sped their 12,000-pound bombs, the heaviest in the world, in their first use, into the mouth of the Saumur–Parthenay railroad tunnel, the last high speed means of passing the barrier of one of France's great rivers. The tunnel shuddered and then collapsed under the impact of one six-ton bomb after another. Another British agent launched his team and paralyzed the railroad system between Montauban and Toulouse, effectively stopping Das Reich's trains and bridging equipment, the latter being the only remaining means for the division to cross the Loire.

With the railroads shut down, Lammerding was forced to put the division on the road under its own wheeled and tracked transportation. His fuel would give out before he reached the Loire, but OB West had promised a fuel resupply convoy would meet them en route. Das Reich's problems had just begun. Its road march took it into the small valleys, stone villages, and roadside granite outcroppings of that region of Gascony that nature and the hand of man had seemingly designed for the ambush, the mine, and the sniper. The hate-filled French resistance and the SOE's teams made the most of their opportunities, making the SS pay with blood for almost every mile. Tank commanders were shot dead standing up in their hatches, tank and APC tracks were blown off by mines, soft-skinned vehicles and their passengers were machine-gunned and left littering the road, and small detachments were wiped out. Day after day the division bled from a thousand cuts, and losses began to equal those of a serious battle with regular troops. Throughout the region, the French had risen in open revolt and besieged German garrisons. Lammerding was in his element and immediately resorted to reprisal and terror. Somewhere along the way, his taste for blood and his hysterical messages to OKW prompted orders for him to engage in antipartisan and terror operations against the civil population. Both he and OKW appeared to have forgotten why Das Reich was on the road.

On 10 June, the bloodletting caught up with Lammerding in a little brown stone Gascon village with slate roofs. An SOE team led by Captain C.D. Baker of the Scots Guards was waiting there, not for Lammerding especially, but for whatever element they could isolate by blocking the hairpin turns outside the town. The British were reinforced with a few bands of Frenchmen armed with 1914 Lebel rifles and a Sten or two. Just outside the village the road turned sharply around a rocky cut in a hill. Sergeant John Patterson, RE, watched an armoured car and two staff cars go by, then twisted the detonator in his hand, just as the first of several more armoured cars appeared. The blast tossed the first armoured car into the ditch and triggered a rock fall that blocked the road. The dozen Frenchmen with him shot down the Germans who tried to climb out of the cars. In the town, Captain Baker watched as the armoured car disappeared around a corner of the narrow main street. The two staff cars were now helpless. A fusilade of shots at close range ripped through both of them, whipping around the occupants like rag dolls. The first one crashed into the village fountain and the second into the first. One man staggered out of the first car and was shot down. The Frenchmen rushed to the wreckage. One of them climbed on the running board of the second car, took careful aim with his Lebel, and fired. Baker was right behind him and took in the scene with one glance. Dead SS general officers invariably extracted a bloody revenge, even from the grave. Within two minutes, Baker and his men were gone. So were the inhabitants of the village.

Command devolved upon Obersturmbannführer Christian Tychsen, the thirty-four year old commander of the 2nd SS Panzer Regiment whose shaven bullet head and hideously scarred chin made him a chilling sight. Wounded nine times, the brave, battle-hardened, and coldly efficient Tychsen was everything Lammerding was not. Above all he was a good soldier not likely to be diverted from the main objective. Reprisals would be limited to shooting up the towns and villages through which the division passed if it had met with resistance in the area. French attacks did not lessen, but Das Reich stopped wasting time going out of its way to deal with them.

Not everything went against Das Reich during its march north. An SAS detachment of fifty men in armoured jeeps had been air-dropped on D-Day northwest of Limoges. Warned by signals intelligence of an important target of opportunity, they tried to intercept the OB-West fuel convoy, but Tychsen had been faster and swept it up into the protective arms of the division. He cornered the SAS in woods, killed thirty and shot most of the survivors. He authorized only one minor detour when the town of Tulle had risen to besiege its German garrison. A battle group rode to the rescue and committed the usual atrocities after breaking the siege. Another potential detour was barely avoided the next day. A special vehicle had been separated from its convoy and taken a wrong turn down a country lane leading to the village of Oradour-sur-Vayre and been ambushed. As the Frenchmen broke open one of the heavy wooden boxes in the truck, gold bars fell onto the road. They had unwittingly snatched the profits of certain senior officers of Das Reich. French peasants know the value of gold. They have buried enough over the centuries, but even they were momentarily agog at their windfall and did not see the armoured car detachment burst around the bend in the road to sweep them away with their machine guns. The gold was reloaded into the German vehicles which rapidly returned to the safety of the main column. Another detachment had mistaken the name of the village towards which the truck had disappeared and sped into Oradour-sur-Glane. The commander ordered the population to assemble and accused them of hiding explosives. The women and children were marched into the local church and its doors locked. The men were lined up in the square. The officer was an efficient killer. His machine guns were well placed to make short work of the men. The church would burn quickly. Just then he was called to his vehicle by a call from his battalion commander. The special shipment had been found. Rejoin the column immediately. As the last vehicle raced out of town, the men ran to the church to release their families.

The ambushes and the coordinated air strikes continued, but with the fuel carriers in tow, Das Reich cleared the Loire over its own bridges on the night of 12 June. Advance elements reached the front three days later. The SS laagered in the woods and along the hedgerows with a profound sense of relief that they would soon be fighting proper soldiers instead of warding off the maddening stings of swarms of blood-sucking insects. As it was they had lost over two thousand men killed and wounded and a quarter of their combat vehicles to break-downs or combat loss.

The Panzer Lehr Division, much closer to the front, suffered far more from Allied air attack than Das Reich. General Bayerlein himself became quite adept at leaping for safety from his staff car. On one occasion, his driver helped him to safety only to die in the attack that left the staff car a twisted ruin. His orderly officer, Captain Alexander Hartdegen, left these indelible impressions of the division's march to the front:

> Dozens of wrecked vehicles, now no more than steel skeletons, lay by the roadside burning and smoldering. The sector from Caumont to Villers-Bocage was a road of death. Burnt-out tractors, many of them still smoldering with dead bodies strewn alongside, this was the appalling backcloth throughout our journey.
>
> Unless a man has been through these fighter-bomber attacks he cannot know what the invasion meant. You lie there, helpless in a roadside ditch, in a furrow on a field, or under a hedge, pressed into the ground, your face in the dirt – and there it comes towards you, roaring. There it is. Diving at you. Now you hear the whine of the bullets. Now you are for it.
>
> You feel like crawling under the ground. Then the bird has gone. But it comes back. Twice. Three times. Not till you think they've wiped out everything do they leave. Until then you are helpless. Like a man facing a firing-squad. Even if you survive it's no more than temporary reprieve. Ten such attacks in succession are a real foretaste of hell.[2]

Over the two to three weeks following D-Day, Army Group B's and OB

West's reserves stumbled into Normandy trailing similar experiences and losses. Their freshness had been bled away in the countless dashes to the doubtful safety of roadside ditches and the numberless battle drill reactions to ambushes. But they arrived. Awe was the proper term to describe the Allies' reaction to the mass movement of German forces. The red goose eggs on the map of France seemed to move closer to Normandy each day, despite Allied foreknowledge and countermeasures. Hitler had rolled for the whole game. Twenty-four divisions, more than a quarter-of-a-million men, were on the road to Normandy.

The Allies Race

The Allies were immediately more successful in reinforcing their lodgement because of the follow-on divisions already at sea. Elements of the British 51st Highland and the 49th had already come ashore on D-Day. They were followed the next day by the 7th Armoured Division and the patched-up U.S. 29th Division consisting of the two uncommitted infantry regiments of the 1st and 29th Divisions as well as their artillery and trains. The 29th was attached to the British XXX Corps. The loss of Omaha had left all the follow-on divisions of the U.S. V Corps, 2nd Infantry and 2nd Armored Divisions, without a home. Montgomery decided to feed them immediately through Gold and Juno beaches and move them to the right of Gold where the V Corps could resume its attack on the Omaha sector but from the land side.

On the surface the German and Allied build-ups appeared to balance each other out. The Germans reasonably hoped to have about thirty divisions in Normandy by the end of June and the Allies twenty-three. The actual correlation of forces was far more lop-sided. Most of the Allied divisions were effectively twice the strength of the German divisions, especially the infantry. The Allied divisions would be entering the fight with their complete tables of equipment and the ability easily to replace material losses as long as the logistics flow from southern England was unimpeded. The Germans would be entering the fight after suffering personnel and equipment losses equal to a major battle in their road marches. Most of OB West's supply dumps had been placed behind the 15th Army on the Pas-de-Calais and could only be moved at great risk. Concentration of Allied air attacks on the German fuel and ball-bearing industries had multiplied the number of immobilized vehicles awaiting fuel or repairs. The Allies also had the Germans completely outclassed in firepower support. In addition to plentiful Allied artillery, the divisions could rely on unrelenting air support limited only by the weather and by the ships of the Royal and U.S. Navies that could hammer any German attack flat within range of their guns, the outer range of which was about eighteen miles. So thoroughly absent from the fighting was the Luftwaffe that the German troops composed an aircraft identification code: 'If it shows up during the day it's the American

Air Force; if it shows up at night, it's the Royal Air Force; and if it never shows up, it's the Luftwaffe.'

If the Germans on the road to the front had to contend with air attack and ambush, the Allied reinforcements had to deal with the weather, German shelling, and the remnants of German anti-landing obstacles as well as the intricacies of amphibious resupply. Had the Luftwaffe been able to do half of what the Allied air forces were doing to the German ground units, the continued reinforcement of the lodgement might have been crippled. The ordeal of elements of the 67th Armored Regiment, 2nd Armored Division were typical. An LST bearing three tank companies and maintenance elements struck a mine off Gold Beach on the evening of 9 June. The explosion sent a shower of debris into the air as it broke the back of the ship. The ship quickly listed and defied the Navy's attempts to tow her ashore and sank in eight minutes with all equipment. Sixty-six men were killed and wounded; among the dead were two company commanders. Seventeen medium and 14 light tanks, 6 half-tracks, 3 self-propelled guns, and 6 jeeps went to the bottom. So strong was the explosion that the ship several hundred yards away carrying the division commander and staff was jarred and showered with debris. The delays and confusion attendant on such vast and complex logistics had their effects as well. Seventh Armoured Division landed only to discover that the ship carrying the infantry carriers of its infantry brigade had been sidetracked back across the Channel to an English port.

The weather was the great wild card for the Allies. The summer of 1944 was proving to have the worst Channel weather in a century. The invasion had nearly been derailed by the storms of the fourth and fifth, and only Eisenhower's nerve to take the main chance and the skill of the navies had allowed them to leap through the narrow weather window.

Operation ROYAL OAK

Villers-Bocage

Elements of Panzer Lehr's reconnaissance battalion had just passed through Villers-Bocage on the way to Tilly-sur-Seulles at 1030. Colonel Gerhard had reached Villers-Bocage at the same time with the lead elements of his regiment's battle group built around the Panther battalion. The drone of hundreds of aircraft engines had every eye looking upward as wave after wave of transports began spilling their sticks of paratroopers. It occurred to Gerhard that he was experiencing something unique, a ground and air meeting engagement. He had lived through more of the normal kind of meeting engagements on the Russian Front than he cared to remember. Then it had been only two ground forces, both attacking towards each other and in ignorance of the other, the

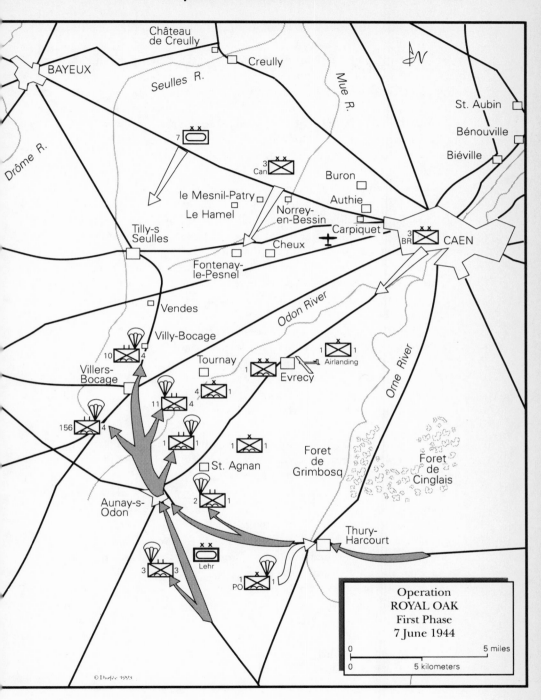

Operation
ROYAL OAK
First Phase
7 June 1944

0   5 miles

0   5 kilometers

kind of situation that put a premium on quick wits and daring, one reason it was such a dreaded situation.

Only when they began their silken descent did the men of the 4th Parachute Brigade realize what had happened. The lights winking up at them from the columns of German vehicles began turning them into bloody bundles that would hit the ground like limp rag dolls. Rifles, machine guns, and the numerous flak guns in the columns passing through the town were practically engaged in target practice. No one was shooting back at them. The bane of the paratrooper was that he was essentially defenceless until he hit the ground. The 11th Parachute Battalion suffered the most. Its drop zone was the open fields south of the town paralleling the road on which the Panzer Lehr was stopped. Dead paratroopers dropped by the scores into those fields. North of the town, 10th Parachute Battalion suffered as well in its descent, saved from the more thorough slaughter of its sister battalion by the fact that the Germans' fields of fire were restricted by the buildings of the town. The 156th Parachute Battalion landed to the southwest of the town beyond the high ground, Hill 213, that was their objective. Gerhard's subordinate commanders had slipped the leash on their men who surged across the fields to hunt down any survivors. It was hardly worth their effort to go after 11th Para; the Germans counted 337 dead paratroopers still attached to their harnesses in the fields. Aside from a few men that had been blown east into wooded terrain, the loss of the battalion was complete. The Germans had also worked through the side streets and into the fields and to pursue 10th Para as well, but the more broken and wooded ground saved many of those who hit the ground alive. Nevertheless, with 193 dead and wounded in the first five minutes of the operation, 10th Battalion was badly hurt.

Only 156th Battalion landed intact and was able to seize its objective of Hill 213 through which passed the road to Villers-Bocage. On the hill were a few buildings including a post office and bus stop. Within minutes they were attacked from the west by a panzergrenadier company supported by tanks. The Germans were confined to the road because of the two streams on either side. Two Panthers led the attack with the infantry behind. Sergeant Willy Acton's section had occupied the post office with a machine gun and two Piats. Acton had enlisted in 1933 and had volunteered from one of the Guards regiments to join an even more elite outfit, the paras. For him the spit and polish of the Guards had only one useful application: keep weapons as clean and perfect as any Guardsman's breastplate. As the Germans pressed forward pushing A Company back up the hill, the first Panther clanked up towards the post office. Acton pushed his men into the cellar of the building. The first Panther swivelled its gun and put a shell into the building, sending a shower of stamps and plaster dust out the windows. The tanks moved on, and Acton rushed his men out of the cellar. The machine gunners set up their piece. Every link of ammo

carefully oiled and ready, as Acton had beat into them. They fired into the unsuspecting panzergrenadiers now separated from the tanks by a dozen metres. The Germans left a tangle of gray bodies in the road as they scampered back down the hill to find cover. Acton rushed out of the building with his two Piat gunners and ran up behind the last tank. The gunner knelt and fired the spring-propelled shaped charge. There was a shower of sparks and the rear engine compartment exploded. Flames spurted out of the grilles on the back deck. The hatches flew open as the crew tried to escape. Acton was on them with his pistol, shooting one and taking the others prisoner. With the remaining Piat gunner he stalked the remaining Panther whose escape was now blocked by its burning companion. Another shot at close range and the Panther began to burn.

Aunay-sur-Odon and Thury-Harcourt

The slaughter at Villers-Bocage was repeated at the other drop zones around Aunay-sur-Odon and Thury-Harcourt, as the British 1st Parachute Brigade fell upon other columns of Panzer Lehr Division. At Aunay-sur-Odon, the 1st, 2nd, and 3rd Parachute Battalions and Division Headquarters landed north, east, and south of the town in the open fields separated by the spokes of roads that led into the town. To their grief those roads were full of Panzer Lehr vehicles. The massacre of the 11th Paras at Villers-Bocage was reenacted three times for 1st Brigade. Even the division commander 'Roy' Urquart was killed in the air and was later found in a vegetable garden on the outskirts of the town. The 1st's brigadier was killed as he tried to escape through the tall corn from a row of tanks and SPWs beating the survivors like an Indian tiger hunt. Nowhere was more than a platoon able to rally itself. A few stragglers stumbled into the wooded safety of the Red-du-Bois, southwest of the town. In an hour, the brigade lost 732 killed and wounded and 306 prisoners and ceased to exist.

The Poles fell with more luck southwest of Thury-Harcourt almost on top of a German supply column. These Germans tried to escape rather than attack. They merely jammed their trucks on the road. Sosabowski's brigade had fallen in three tight drop zones with little dispersion. The former war academy professor's battalions rushed upon the stalled German convoys and began killing Germans. Most had already had the good sense to abandon their vehicles and flee back into Thury-Harcourt with the Poles baying after them. That was all the encouragement the Germans needed to keep running over the Orne River bridge so the town was quickly cleared. In less than an hour Sosabowski had taken his objective, killed or captured several hundred Germans, lost only seventeen men, and put the objective in state of all-round defence.

Evrecy

A German flak battery at Evrecy was the only opposition to the 1st Airlanding

Brigade's assault around the town. For the slow plywood Horsa gliders, it was more than enough. The gunners were adept and cool, pulling out of the sky at least fifteen of the fragile gliders and a half dozen transports in their slow, straight approaches. Oberleutnant (First Lieutenant) Wolfgang Priller was amazed how easily the gliders splintered and disintegrated, spilling bodies and equipment into the sky. His two 88mm and four 20mm anti-aircraft guns could not fire fast enough at all the targets that kept landing around the town.

Within minutes the targets were gone from the sky. Scores had landed for every one shot down. Now the British organized their battalions and pressed into the town from east and north. Companies of the 2nd Battalion of the South Staffordshire Regiment and 7th Battalion of the King's Own Scottish Borderers closed in on Priller's battery. The 1st Battalion of the Border Regiment set up defensive positions south of the town. Priller ordered an immediate retreat. Luftwaffe flak units without infantry support were easy game at times like this. His battery ran into the Border Regiment's ambush south of town. Priller survived simply because he was the last man out of town having made sure every one of his men had escaped. The enemy fished him out of stream and marched him and the other prisoners back into town.

With Evrecy as its apex, the British should have had a good grip by now on a large triangle of territory into which the ground forces could flow. Instead, the stout door they had designed had been smashed at Villers-Bocage and Aunay-sur-Odon leaving only the Poles as a lonely outpost at Thury-Harcourt. The destruction of the 1st and 4th Parachute Brigades had fallen upon them with such speed that barely a hint of it had reached outward. Only the Poles and the 1st Landing Brigade had reported successes. Leaving the Staffords holding the town, Brigadier G.W. Lathbury assembled the brigade on the road heading south to Aunay-sur-Odon. Luckily the jeeps and their towed 6-pounder anti-tank guns had survived the glider landings. He put them near the head of the column and set off. It was now almost noon.

Along the forward edge of the battlefield reconnaissance regiments of three of 2nd Army's divisions crossed Highway 13, almost two hours after the air drop, far behind schedule. They were lucky to have begun even that soon. Bad weather had delayed the landing of 7th Armoured Division's 22nd Armoured Brigade, the main exploitation force for Operation ROYAL OAK.

On the right part of 8th Hussars led the way for 22nd Armoured Brigade – 1st and 5th Royal Tank Regiments, 4th County of London Yeomanry, and 1st Battalion the Rifle Brigade (Motor) with the 5th Royal Horse Artillery toward Tilly-sur-Seulles and Villers-Bocage beyond. Much of Major General Erskine's Division had not yet arrived including his 131st Infantry Brigade, and the 56th Brigade from 50th Division was attached in its place. Next in line came the Canadian 3rd Division's 17th Duke of York's Royal Canadian Hussars (7th Reconnaissance Regiment) ahead of the Canadian Scots of 9th Brigade still supported by the Sherman tanks of the Sherbrooke Fusiliers, and 8th Brigade in echelon to the rear. Out of Caen rode the 3rd British Division's 3rd Reconnaissance Regiment toward Evrecy. Behind rode the much reduced 8th Armoured Brigade and behind them marched Brigadier Cunningham's 9th Brigade still exhilarated from their conquest of Caen the night before.

An hour later Bayerlein was driving past columns of survivors of the two parachute brigades to meet with Colonel Gerhard in Villers-Bocage. The fields he passed were dotted with fluttering white silk parachutes still attached to dead paratroopers. His own men seemed in excellent spirits. It had been a lucky day so far. An apple had fallen out the sky right into the division's lap. Gerhard had more good news. He had learned from prisoners that a large ground operation was on its way to link up with the airborne forces. One of their objectives would be Villers-Bocage. They pored over the map. The unexpected halt had allowed most of Panzer Lehr's combat power to concentrate between Villers-Bocage and Aunay-sur-Odon. Bayerlein realized he could strike with a closed fist at what ever was coming towards Villers-Bocage.

The advance of the 7th Armoured had gone well for some five miles until the 8th Hussars bumped into a reconnaissance element of Panzer Lehr on the outskirts of Tilly-sur-Seulles. The tank of the first troop leader was brewed up. The Hussars deployed and called in a battalion of the 56th Brigade to clear the town. The Germans stayed in contact long enough to delay the British for an hour before they slipped out of town. Similar delays in the thick hedgerow country slowed 7th Armoured down on the road towards Villers-Bocage. Erskine planned to send 1st Tanks to occupy the high ground a mile or so north of the town and the 5th Tanks on a similar mission south of the town. The County of London Yeomanry and 56th Brigade would advance through the town itself. He was advancing straight into the jaws of the trap set by Bayerlein and Gerhard. They could tactically read a map as well as Erskine and had had the forewarning the British officer had not. The Panther Battalion's tanks each supported by panzergrenadiers of the 902nd were on the same two pieces of high ground selected by Erskine for his two tank regiments. Panzergenadiers were in the town and surrounding hedgerows. In the woods just to the north of the town were the Tigers of Heavy Battalion 101. Echeloned back towards Aunay-sur-Odon was the Mark IV battalion, the 901st Panzergrenadier Regiment, and the divisonal assault gun battalion.

The 8th Hussars had pushed to Villy-Bocage, a hamlet barely a mile from Villers-Bocage, when the Germans in their front seemed to melt away. There was still no contact with the paratroopers. Lieutenant Colonel the Viscount Cranley, Commanding Officer of the Yeomanry, was worrying and had wanted a thorough reconnaissance of the area. He was told to push on regardless. There should have been patrols from the 1st Airborne at the very least. There was only a little gunfire to the south of the town, it seemed. A Troop of the Hussars

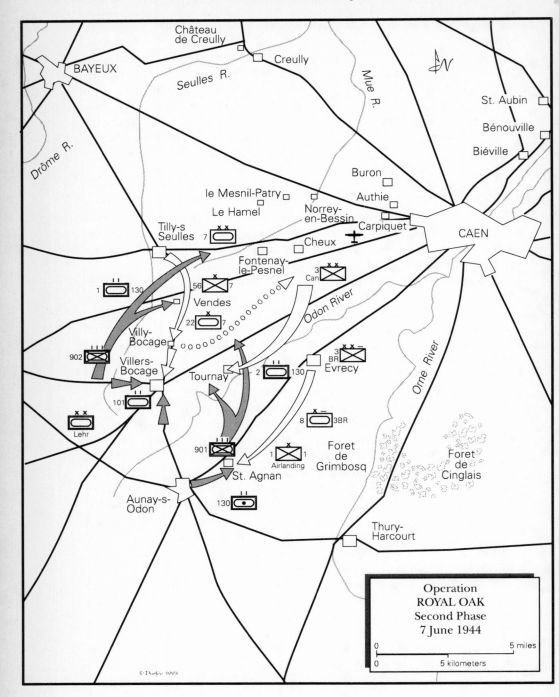

Operation
ROYAL OAK
Second Phase
7 June 1944

0   5 miles

0   5 kilometers

drove warily into the town followed by the Yeomanry and behind them in trucks the 2nd Battalion The South Wales Borderers from 56th Brigade. Cranley was at the head of his column in a scout car, standing up in the hatch, when the Hussar's tank in front of him exploded as it passed a side street. Out of the street lumbered a Tiger. It pivot steered to face down the street, its huge 88mm pointing right at Cranley. The Viscount's driver was faster than the Tiger's gunner and accelerated forward and between the tank and nearest French house. As they passed, Cranley read the red-outlined number 200 in white on the tank's turret rear. The gunner fired anyway and brewed up the first Cromwell in line. Behind the first Tiger another appeared and turned right to shoot up the Hussars. The Desert Rats had stumbled into the trap set by the Tyrannosaurus Rex of the tank world, the 57-tonne Mark VI, Tiger I. The most feared tank in the world, its high velocity 'long as a telephone pole' 88mm gun could punch holes through any Allied tank with ease. Its frontal armour was proof against anything the Allies had except the 17-pounder antitank gun. Its only drawbacks were a certain clumsiness and mechanical unreliability.

Tiger 200 ground down the street brewing up one Cromwell after another. Two more followed. The Cromwells with their useless 75mm guns were in a deathtrap. There was enough room for the Tigers to drive past them but not enough for the Cromwells to turn around. One after another the tanks of B Squadron burst into flames as the 88 tore holes through their inadequate armour. Here and there a Yeomanry tank backed into a side street, but Tiger 200 or one of the following Tigers calmly swivelled its turret and destroyed it. The Cromwell commanded by Captain Pat Dyas backed off the street into a front garden as Tiger 200 passed. Dyas's gunner was facing forward when the second Tiger passed, in effect crossing the Cromwell's T. The gunner fired at the more vulnerable side. The tank lurched to the side and crashed into a building as smoke and flames erupted from its hatches. Dyas was to have the only such piece of luck in the Yeomanry that day.

Another dozen Tigers had emerged at the same time from the woods to attack the rear of the Yeomanry on the outskirts of the town. The range was so close that the first salvo left a dozen British vehicles burning, extinguishing B Squadron in thirty seconds. A second Tiger company followed the first and broke off to strike for the road leading to Villy-Bocage. C Squadron was manoeuvring wildly to escape the Tigers' close-range killing. The second Tiger company cut the road behind them and swept upon the South Wales Borderers truck column. The firing ahead in the town had warned the Welshmen to dismount and deploy on either side of the road or they would have been destroyed along with their transportation. The few 6-pounders fired and watched their shot bounce off the Tigers' frontal armour and then quickly lost the gunnery duel to the 88s. One gun crew had been lucky enough to fire at an impossibly close range and see the Tiger stop and burn. An 88 shell from another Tiger then sent the gun spinning backwards and scattering its crew. The other Tiger rode up and down the road over the trucks and other vehicles in the column. The Borderers pulled back where they could or slipped into the dense protection of the hedgerows. From there they fought back with Piats and the one or two surviving 6-pounders. Without infantry the Tigers could not advance very far in such country and pulled back toward the town where forty-three Cromwells and thirty-seven other vehicles of the Yeomanry and Hussars burned. Viscount Cranley had survived to be taken prisoner. As he was being interrogated, he asked who was in Tiger 200 that had trapped his battalion in the street. The Germans present all grinned and said at once, 'Michael Wittmann!'

To the north of the town, 5th Tanks was stopped in its tracks by tank gun fire that destroyed its lead five tanks. Attempts to manoeuvre around the Germans failed, leaving more tanks wrecked in the small fields. A line of Panthers burst out a wood line. 5th Tanks fire was accurate but stopped only two tanks. The 45-tonne Mark V Panthers were well armoured and easily resisted most frontal shots from Allied tanks. Their high-velocity 75mm guns furthermore made short work of anything the Allies had, Shermans as well as the British Cromwells in front of them. Now the rest surged on stopping for quick engagements which picked off more and more and more Cromwells. More tanks and mounted panzergrenadiers were seen manoeuvring. Fifth Tanks had no infantry, and the absence of its own APC mounted infantry battalion was sorely missed. The battalions of 56th Brigade were all on foot except for the Borderers and could not have kept up with the tanks. Now without infantry, 5th Tanks would be at the mercy of the enemy's infantry in the hedgerows. Having lost eighteen Cromwells, 5th Tanks broke off the action and withdrew in the direction of Villy-Bocage. There they found the survivors of the County of London Yeomanry and the South Wales Borderers ready to bolt back to Tilly. All it would take was a sharp push by the Germans.

That is just what Bayerlein had in mind. His trap had worked, the second apple to fall into his lap that day. Now he would finish the job. He aimed his attack straight up the road to Villy-Bocage led by the Tiger battalion reinforced with infantry. The northern Panther battle group would strike behind the village to cut off the enemy's retreat. The Mark IV battle group to the south had been equally successful with 1st Tanks and would form the other arm of the pincer that would cut off the English. At 1630 the attack began with the heavy support of Panzer Lehr's artillery regiment. Many vehicles in the 22nd Armoured Brigade's area were destroyed. Hull-down positions were hard to find in the dense woods and orchards and unfavourable ground. The Tigers attacked down the road and fields on either side supported by panzergrenadiers. A squadron of 1st Tanks fought a rearguard action supported by C Company from the 2nd Battalion The Essex Regiment. To the north, 5th Tanks with two companies of the 2nd Battalion The Gloucestershire Regiment was trying to hold off the Germans who were throwing in one sharp attack after another. The road back to Tilly was crowded with support vehicles, many of them set afire by German artillery. The 5th Royal Horse Artillery was burning up its guns in support of the hard-pressed tanks and infantry. The German guns found them eventually and destroyed several guns before they could displace to another position.

The Tigers were slowed by the rearguard of the 1st Tanks and Essex in the hedgerows but not stopped. They steadily advanced but left one after another of the huge tanks burning in the sunken roads or small fields. The panzer-grenadiers took heavy losses as they experienced British tenacity in the defence. Corporal Bill Dawson of the Essex was a patient man, almost cold-blooded, his mates thought. He held the bead on the German squad working its way along the edge of the hedges till they were so close none could escape. He pulled the trigger and swept the file of seven men into the grass. One moaned and tried to crawl away. Dawson waited for the next lot. That was the undoing of 7th Armoured Division. If the Tigers had pressed faster, the division would have withdrawn faster and escaped the Panthers slipping around the flanks of the division.

At 1715 the Panther battle group, which had swung around the flank of the delaying 5th Tanks, cut the road to Tilly-sur-Seulles. The Panthers burst upon the backed up trains of 7th Armoured and the accompanying corps artillery all in column. Private Erich Schmidt manned the MG-42 machine gun on an SPW that accompanied the tanks.

I fired into one truck after another. They just sat there, trapped on the road. I remember the crews spilling out and running into the ditches and field and then crumple. The tanks just rolled over the trucks and seemed to chase the English into the woods and orchards and fields.[3]

A battalion of 25-pounders became the special target of the Panthers' guns. Trucks are soft kills, but guns were special. They could kill tanks as well as any antitank gun. Now they were just as helpless as the trucks. Now the guns and truck transports disintegrated as the Panthers concentrated their fire into them. Exploding ammunition carriers added to the carnage. At the tail of the column behind a turn in the road two guns were unlimbered and run up against a protecting bulk of a hedge. The gunners sighted down their gun tubes, the range was so close. 'Fire!' the heavy projectiles slammed into the nearest two Panthers. The turret blew off the near one and the other staggered under the impact and began to fly apart with its exploding ammunition. The gun crews had loaded their guns before the Germans could react. 'Fire!' and two more Panthers were hit. The guns recoiled and the breaches thrown open to accept the next pair of heavy shells carried by the loaders. To their left an SPW came out of the hedge, the machine gun spraying over the guns. Schmidt saw the gunners twist and fall in the bullet stream, the 25-pounder projectiles falling to the ground. The SPW drove between the trucks and the guns shooting at the rest of the crews. The other grenadiers were firing over the sides of the SPW at anyone they could see. The English were not giving up their guns easily. An officer dashed toward the vehicle and tossed a grenade into the open squad compartment, killing and wounding the whole squad. Schmidt sagged to the floor bleeding from neck to waist. Another gunner fired through the driver's vision slit, wounding him again. Another SPW drove up and dismounted its squad which overwhelmed the remaining gunners.

Major Markowski, commander of the Panther battalion, surveyed the chaos and destruction from the turret of his command tank, pleased with the day's work. Of more than eighty Panthers he had lost between ten and fifteen to smash up an enemy tank battalion and close his half of the trap on the enemy. Now everything depended on the commander of the Mark IV battalion, Lieutenant Colonel Prinz Wilhelm von Schönburg-Waldenburg, to close the other half.

The Canadians at Tournay

He was doing just that. The weight of more than ninety Mark IVs of the 2nd Battalion, Panzer Lehr Regiment, and the entire 901st Panzergrenadier had the 1st Tanks at a grim disadvantage in numbers. The British had been pressed back by the weight of the German attack, but its Cromwells were a match for the Mark IVs. The Desert Rats expertly fell back to one defilade position after another long enough to fire and brew up a few tanks or SPWs. Only the constant flanking pressure of the panzergrenadiers jimmied them out of each position before they could do more damage. By the time 1st Tanks had drawn back to a line parallel with the main column, they had traded eight Cromwells for twenty-three Mark IVs and a dozen SPWs. Most of the pressure on them now seemed to shift from the tanks to panzergrenadiers. The panzers were skirting 1st Tanks to swing around the open flank to link up with Markowski's tanks.

They had crossed the Odon River and found an open road to the enemy rear near Tournay when the first three tanks were struck. All hell broke loose as concentrated fire swept over the head of the column. Fifteen Shermans of the Canadian Sherbrooke Fusiliers cut through the centre of the column firing up and down the road. In their speed to close the trap on the 7th Armoured, they had driven across the front of the armoured advance of the Canadian 9th Brigade. The Germans recoiled off the road and into the hedgerows and small fields in small groups of vehicles. The head of their column was trapped by the Sherbrookes who left eight Mark IVs and several SPWs and flak vehicles in flames in the sunken lane.

The Highland Light Infantry of Canada were attacking with the Sherbrookes and followed them into the maze of fields and hedgerows to hunt for the Germans. The fighting became a hundred little engagements as squads and individual tanks hunted each other. The North Nova Scotia Highlanders entered the battle from the west lapping around the Caen highway to take the Germans from the flank. The ferocity of the Canadian attack pushed the Germans east away from the 7th Armoured struggling to get out of the trap. The Canadian 8th Brigade led by the Shermans of the Fort Garry Horse came into the line to the west of 9th Brigade and made contact with the retreating 7th Armoured. The Canadians were now holding the open door for the Desert Rats. With the road to Tilly shut, Erskine ordered a retreat down the Caen highway, and his wounded battalions were eventually able to break contact with the slow pursuing Tigers and straggled through Canadian lines. By the time Bayerlein realized that the southern jaw of his trap had been hammered back, the Desert Rats had oozed out of his grip.

It was a sad husk of a great division that had escaped. Three Cromwells and thirty-seven infantrymen were all that survived of the rear guard's tank squadron and infantry company. The County of London Yeomanry had been for all intents and purposes wiped out as a fighting battalion and was represented by only four tanks that had escaped from Villers-Bocage. The battered 1st and 5th Tanks and 8th Hussars were down to fewer than sixty tanks. The Desert Rats had lost 117 tanks out of the almost 180 with which they had begun the day. Personnel losses, including 56th Brigade, exceeded 2,700 men. While half the losses had been in the trains and artillery, the loss of experienced tank crews had been crippling. Few of the survivors of brewed up tanks were able to escape with the division. The Desert Rats would be out of action for a long time.

Advance from Evrecy

As the Canadians entered the battle in the centre, the 1st Airlanding Brigade emerged out of the dense cluster of villages south of Evrecy and headed for Aunay. At the same time, 3rd Division's 8th Armoured Brigade cleared Evrecy and followed in their wake. At 1612 the advance guard of the 1st Airlanding crossed the small river that fed downstream a few hundred metres into the Odon outside Aunay. There was some question next as to which force was surprised more, the King's Own Scottish Borderers in the lead or the 130th Assault Gun Battalion, Panzer Lehr's division reserve, waiting on the outskirts of Aunay. German battle drill took the opening point. The battalion had been waiting for a momentary order to join the rest of the battle and was ready, and their commander was quick. The assault guns shook out of their assembly area and attacked with two companies on line, twenty assault guns, followed by the third company and one company of grenadiers.

The first wave of assault guns rolled over the lead platoons of the Borderers and crossed the river scattering the first company of the battalion. Then they ran into the half-dozen 6-pounders that Colonel Lathbury had placed near the head of the column. One! Two! Three! . . . Six assault guns staggered under the antitank counterpunch and burned. The rest backed up and found defilade positions from which to return fire. 1st Airlanding deployed among the orchards and hedgerows to either side of St.-Agnan-le-Malherbe, trying to work around the Germans. They were able to call in strikes by RAF aircraft which hovered over the fighting. Within an hour, 8th Armoured Brigade arrived and attacked straight down the road with a heavy artillery concentration. The Shermans of the 24th Lancers led the way followed by the 13/18th Hussars, at half strength from their ordeals of the sixth. Lieutenant Herbert Ronson of the Lancers watched the orchard ahead erupt as a heavy artillery stonk (short but intense pinpoint strike) hit the Germans.

> We shook out with B and C Squadrons on line and A in reserve. It looked like we would ride through on the very edge of the stonk before the Germans could recover. I don't know how they did it, but they fired coolly with the artillery bursting around them. My tank was hit and we barely got out before it caught fire.[4]

Ronson and his crew peering out of a ditch were spectators as the rest of the battalion crashed into the German position leaving a trail of burning tanks. The 13/18th Hussars followed. Apparently once in among the guns, the Sherman's ability to traverse its turret rapidly was the deciding factor in close quarter engagements. The assault guns had to pivot the entire vehicle to move the gun and came off second. The Shermans finished off the ten assault guns that had survived the concentration. They reassembled and tried to bounce the river but were stopped by the last assault gun company positioned on the other side. Firing from good positions, the German gunners avenged their slaughtered companies. Now it was the turn of the Germans to give the British a good stonk as Panzer Lehr's artillery regiment chimed in.

The Lancers and Hussars lost five tanks trying to force the river. Bayerlein was on the point of committing his last reserve, the special tank company of the panzer regiment with its six Tigers and nine assault guns, when the British withdrew and pulled back to St. Agnan. Brigadier Cunningham's 9th Brigade arrived an hour later and was fed into the line to the east until its patrols made contact with the Poles in Thury-Harcourt. ROYAL OAK was finished.

On the Flanks

While the British had eliminated the surviving German strongpoints along their three beaches, fighting on the flanks had been heavy and without gain.

East of the Orne River, 6th Airborne and 51st Divisions were successful only in linking up with isolated paratrooper battalions. They failed to advance against the remnants of the 716th Coastal Defence Division reinforced by the equally second-rate 711th Costal Defence Division who pulled out their beach defences and marched inland. They were reinforcement for the heart of the German defence, Colonel von Luck's 125th Panzergrenadier Regiment. That they fought surprisingly well was a testament to the German Army's ability to transform even second-rate material into an acceptable if not good combat unit. Nightfall hid the arrival after forced marches of the lead battalions of the Luftwaffe 17th Field and 346th Infantry Divisions.

The 50th Northumbrian Division had been severely tested that day as well. An early morning attack by 231st and 69th Brigades had been checked almost immediately by the Germans. The 352nd Division was in strength from Port-en-Bessin to just outside Bayeux, supported by a rocket launcher brigade. Everywhere the Northumbrians seemed on the point of breaking through, they were thrown back by vicious combined tank and infantry counterattacks by Hitlerjugend battle groups held in reserve. German artillery from these two divisions energetically shelled the beaches, delaying the landing of the U.S. 29th and British 49th Divisions. The Royal Navy had done its part to change the balance by pouring fire down the length of the German positions at right angles to the coast. Still the Germans hung on. As night fell, the 12th SS Panzer began slipping out of the line and to an assembly point in the Cerisy Forest west of Balleroy. They had been pulled out unexpectedly. Kurt Meyer waited until the early morning hours to receive his orders.

Amid the chaos and fighting, there was still room for the surreal. The British correspondent, Alan Moorehead, recorded his impressions:

> We went on into the town of Bayeux. For a moment a few German officers had fired from the post office, but the town had fallen intact. It remained exactly as it had been through the last four years; the soaring cathedral, the Camembert cheeses in the shops, the wine carts going up the Rue St. Jean; the evening gowns in the shop marked 'haute couture.' . . . there was a commotion in the square outside. A crowd came yelling up the Rue St. Jean, driving an old man in front of them. His shirt was torn off to the waist. There was blood running down his face, his eyes were wide with fright. Every now and then a man or a woman would run forward to beat him or scratch him. They did this viciously, with an evident sense of gratifying some pent-up desire for revenge. It was difficult to get much sense out of the crowd. They merely shouted, 'Collaborateur.' Presently more victims were brought out and beaten in the square in front of the hotel. Excited young Frenchmen were running about carrying tommy-guns.[5]

As darkness and exhaustion put an end to the day's fighting, the British had cause for severe dismay. Even Montgomery could not find a silver lining in the

outcome of ROYAL OAK. His plan to retrieve at one stroke the failure of the
Americans at Omaha could only be termed a near disaster because of the more
awful and complete disaster barely avoided. The only advantage gained had
been the doubling of the area of the lodgement, which now ran from Bayeux to
the north of Tilly then Tournay, St. Agnan, and finally to Thury-Harcourt. But
the cost had been appalling. It was sinking in that not only had 7th Armoured
been badly mauled but that 1st Airborne had been gutted as well, and would
have to be written off. The slaughter of two of the best veteran divisions in the
British Army in one day had thrown a pall over the chain of command all the
way up from I and XXX Corps to 21st Army Group to the Chiefs of the
Imperial General Staff. Churchill was stunned at the defeat, not having had so
bitter a taste since Tobruk, two years before. The Government would be hard-
pressed to defend this day in Parliament. In this fifth year of the war, Britain
had scraped the bottom of the manpower barrel. There were no significant
replacements for losses at this rate. Almost ten thousand men had been killed,
wounded, or taken prisoner, three times the rate of the assault on the beaches
the day before. The British could not afford many more days like this.

The American Sector

For Rommel it had been, to say the least, an intriguing night. He had fre-
quently hosted captured enemy generals at his mess table in France and North
Africa. Now he was the guest of fifteen American paratroopers in warpaint and
Mohawk haircuts and dined royally on something called C rations. He felt right
at home. It was a soldiers' mess. They were surprised and delighted when they
discovered that he spoke English well and had a thousand questions, mostly the
kind that soldiers do, and his answers were the honest ones that he would have
told his own men. Long ago he had learned that the human heart is the
foundation of all things military.

The morning found them still speaking when the guards came running into
the barn as the doors splintered above them. German shouts of command and
heavy engine noises came from outside. Lieutenant Eberly was going to fight it
out in the stout stone barn, until a shell blew a hole in the wall and wounded
four of his men. He surrendered. The German sergeant commanding the patrol
was an experienced soldier. He had survived a great many things in Russia. Still,
he was not quite prepared to hear a clear German voice of command thunder
from the barn. Then out stepped a field marshal.

The German medics attended to the wounded as the others were searched.
Twenty minutes later an escort arrived from Hitlerjugend's reconnaissance
battalion. Rommel was on the radio in animated conversation when he stopped
and pointed to Eberly who stared, holding his breath. 'That one comes with
me,' he said to the SS officer commanding the escort. Eberly was hustled into

another armoured car. Through the port he could see Rommel shaking hands with each of the other captured paratroopers.

Ste.-Mère-Eglise Again

Fritz Witt had not heard of Rommel's rescue when he began the second round of his duel with Matthew Ridgway. His plan to break the American pocket in Ste.-Mère-Eglise had been knocked twice out of his hands the day before. At 0500 he attacked from three sides preceded by a sharp artillery bombardment. From the north came the 91st Division's reinforced 1058th Regiment and from the south a battalion of its sister regiment the 1057th. From the east, Witt led the attack of his 12th SS battle group.

The gliders that had landed the previous day had resupplied Ridgway with more than just antitank guns and ammunition. They had brought in functioning radios. The disasters and disappointments of 6 June had concentrated all the anxiety of the American chain of command on the rump of the 82nd Airborne Division standing siege in Ste.-Mère-Eglise. Everything that could fire was put in support. Counterbattery fire from the 8th Division artillery and the Navy smothered the two German self-propelled battalions north of the town and forced the surviving pieces to displace. The 91st Division never got beyond the 82nd's listening posts, so heavy was the curtain of fire around the town. Witt's Hitlerjugend were no more proof in the open to the concentration of high explosive than the 91st's infantry. He was trying to pull his battle group back when Stempel's anti-aircraft section started firing at a new target, small observation aircraft. A few minutes later, the ground heaved with incoming artillery of huge calibre. He watched as vehicles were flung about or dissolved in the enormous spouts of earth and flame. Any dismounted man who hadn't thrown himself in a ditch or hole was dead. After a ten minute workover, the guns stopped. Huge craters dotted the area amid splintered stumps of trees. Vehicles that air strikes would have left burning were now overturned or twisted piles of metal. There was little other evidence that some vehicles had existed at all. As for the men, it was as if the contents of a butcher's shop had been scattered all over.

Some of that artillery had fallen on the Georgian Battalion nervously holding the blocking position to the east of Ste.-Mère-Eglise. Witt had depended on them to hold the Americans long enough for him to overrun the town. The battalion had been in a state of sustained panic and had only repulsed the first attack of the 4th Division the day before because their German officers and NCOs were ready to shoot them on the spot. Today that fear had evaporated. Instead they shot most of the Germans among them and then fled into the arms of the attacking 8th Infantry Regiment. The few surviving Germans ran in the opposite direction and warned Witt who had his hands full trying to reconstitute his battle group. His men were slowly coming back to life, as the clanging of the bombardment faded. With that wonderful resilience, the elements of the battle group were reconstituting themselves, of course, with a certain amount of energetic prodding from Witt. As they became ready, a single tank or antitank gun, an infantry platoon, Witt sent them west into the hole left by the Georgians. Witt sent his operations officer to guide them into position. There was no time for anything fancier than finding a suitable fold in the ground or stone wall. They barely beat the Americans to the punch.

The Shermans of the 746th Tank Battalion had shot forward with infantry clinging to their backs through the new hole in the German lines. Their orders were to break through to the 82nd Airborne regardless. Ste.-Mère-Eglise was barely a mile and a half away and seemed to be in their grasp already. They passed through and around Turqueville and were approaching Ecoqueneauville when the first three tanks were hit. The riding infantry were thrown off by the hits, leaving the burning tanks surrounded by a ring of crumpled men. The battalion kept on going. Short intense actions were fought between groups of Shermans and Mark IVs that were struggling into the gap. An 88 on the edge of the village picked off four tanks in succession. The infantry had already dismounted and were following the tanks when they were hit. Their officers led them past the burning tanks when machine gun fire cut a swath through them. The rest disappeared into the nearest fold in the earth. More tanks appeared and more dismounted infantry followed. The 88 took another kill, but its crew was shot up by the riflemen edging forward. The Americans broke into the village and reduced it house by house. The Hitlerjugend counterattacked wherever they could but were beaten back. Still the men of the 8th Infantry had to kill every one of them, and it took time. General Barton committed his reserve, the 359th Infantry Regiment of the follow-on 90th Infantry Division. Led by the 70th Tank Battalion, they swung north of the fighting between the Hitlerjugend and the 8th Infantry. The few tanks that Witt had on that flank were brushed away. The Americans also were covering the flank of their attack with heavy artillery fire. It fell upon Witt as he led a tank platoon and some infantry into a counterattack, and he died with his teenagers.

The 359th Infantry and tanks rode straight into Ste.-Marie-Eglise. The 82nd Airborne was relieved. Witt's operations officer took over the shrunken battle group. As soon as the Americans broke the ring around town, it was the battle group that was in danger. He pulled back through Fauville south down the road to the slightly higher ground around les Forges along with the battalion of the 1057th. Les Forges tied in with the Merderet River to the west and the inundated area to the east, with only two miles between them. It was a better defensive position than most with water on either flank. In the late afternoon, they were treated to the sight of another large glider landing, this one safely executed near Ste.-Mère-Eglise. Later patrols of the 359th Infantry approached les Forges but were driven off. By nightfall the Americans were in position in strength.

The Batteries at Azeville and St. Marcouf

There was another battle that day in the Cotentin. The 12th and 22nd Infantry Regiments of the 4th Infantry Division began their struggle against the German army battery at Azeville and the naval battery at St. Marcouf. At 0700 Lieutenant Kattnig, commanding the Azeville Battery, called his counterpart at St. Marcouf, Lieutenant Ohmsen, to report that his No. 3 gun had been smashed by a direct hit that had broken through the ten-foot-thick concrete roof to bury gun and crew. Suddenly Ohmsen heard machine gun firing from his own position and the shout, 'Alarm! Enemy attack from direction Crisbecq.' A battalion from the 22nd Infantry had approached close to the battery before the Germans were alerted. The battery's barbed wire and trench system had been swept away by two days of naval bombardment, and the Americans quickly flooded the battery position, their engineers rushing towards the bunkers with their demolition equipment. Ohmsen reacted quickly, 'Signal to Azeville battery: request gunfire on my own position. Ohmsen.' The signalman hesitated in disbelief, 'Get on with it, man! We shall have some losses ourselves. But it's our only chance.' At the Azeville Battery, Lieutenant Kattnig understood immediately and said to one of his NCOs, 'Schurger, we're going to make those fellows dance.' He planted a few shells precisely in the middle of Ohmsen's battery, blowing away the Americans who had climbed on top of the bunkers. Ohmsen rallied his gunners to counterattack, and they boiled out of their bunkers just as a company of the 916th Infantry Regiment arrived as reinforcements. Together they threw the Americans out of the battery position and pursued them so vigorously that the American retreat became a rout that not even the commitment of a reserve company could stop. The Germans returned in triumph with ninety prisoners.[6] Clearly, greater forces were necessary to reduce these batteries.

Despite this black eye, at the end of the day, the American chain of command breathed a collective sigh of relief. The disaster at Omaha had galvanized everyone into a supreme effort today in the relief of the 82nd. The battered 8th Infantry and the 359th Infantry and their supporting tank battalions had shown real drive. The coordination of artillery had broken Witt's grasp on Ste.-Mère-Eglise for the third and last time and rolled the Germans south. Now the Utah lodgement was a broad triangle running east from its blunt two mile wide point on the Merderet River. The rest of the 90th Division was coming ashore and was deploying in the southern half of the lodgement. The 4th Division, with elements of the 82nd and 101st attached, was concentrating against the German forts on the northern edge of the lodgement. VII Corps was now fully operational. The Americans, now at last, had their firm toehold on the Continent.

The Germans Regroup

German communications definitely warmed up with the news that Rommel was back. The dissemination of the Ultra intercepts to that effect had the opposite effect. Montgomery was disappointed but did not show it. Chivalrous and generous as a reflection of his stern Christianity but also because it made good policy, Montgomery was not above more practical considerations. As much as he admired Rommel, he also understood that for just that reason, the sooner he was dead, the fewer British soldiers would die.

Rommel's return short-circuited all of the emergency command arrangements that had been half-implemented by the elimination of the Army Group to Army to Corps chain of command in Normandy. His presence was felt immediately. He stopped first at St. Lô to get in communication with Speidel and be briefed on the situation. His hopes soared when he learned that the old Prussian, von Rundstedt, had prised Case Three out of Hitler. He transferred General der Artillerie Fahrmbacher from his command in Brittany to be the new LXXXIV Corps Commander and Pemsel as acting 7th Army Commander. He then requested and received the assignment from the OKW leaders reserve of Lieutenant General Dietrich von Choltitz to command the three divisions fighting east of the Orne under the recently arrived LXXXI Corps Headquarters. If anyone could keep the British pinned to the Orne it was the daring and tenacious von Choltitz. He had been the first German officer in the invasion of the Netherlands in 1940 and was the conqueror of the mighty Soviet fortress of Sevastopol in 1942. Rommel then ordered the concentration of 12th SS Panzer in the Forest of Cerisy after nightfall. There he met Kurt Meyer and informed him of the death of Fritz Witt and his new appointment as division commander. Stabbing the map with his finger, he emphasized the place where the Hitlerjugend would make its mark in the next few days.

Notes

1. Gerd von Rundstedt, *Mein Leben* (Potsdam and Leipzig: Verlagshaus Hindrichs, 1949) pp.312–313.
2. Paul Carrell, *Invasion: They're Coming*, tr. E. Osers (London: George E. Harrap, 1962); (New York: E.P. Dutton) pp.114–116.
3. Erich Schmidt, *Hitlerjugend!* (Dresden: Verlag Edelsheim GmbH, 1952) p.174.
4. Herbert H. Ronson, *A Subaltern With the Hussars* (London: Collins, 1948) p.149.
5. Alan Moorehead, *Eclipse* (London: Hamilton, 1945); (New York: Harper & Row, 1968) p.113.
6. Paul Carrell, *Invasion: They're Coming*, tr. E. Osers (London: George E. Harrap, 1962); (New York: E.P. Dutton, 1964) pp.131–132.

CHAPTER 6

Operation SPANNER
8 to 11 June

The British Sector

Operation ROYAL OAK did more than wreck two of the British Army's best divisions and Montgomery's hopes. The end of the battle perversely had almost doubled the size of the lodgement. The gain in ground was, in fact, a deadly prize. Most of the new ground was in the shape of a deep salient that ran down the Orne River to Thury-Harcourt. It did nothing to expand the operational depth of the lodgement to support the build up and would be difficult to defend. Much of it was beyond naval gunfire support range. It was a major operational liability.

For all these reasons, the Thury Salient also begged to be attacked. Rommel had instantly recognized its importance. Bayerlein's victory at Villers-Bocage had bought him the time he needed to concentrate the forces necessary for the counterpunch. Kurt Meyer's 12th SS Panzer Division had slipped out the fighting around Bayeux and taken up positions between Tilly and Villers-Bocage where the battle group that Witt had taken to fight the Americans joined it. Panzer Lehr sidestepped to the east and occupied the front between Villers-Bocage and Thury. The British had not stirred much on 8 and 9 June after Bayerlein's drubbing, which was fine for Rommel. They were giving him a gift of time.

The time was paying for the arrival of his Case Three reinforcements. SS General Sepp Dietrich arrived with his I SS Panzer Corps staff to provide the operational command and control for the panzer divisions. General Geyr von Schweppenburg also arrived with his Panzer Group West staff and began busily preparing the operational plans of the attack. On the evening of the 8th, 2nd and 116th Panzer Divisions' last elements arrived at the front. 2nd Panzer was hidden southeast of Caen in the Forest of Cinglais. 116th Panzer Division, stationed on the Seine, was closest to the front and was passed behind the two panzer divisions to fill the gap between the 352nd and Hitlerjugend. The *Landsers* (German Tommies or GIs) of the 84th Infantry Division were filtered across the front of Panzer Lehr while the advance elements of the 77th Infantry Division took positions in front of Hitlerjugend. Now the mobile units could pull out of the line to regroup. Northeast of Caen the 346th Infantry and 17th Field Divisions had been thrown immediately against the Orne River bridgehead as soon as they arrived. Von Choltitz had arrived to take over LXXXI Corps there late on 8 June, having driven at breakneck speed from Germany. By 10 June, the Germans had concentrated four new infantry and two new panzer divisions against the British sector, a healthy accomplishment. There had been a price. The constant air attacks and ambushes by the resistance had taken the edge off every unit and reduced combat power by anywhere from 10 to 15 percent. Resupply efforts had been even more badly hurt: a truck load of ammunition, food, or fuel cannot jump out of its truck and run to safety in a ditch or woods.

Not all of the British forces had been relatively quiet. The Canadians launched a sharp attack on Tilly-sur-Seulles the day after ROYAL OAK and retook the town. Elsewhere the action was on the flanks of the lodgement as Montgomery attempted to, as he liked to say to the intense irritation of the Americans, 'Tidy up the battlefield.' The Canadians had already removed the bothersome German hold on Tilly. Now he shifted 50th and 49th Divisions to the line Bayeux to Tilly and fed the newly arriving American V Corps into the fight against 352nd Division. The U.S. 29th Infantry Division with its two orphan regiments and the 2nd Infantry Division attacked almost immediately. On the other flank, Montgomery responded to the German attacks on the Orne River bridgehead by reinforcing it with the remainder of 51st Highland Division, 4th Tank Brigade, and 13/18th Hussars. Two armoured divisions, the U.S. 2nd as part of V Corps and the British 11th, the lead division of the British VIII Corps, were arriving as well. If General Dempsey, 2nd Army Commander, was bothered by Montgomery's effective usurpation of his role as army commander, he did not let on, in public. More and more, this became Montgomery's battle, as it was becoming Rommel's on the other side of the hill.

Geyr von Schweppenburg was much less accommodating than Dempsey. He had already clashed with Rommel before the invasion on the positioning of the panzer reserves. Now he opposed the deployment for the counterpunch that Rommel had set in motion. He insisted that it was not bold enough and that Rommel had become gun shy about Allied air power. That act of hubris was about to be punished. Ultra quickly identified the location of the headquarters of Panzer Group West at la Caine. On the evening of the 10th, the Royal Air Force's Typhoons of 83 Group and the Mitchell medium bombers of 2 Group paid Geyr von Schweppenburg a visit. Between the rockets of the Typhoons and the bombs of the Mitchells, Panzer Group West ceased to exist as a functioning headquarters. Geyr von Schweppenburg was wounded and seventeen of his staff officers, including his chief of staff, Colonel von Dawans, were killed. Their bodies were given a mass burial in one of the bomb craters. Rommel was not sorry to see the troublesome Geyr von Schweppenburg carried off to a hospital in Paris; he was alarmed at the loss of a highly trained and expert staff that had been carefully prepared for this very moment in the

15. Tanks and infantry of the 29th Infantry Division. Formed from the remnants of the original 1st and 29th Divisions, they smashed the anchor of the German line in their first attack at Port-en-Bessin. Here they attack west of the town. *U.S. National Archives*

16. The German infantry that struggled into Normandy under Case Three were absolutely vital to Rommel's conduct of the battle. Without them, his armoured divisions would have been burnt out in defensive battles. *U.S. Army Center for Military History*

17. The attack of the 3rd Canadian Division in Operation SPANNER went through hedgerow country like this, with the German defenders staggered in depth. Few military engineers could have devised better defences to soak up and defuse the power of an enemy attack. *U.S. National Archives*

18. Hitler's order to execute Case Three put quarter of a million German troops on the roads leading to Normandy. They were hammered relentlessly from the sky by the Allied air forces. Here Tiger tanks and other armoured vehicles have literally run themselves in circles to escape the torment from the sky. *U.S. National Archives*

19. A GI from the 29th Infantry Division fires from behind a hedgerow. Normandy's natural defensive works, the hedgerows were so high that the soldier had to stand on a ration box to fire over the edge. *U.S. National Archives*

20. The debris of the 2nd Armoured Division's great riposte, which saved the British lodgement from being caved in from the west as it had been elsewhere under Rommel's counter-attack. *U.S. National Archives*

21. Flail tank from Major General Hobart's 79th Armoured Division, thrashing a safe path for the follow-on infantry. The flail tank was only one of many ingenious pieces of equipment, called Hobart's funnies, that provided a decisive margin of victory for 2nd Army's landings. *U.S. National Archives*

22. Dead American gliderborne infantrymen spilled out from one of the gliders that did not survive the tricks the Germans had strewn through the likely landing fields. *U.S. National Archives*

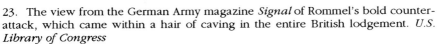

23. The view from the German Army magazine *Signal* of Rommel's bold counter-attack, which came within a hair of caving in the entire British lodgement. *U.S. Library of Congress*

24. The wreckage of the American Mulberry on 24 June after the great storm. *U.S. National Archives*

25. Young SS troops of Hitler Jugend just before the attack on the Canadians at Fontenay-le-Pesnel and Cheux. *U.S. National Archives*

26. A burning German assault gun outside Carentan. The rush of the 17th SS Panzergrenadier Division into the city to bolster the 6th Fallschirmjäger Regiment prevented the U.S. VII Corps from taking the city. *U.S. National Archives*

27. The glider swarm of the 82nd Airborne Division's follow-on 325th Glider Infantry Regiment landing near les Forges. *U.S. National Archives*

28. Eisenhower pays Montgomery a visit at his headquarters at the Château de Creullet after Rommel's great counter-attack. *U.S. National Archives*

29. Anti-tank gunners of Colonel Birk's 120th Infantry Regiment turned back 9th SS Panzer Division's attempt to stop the escape of the trapped British forces over Pegasus Bridge. *Painting by Keith Rocco; U.S. National Guard Bureau*

invasion battle. Responsibility for the operation shifted down to I SS Panzer Corps to Sepp Dietrich's dismay. He liked to be near the troops, and army level command would take him in the opposite direction.

On the Flanks

Crisis on the Orne

To buy his time, Rommel decided to keep Montgomery busy on the flanks of the British sector while he prepared his own attack on its centre. East of the Orne German resistance had already sucked in 153rd Brigade of 51st Division on 7 June. On the morning of the 8th, the brigade, temporarily attached to 6th Airborne Division, was ordered to push eastward on an arc from Bréville to Touffréville. The 5th Black Watch's objective was Bréville. Within a mile they ran into a hornet's nest.

> The ditches at the side of the road were full of Germans, and the whole of the front was swept by very accurate fire. The result was that 'A' Company was practically wiped out; in point of fact, every man in the leading platoon died with his face to the foe. Lt.-Col. Thomson then decided to occupy the ground south of the Chateau de Bréville some half-mile south of the village. The Germans put down a very heavy attack on the chateau and grounds and then put in a strong frontal attack. The enemy were extremely brave and, as a result, made good targets. They were literally killed by the hundred. But despite everything the Germans could do, the much-depleted 5th Black Watch stood their ground, and the Germans withdrew.[1]

The 1st and 5/7th Gordons were luckier. They easily occupied Touffréville by 0800, and 5/7th Gordons just as easily threw back another strong German attack. Sergeant Aikenhead of B Company had been captured in the attack but escaped in the night by killing his guard with a pocket knife that had been overlooked when he had been searched.

The Highland brigade had tangled with elements of two new German divisions, the 346th Infantry and 17th Field Divisions. Von Luck's 125th Panzergrenadier Regiment had been reinforced with surviving elements of 21st Panzer Division and now formed a respectable battle group with a company's worth of Mark IVs and some assault guns, two batteries of self-propelled artillery, and a few platoons of engineers. With von Choltitz's arrival, German LXXXI Corps headquarters immediately began preparing a bigger party for the British. The stocky little general seemed to be living on adrenalin as he drove his new staff to organize the attack. He did not believe in written orders where speed was vital. Mission orders were given directly to his subordinate division commanders. He had sized them up quickly. Major General Oscar Kreutz of the 346th was a fighter; he had known him in Russia. Colonel

Liebknecht of the 17th was just bewildered, one of the few Luftwaffe officers the Army had not replaced when it took over control of the Luftwaffe field divisions early in 1944. Von Choltitz relieved him on the spot and replaced him with one of his more alert regimental commanders. On the morning of 9 June, the corps attacked with the 17th and 346th on line north to south. Von Luck's battle group led the attack on the northern flank with the objective Ranville, which was the headquarters of the British 6th Airborne Division. Coming out the Bois de Bavent, a German tank crewman remembered:

> We rolled forward in attack formation . . . Suddenly, the enemy artillery opened up. The grenadiers were halted and began to dig in, the screams of their wounded mingling with the ceaseless detonation of the shells. Even inside the tanks, we ducked, surprised by this unexpectedly strong defence. But we drove through the fire, on and up the hill to the glider field, where we met such a hail of shells that the tanks turned off to the left towards Longueval. Now prisoners began to appear and when we sprayed the tree-tops, wounded Englishmen fell out of them. Unsupported by our own artillery and infantry, we were in the middle of enemy anti-tank and infantry positions, where every hedge and ditch spat fire, their occupants determined not to be overrun.[2]

If the little company of Mark IVs were in a state of anxiety over their position in the middle of an antitank cauldron, von Luck was elated. By 1015 the tank spearhead had penetrated almost to the Orne River, splitting the British bridgehead, but they could not survive much longer unsupported. He moved heaven and earth in a few minutes to get his grenadiers moving forward to catch up with the tanks. They were just in time. Seven Mark IVs were burning. The grenadiers rode into action behind the assault guns, bringing heavy small arms fire onto the British antitank guns. One after another, the antitank guns were silenced. The bridges over the Orne were barely two miles away to the north.

Meanwhile the 17th Field Division was attacking strongly against Lovat's Commando Brigade and the 5th Black Watch of 153rd Brigade around Bréville. South of the Bois de Bavent, 346th Division struck the two battalions of the Gordons in Touffréville at 0530. The Gordons held off their attacks all morning as the Germans seized and lost foothold after foothold in the village. Much of the village was in ruins from the German artillery. The last attack had been led by two self-propelled guns. Both lay smoking just inside the village with a platoon's worth of Germans sprawled dead in files behind them. By noon their battalions were sweeping northwest of the village to cut it off. It was now or never for the Gordons. Rather than see the battalions cut off, 6th Airborne Division authorized them to abandon the village and retreat back upon the parachute brigades. The 5/7th Gordons were first, followed by 1/7th as rear guard. They had just missed the gate. The lead platoon of 5/7th was cut up by the fire from several machine guns crews that the Germans had infiltrated. B Company tried to manoeuvre its other platoons to the left. One of its platoons manoeuvred close to one machine gun. First Lieutenant George Carver led one section in a dash towards the gun. The rest of the platoon covered them with fire. The Germans kept their heads down a moment too long. Carver was in the lead throwing grenades, one and then another right into the German position. He followed the last blast over a fallen log guarding the gun and finished off the crew with his Sten. The section followed after him into the position to examine their kill, when a stream of fire from another gun sliced through them, killing Carver and three other men. More Germans were infiltrating the area and took rest of the platoon under fire with heavy casualties. A German platoon supported by several machine guns attacked and was thrown back leaving a dozen men on the ground. By now a whole company had the platoon surrounded. Another attack washed over them. All but seven men of the twenty-eight who had started that morning were dead or wounded.

With its lead company badly hurt, the commander of 5/7th Gordons ordered a charge by his remaining companies to break open the rapidly thickening German opposition. They were knocked almost immediately back to their starting positions by the volume and accuracy of the German fire. The Germans followed with company-sized attacks on his flanks. With what appeared to be several battalions in front of them, 5/7th could go no further. Now this wounded battalion formed the rearguard as the column turned around to return to Touffréville about three in the afternoon. The 1/7th now had to fight its way back into the village, throwing out the German company that had followed them on the way out. More attacks followed, probing for the soft spot. It was a grim fact, that the men they had been fighting all day were not coastal defence troops. They just kept coming back, always aggressive, always attacking. German dead littered the outskirts and streets of the village, but so did those of the Gordons. By nightfall, there had been over five hundred casualties in the two battalions.

The Gordons were trapped and almost out of ammunition. Kreutz and his 346th Division smelled victory and kept up the pressure all night. Von Choltitz also succumbed to the chance of overrunning most of a British brigade and failed to make the 346th mask Touffréville and press on with its attack towards the Orne. Instead of striking 6th Airborne's southern flank with two full regiments, the 346th struck with barely one. Luck should not have rewarded that attack but perversely did just that. The German regiment struck at the join between 3rd Parachute and 6th Airlanding Brigades shortly after eleven in the morning and broke right through, cutting off the 3rd, which had been in the apex of the British position facing the Bois de Bavent. The fighting now settled down to attack and counterattack as the 3rd and 6th Brigades tried to reestablish contact. The Germans hung on and were supported by 17th Field Division which pressed down on 3rd Para from the north.

Von Luck's success was followed up by an attack north to seize the Orne bridges. By now the British were seriously alarmed over the strength and success of the German attacks east of the Orne. The bridgehead appeared to be in a rapidly closing vice. With the 3rd Parachute Brigade and most of the 153rd Brigade cut off, the situation reminded too many officers around Montgomery of Tobruk. The 3rd Division artillery and priority air support and naval gunfire support were thrown onto the scales. The I Corps reserve was also thrown into the battle, the 4th Armoured Brigade and the 152nd Infantry Brigade from 51st Division as well as 13/18th Hussars from 8th Armoured Brigade. The 51st Division's third brigade, the 154th, was given priority on landing over the beaches.

The tanks of the Royal Scots Greys were first across the Pegasus Bridge and then the Orne River bridge at 1725, then turned south. They met von Luck's battle group half a mile from the bridge, nailed to the ground by the guns of the Royal Artillery and the Royal Navy. When the fire lifted, the Greys attacked right into the churned earth and splintered trees that held the stunned Germans. Overturned tanks, smashed guns and SPWs, and corpses were everywhere. Prisoners began stumbling forward, dazed, their ears bleeding. The Greys were shooting up any of the survivors that still had any argument in them. Rushing two 88s forward, von Luck was able to buy the time needed to pull back perhaps half of his original force before it was swept away by the British tanks. The 88s brewed up half a dozen of the Greys' tanks before the concentrated fire of the battalion destroyed the guns.

The attack of the Luftwaffe 17th Field Division had been less expert than that of the 346th, but it had the weight of numbers behind it and an enthusiastic new commander. The 5th Black Watch was shoved back from the outskirts of Bréville and managed to link hands with the Lovat's Commandos just outside 6th Airborne's Ranville headquarters by 1000. Where the regular German infantry of the 346th had expertly used infiltration and fire and movement tactics to pry the British out of many positions, the 17th showed the clumsiness on the battlefield to be expected of air force personnel pressed into the infantry. Their attacks were straightforward affairs, usually across open fields, much like 1914, and with the same results. The Black Watch and Commandos tore great holes in their ranks with every step backward. Just outside of Ranville, the 17th Field Division ran out of steam, their 'culmination point' as Clausewitz would have put it. So they did not expect the immediate counterattack delivered by the tanks of the 44th Battalion, Royal Tank Regiment, which had crossed the Orne Bridges behind the Greys. The first squadron rolled over the Germans disorganized by their own advance and casualties. The German battalion in their path dissolved into a mass of fugitives. The remaining squadrons followed swinging left and right to roll up the rest of the leading German regiment which broke down in the ensuing panic. It was the tanker's dream, the pursuit of broken, terrified infantry. Captain Archibald Clarke led his troop through the fleeing enemy, the turret machine guns cutting them down as they rode through and over them. 'They just ran, throwing away their weapons and helmets, and we just murdered them by the hundred. More of them were surrendering in clumps or one by one, their hands and arms poking up out of the tall grain. We left them to the infantry coming behind.'[3] It was inevitable that the advance would bounce into something. That was the antitank battalion of the 17th which had been moving up behind the infantry regiments. They announced their presence when Clarke saw three of his tanks blow up and gush fire out of their hatches. Four more followed, and then came the German artillery landing in the middle of his shrinking formation. He pulled his squadron back behind the last tree line he had passed.

A Save and a Loss

Already the crisis of the battle in the Orne bridgehead had passed, a fact that was to elude 2nd Army for several more days. The British had been given a terrible fright, and for good reason. Their whole position east of the Orne had been battered and staved in, and two brigades were still cut off behind German lines. The German LXXXI Corps was in a similar mood by this point, though arrived at by a different route. Von Choltitz's attack had come within an ace of completely cutting up and eliminating the Orne bridgehead, only to be beaten back at the last minute by arrival of the British 4th Armoured Brigade, the tank equivalent of a strong panzer division. The Luftwaffe field division had come close to disaster and was incapable of further offensive operations for the moment. The corps reserve of the 711th Coastal Defence Division was backing it up. Von Luck's battle group had been beaten back from the outskirts of the Orne bridges and was sadly depleted. He was lucky to have the strength of a battalion. Only the gains of the 346th Infantry Division seemed solid with the added profit of two British brigades isolated in its rear.

Those two brigades became the preoccupation of both sides, the Germans to eliminate them and the British to rescue them. The Gordons holding Touffréville, by far were in the greatest danger. Of the 1,300 men that crossed the Orne bridges on the 7 June, there were fewer than 600 unhurt men on the morning of the 10th. They were also nearly out of ammunition and were using German weapons stripped off the dead. All night the Germans probed and attacked. After midnight, they sent in their first demand for surrender. It was politely refused. At first light, the village disintegrated in the heaviest artillery barrage the Gordons had experienced. Immediately behind it came an attack from two directions led by assault guns. This time the Germans were in the village to stay. House by house, the Gordons resisted. The Germans would then bring up an assault gun and demolish the house. By now the British had no more ammunition for their Piats or their antitank guns. The German attack paused, and another party advanced with a white flag. With more than two hundred wounded on his hands and next to no ammunition, the senior British officer recognized the obvious and surrendered at 1142 that morning. The Germans rushed their medical personnel into the village to care for the British wounded. The German division commander personally saw to the arrangements and shook hands with the British officers. He had reason to be elated; 512 unhurt and 233 wounded British prisoners from a famous regiment were his trophies of war.

He had other reasons to be glad that the Gordons had surrendered. The regiment that had been tied down reducing their pocket was desperately needed to hold off the British relief force. Shortly after he began his final assault on the Gordons around ten in the morning, the British relief force had also attacked to relieve both trapped brigades. Fourth Armoured Brigade and 152nd Brigade formed two task forces to relieve the 3rd Paras and the Gordons respectively. The 4th Brigade controlled its own Royal Scots Greys and the brigade's motorized battalion, the 2nd Battalion, the King's Royal Rifle Corps (Motor) and was reinforced with the Highlanders' 5th Battalion, the Queen's Own Cameron Highlanders. The 152nd Brigade controlled its own two battalions, the 2nd and 5th Battalions, the Seaforth Highlanders, which were reinforced by the tanks of the 3rd County of London Yeomanry (Sharpshooters).

Both attacks were preceded by heavy artillery and air support. Both immediately ran into an interlocked defence of strongpoints that the Germans had thrown up overnight. It was slow going for both task forces. The Germans had hoped to force the surrender of the 3rd Parachute Brigade behind the defensive screen as they had the two Gordon battalions. If they had known anything about the commander of the 3rd Paras, they would have been far less hopeful of success. Brigadier James Hill, DSO, MC, was not the man to let the enemy determine events or to quit.

Most people were frightened of him, not because of his rank or because he was a bully, but rather by reason of an indefinable quality which the man possessed setting him above others. Supremely intelligent, very tall, taut as a steel spring, aristocratic in looks and demeanor, he was a most dominating and fearsome character. He had within him the virtue of physical courage of the highest order coupled with great moral integrity. The war to him was a crusade which he pursued with almost fanatical fervor. The Brigadier did not really have to issue orders as such or resort to barking out instructions. In a quiet way he would simply tell people to do things he believed in and they jumped to it.[4]

The Brigade's situation was obviously serious. Hill did not believe the 1,100 men in the pocket on the edge of the Bois de Bavent could survive a long siege. Each battalion had barely 300 men after four days of heavy fighting. They were too weak to defend their position for several more days. There was then no alternative. They would attack and break out of the pocket in one short but sharp effort to coincide with the attack of the relieving force. Luckily he was not burdened with many wounded and his ammunition was adequate. He was also lucky that the Germans were beating up the Gordons first before they turned on the Paras.

The 1st Canadian Parachute Battalion led the breakout at 0530, coincidently just when 346th Division was moving in on the kill against the Gordons. The Canadians were followed by the 8th Paras with the 9th Paras as rearguard. The German cordon around the Paras was more of a holding force than one powerful enough to break into the pocket, and the Canadians snapped it in the first onrush. The Brigade quickly made its way through the woods and fell upon the stronger German force holding off the relieving 4th Armoured Brigade. Moving quietly the Paras were on top of the Germans before they knew they were there. They crawled up to the German positions and were upon them in a short rush with grenades and Sten guns firing. One by one the German positions winked out. The defending battalion launched its reserve into a counterattack which struck the 8th Paras in the woods. 'Whenever the Germans attacked they all shouted to each other, it being obviously part of their drill, and above their shouts could be heard the voices of their NCOs cursing and swearing and urging them on to battle. This shouting sounded eerie in the woods.' While the paras were gutting the German battalion from behind, the tanks of the Scots Greys surged across the fields with the tracked personnel carriers of the King's Rifle Corps behind them. A few German antitank guns were still firing and left a few of the Greys' tanks burning before the concentrated fire of the tanks destroyed them. The infantry dismounted behind the tanks and worked with them to overwhelm the few surviving positions. The defence had collapsed by 0920. The King's Rifle Corps and the Paras met a hundred yards inside the woods. Hill waited on the edge of the wood as the Brigade marched out under the protective guns of the 4th Armoured. His casualties had been small, but the column had actually grown, swollen by the two hundred prisoners taken in the woods.

The 152nd Brigade task force was in serious trouble. Its drive to relieve the Gordons had stalled almost immediately in the face of a stiff German defence. Von Choltitz had thrown his reserves into the fight, a company of assault guns and a battery of 88s. Despite the determined support of the RAF, the Germans were firmly planted between 152nd Brigade and the Gordons in Touffréville. The 2nd and 5th Seaforth Highlanders were each supported by two tank squadrons of the London Yeomanry. Three separate attacks had been repulsed leaving too many burning tanks and dead infantry in the fields. Among the German positions, there were also wrecked assault guns and twisted 88s and dead infantry, but there were still enough of them to shoot up any more British attempts to cross that wide beaten zone. As they were preparing for the fourth attempt in the early afternoon, a German party came down the road from Touffréville under a white flag. With the German officer in charge was a lightly wounded officer of the 1/7th Gordons. With evident mortification the young officer confirmed that the two battalions had surrendered. The historian of the 51st Division was to write of that moment, 'The fact must be faced that at this period the normal very high morale of the division fell temporarily to a low ebb.'[5]

Revenge for Omaha

The two infantry regiments of the U.S. 1st and 29th Infantry Divisions that had been at sea when the Germans crushed Omaha landed on 7 June on Gold Beach. They were followed by the artillery and support elements of both divisions. The 26th and 175th Infantry Regiments now were the manoeuvre strength of the patched-up 29th Infantry Division. The survivors of Omaha were being formed into a reconstituted 115th Infantry Regiment that would land in a few weeks. There had been some argument at 1st Army whether to have this reconstituted division under the flag of the 29ers or the Big Red One. The former won out because of the loss of the commander and staff of the 1st Division. The 2nd Infantry Division also began landing that day on schedule, also diverted to Gold Beach. U.S. V Corps was getting ashore after all, courtesy of the British 50th Division which had won its foothold on Gold. The decision to land the American divisions scheduled for Omaha had put a bad strain on the landing operations in 2nd Army's already crowded lodgement. The British and American forte in logistics management lubricated with a good deal of ad hoc improvisation paid off. The price had been greatly increased congestion along the beaches and among the inland assembly areas and supply dumps. Behind the infantry divisions the 2nd Armored Division was next in line to land.

Major General Gerhardt was not a man to forgive past injuries, and his nemesis was General Kraiss, his counterpart in the 352nd Division. He blessed the luck that gave him a second chance against Kraiss. That chance lay in the V Corps assignment to replace 50th Division between Port-en-Bessin and Bayeux, to destroy German resistance between that line and St. Lô and Carentan, and to link up with VII Corps pressing down from the north. Much of this was the original corps mission. Now it would be jumping off from the land rather than the sea. Gerhardt's first objective was to reduce Port-en-Bessin which had held out against the Royal Marine Commandos and been heavily reinforced after the German success at Omaha. The port itself would relieve the strain on Allied logistics over the shore. It was also the anchor on which the

352nd held the short line from Bayeux to the sea. Cut the anchor cable and the 352nd would be find its flank in the air. That was a serious consideration for Kraiss. He had started the battle with a division strength of 7,500 men that had been depleted by the fighting of the last two days. The Hitlerjugend had staved off disaster acting as a fire brigade on 7 June when 50th Division had attacked. Now the SS had been pulled out the line, and Kraiss was holding a five-mile front with barely two-thirds of his original manpower.

By 9 June the two V Corps divisions had relieved 50th Division. The 29ers were on the north and the Indian Head Division south to Bayeux. That morning the attack went in. Eight U.S. divisional artillery battalions, three V Corps artillery battalions, and eight British regiments of artillery, 243 guns in all, thundered on the dot at 1530. The Royal Navy added its weight of naval gunfire at right angles to the ground artillery. When the fire lifted, 2nd Infantry Division's commander, Major General Walter Robinson, slipped the leash on all three of its regiments (9th, 23rd, and 38th) in line. Each regiment was reinforced with a company of the 741st Tank Battalion. Gerhardt decided first to isolate Port-en-Bessin before attacking it. Preceded by the artillery barrage, the 175th Regiment broke through the German defences outside the port. The 175th wheeled northwest to keep the German flank from finding another anchor. The 26th Infantry then attacked the port from the south along the road to Bayeux supported by all the artillery battalions. British destroyers sailed almost into the little harbour pounding the defences from the rear. The outer circle of machine gun nests and gun positions resisted desperately. The 26th Infantry was motivated by more powerful motives: revenge and shame.

The day before the V Corps attack, Eisenhower did something that was not in the books. He sent General George Patton to Normandy to get a first-hand look at the patched-up 29th and report back on its state. His visit to the Big Red One's orphan regiment, as the 26th now called itself, would become the stuff of legend. For the 26th, Patton, was family. He had commanded them in North Africa and Sicily. After the slapping incident when he had been ordered by Eisenhower to apologize to each and every regiment in the 7th Army, they had practically mutinied when ordered to form to hear the old warrior's humiliation. They were entirely on his side. No vile skulker in a hospital tent deserved any more consideration than the old man had given him. Now he came to them, a cross between a common father and a comrade. He spoke to them of things that touched their memories and every man's heart: trust, loyalty, and love. Grown men, he among them, were in tears. Then they started cheering, something they had not done in years, rifle butts stamping on the ground. The Tenth Legion never honoured Caesar more, beating sword on shield. The white-haired old man had brought them back to life. They were the remnant of a great fighting division whose brother regiments had perished a bare three days before. They could not let that stand as the Big Red One's last act. The division was too much part of them after three years in that singularly male activity of war. They had to live with themselves, and to look into each other's faces and know that they had not measured up was more than they could bear. More valuable than gold was each man's worth measured in the eyes of his comrade. Homer knew it three thousand years ago when he put these words in the mouth of Menelaus:

> Now be men, my friends! Courage, come, take heart!
> Dread what comrades say of you here in bloody combat!
> When men dread that, more men come through alive –
> When soldiers break and run, good-bye glory, good-bye all defences![6]

Patton's simple report to Eisenhower on his visit: 'God help the Germans.'

It was the Germans who said goodbye to glory and all defences that afternoon. The 26th was nothing less than savage, taking few prisoners in cracking the outer defences. Stories were rife among them that there had been a general massacre of prisoners by the Germans at Omaha, and they were set on rough justice. Men seemed to throw their lives away to get at the Germans with grenades and bayonets. No scene from the *Iliad* dripped with more gore than that written by the 26th that day. With the outer ring gone, and the 26th in its killing frenzy, the courage drained out of the Germans. They began surrendering in large groups. Had it not been for Gerhardt's presence with the forward elements of the 26th, few prisoners would have been taken. With his hand to steady them, the frenzy of the 26th drained away as quickly as the port defences collapsed. With a grim satisfaction, matched only by General Gerhardt's, the revenge-sated remnant of the Big Red One watched over seven hundred prisoners trudge out of the port. Gerhardt took particular pleasure in the number. Seven hundred was his estimate of the number of 29ers taken prisoner on Omaha. That was only the principal. Now for the interest.

With the 175th wheeling on the right of the V Corps line constantly lapping over the rapidly backpedalling Germans, it was also a day of sweet revenge. There are few things more exhilarating than the pursuit of an enemy so eager to get away from you that he throws away everything but his weapon. Swept up in the rush to the rear was the 352nd's '1A' or operations officer, Lieutenant Colonel Fritz Ziegelmann. He had just arrived on the coast intending personally to assess the situation at Port-en-Bessin. The trip should have taken less than an hour. Allied fighter-bombers were so numerous and hungry that the trip took five hours instead. After arriving in the port, one look at the Allied fleet in its vastness convinced him the situation was hopeless.

> The sea was like a picture of the 'Kiel review of the fleet.' Ships of all sorts stood close together on the beach and in the water, broadly echeloned in depth. And

the entire conglomeration remained there intact without any real interference from the German side! I clearly understood the mood of the German soldier, who missed the Luftwaffe. It is a wonder that the German soldiers fought hard and stubbornly here.[7]

Ziegelmann didn't have to worry much more about German morale. He was swept up by the 175th and taken prisoner.

While Gerhardt was tearing the 352nd loose from its anchor on the sea, Robertson was landing roundhouse punches at the rest of the enemy division. Even after the heavy artillery barrage, there had been enough antitank guns and machine guns in staggered resistance points to make the first few hours fighting intense for the Indian Head Division. But when these were gone, the whole front seemed to unravel. The 741st Tank Battalion's companies were punching through with the infantry close behind them. The few assault guns that tried to block their paths got a few kills and then were knocked aside to be left burning on the roadsides. By early evening, the situation was fluid. V Corps now had four regiments wheeling west with Bayeux as a pivot driving the remnants of Kraiss's division ahead of them. Many of the prisoners among them amazed the V Corps troops as well as their intelligence officers. They represented a real tower of Babel, speaking almost any language but German. They were members of the *Ostruppen* battalions that had fought surprisingly well in many cases, more fearful of their German officers and NCOs than of the Americans. At first the number of oriental-looking prisoners were taken for Japanese to teach the Germans infiltration tactics, as if they needed it. Actually they were Mongols and other peoples from the eastern Soviet Union, taken prisoner by the Germans and given the opportunity to fight for the Reich or starve to death in a prisoner of war camp. Among Mongols, Kirghiz, Koreans, and Uzbeks, there were two prisoners whose origins could not be determined until long after they were sent to a POW camp in the United States. There a search through the oriental language departments of numerous universities finally found someone who could speak to these two barrel-chested men. They were Tibetan shepherds who had been press-ganged by the Red Army, none too concerned by borders in that region of the world. Seemingly betrayed by Allied propaganda which portrayed the enemy as the Aryan caricature, one soldier of the 175th exclaimed to his company commander, 'Captain, just who the hell *are* we fighting anyway?'

Kraiss had alerted his chain of command to the seriousness of the situation shortly after V Corps attacked. If collapse of the front was to be avoided, reinforcements were needed immediately. Already one regiment of the 3rd Fallschirmjäger Division was approaching the sector. More was needed. Rommel ordered that the 116th Panzer Division leave one of its panzer-grenadier regiments in place to hold the line and swing around Bayeux and counterattack. The 77th Infantry Division in front of Hitlerjugend was ordered to extend its front west to pick up some of the slack left by the 116th's move. By morning these two formations were in place ready to intercept the Americans between the St. Lô to Bayeux road and Highway 13 some five miles outside Bayeux. They had scooped up retreating elements of the 352nd and incorporated them into their positions. The 3rd Fallschirmjäger, which was being ferried from Brittany one regiment at time because of a shortage of trucks, was about to be a particularly unwelcome surprise for V Corps. These German paratroopers were an elite fighting force. Not only were parachute units the best equipped of any German ground force unit, they were imbued with a special paratrooper spirit or *Fallschirmjägergeist* that built a cohesion that was superior to any other in an armed forces that excelled in instilling cohesion. Their training emphasized initiative and improvisation and constantly hammered home that they were an elite. Their armament was superior to even comparable SS units, being the special concern of their patron, the head of the Luftwaffe, Reichsmarshal Hermann Göring. Unit for unit, they had more firepower than any army in the world. The 3rd Fallschirmjäger Division had eleven light machine guns for every one in the 2nd Infantry Division, making a total of 930. Where a U.S. rifle company would have two Browning air-cooled machine guns and nine BARs (Browning Automatic Rifles), the German Fallschirmjäger company would have 20 MG-42s and 43 submachine guns. The American rifle squad would have a single BAR whereas the Fallschirmjäger squad had two MG-42s and three submachine guns. Added to the combat power of the 116th's fifty-eight Mark IV tanks, the Germans had assembled a force to block V Corps that was clearly more formidable than the broken 352nd.

The morning of 10 June saw V Corps quickly off the mark in resuming the attack with four regiments abreast. The 26th Infantry had gone into corps reserve. Since the Germans had moved entirely by night, the Americans were unaware of the stone wall that faced them inside of whipped stragglers. They slammed into it almost immediately, completely surprised by the volume of fire that blew up their leading tanks and cut down the leading platoons in every column. By noon, heavy casualties told V Corps commander, General Gerow, that he did not have enough combat power to budge the Germans. His four regiments were up against a powerful Fallschirmjäger regiment, a panzer-grenadier regiment, and the single battalion of the panzer regiment (the other was being reequipped with Panthers in Germany). Instead of having a ratio of three to one over the defence, he had, in practical firepower terms, mere parity, even in tanks. He would have to wait for the 2nd Armored Division, which had just begun landing.

No Quarter: the Canadians and Hitlerjugend

As the fighting simmered on the flanks of 2nd Army, Montgomery threw another punch on 11 June, this time from his right and centre, codenamed SPANNER: XXX Corps's two divisions (49th and 50th) and I Corps' 3rd Canadian. The objective was to wheel southwest pivoting on Bayeux to out-flank the Germans holding up V Corps. If successful in rupturing the front, the 11th Armoured Division now beginning the landing of its advance elements was expected to be able to exploit the opening by 13 June. 7th Armoured Division was being reconstituted with new tanks, but the loss of so many crews could not be made good as easily. By the 13th, the Desert Rats would be able to muster about half the manned tanks with which they had landed. The division's 131st Infantry brigade and other supporting arms had by now landed.

The opening artillery storm swept over the hedgerows and villages where the Germans were known to be. Most of them were missed in their carefully camouflaged positions. The two XXX Corps divisions attacked at 0630 in the time-honoured fashion with two brigades up and one back. The corps boundary was the Seulles River. Their attack took them southwest. The 3rd Canadian Division attacked more in a southerly direction, constrained by the corps boundary on one side and its division boundary, the Odon River, with British 3rd Division on the other. The territory between these two rivers narrowed to the south until they passed within three miles of each other. In between them at this point was Villers-Bocage. The Canadians would attempt what the 7th Armoured had failed. Because of the narrowing sector, the attack would be delivered by one brigade, the 9th, followed by the 7th, with 8th Brigade in reserve.

The 11th of June was slow-going for all three divisions. They were deep in hedgerow country and up against good German infantry in the *Landsers* of the 77th Infantry Division and the panzergrenadier regiment of 116th Panzer Division. The Germans had staggered their defensive positions in depth rather than in a single line. The small, irregular fields with the built-up mounds of earth in each hedgerow were a natural defence unparalleled in complexity and danger for the attacker. It was impossible to mass an attack. Squads and platoons had to carry the fight forward against hidden machine guns and antitank guns that made each small field a killing field. Tanks could only be employed individually and then were in great danger from the concealed antitank gun that could engage them at close range with little chance of missing. The three divisions seemed to be suffering the death of a thousand cuts as casualties of hundreds of small squad actions piled up. That day's advance was measured in yards.

For Rommel that was all for the best. The fighting on the British flanks had sucked in their reserves. Now this attack would commit those divisions that were still fresh at the western end of the British sector. Montgomery had done him a favour by driving his fist right into the tactical equivalent of the tar baby of American folklore. He needed that time. His hopes to launch his attack by

11 June had been withered by the Allied air interdiction campaign that was seriously interfering with German attempts to build up the necessary supplies for a major German counterattack as well as delaying the supporting artillery and engineer battalions he needed. Too many horse-drawn artillery columns had been slaughtered on the roads by the swooping Allied birds of prey. The bridging units were critical. With their bulky equipment they had been repeatedly delayed or damaged. Operation SPANNER presented only one danger. Should the Canadians take Villers-Bocage, they would steal the pivot on which the German counterattack would turn. He had no choice but to commit Hitlerjugend prematurely.

On the night of 11 June Kurt Meyer infiltrated his division into jumping-off positions in the forward positions of the regiment of the 77th Infantry Division in his sector. The Canadians would be expecting more hedgerow fighting against a defending infantry division. That would be the first in a series of dangerous assumptions. There was a new enemy out there for the Canadians. War correspondent Ralph Allen wrote, 'These Hitler Youth were beardless killers whose highest aim was to die, whose only god was Hitler, who came rustling through the spring wheat, a screaming curtain of mortars just ahead of them, and the fearsome clanking of their tanks behind.'[9]

The 9th Canadian Brigade attacked down the road toward Villy-Bocage, past the wrecked vehicles and bloated bodies of the 7th Armoured Division's defeat the six days before. The Shermans of the Sherbrooke Fusiliers led off with the North Nova Scotia Highlanders and the Highland Light Infantry. They rode straight into killing zones of the Mark IVs of 12th SS Panzer Regiment. A dozen Shermans were burning in minutes. Still stunned by the tank ambush, the deployed Canadian infantry was struck by German artillery. Even before that lifted the tanks and the panzergrenadiers of 26th Regiment rolled forward. The Sherbrookes were fighting back, but too many of them had been brewed up in the first few minutes. They were pulling back in sections by bounds, shepherding the infantry of the North Novas with them until they found the refuge of the little hamlet called Fain. Then the Germans were upon them. Will R. Bird described that fight:

There were Germans everywhere . . . A terrific artillery barrage filled the air with earth and shrapnel and bits of wood. Tanks fired as fast as guns could be reloaded, machine guns chattered . . . More and more Germans appeared in the smoke and dust. Time and again they seemed only yards away but were hurled back. Then men screamed that the enemy were coming in from the other side . . . C Company was being surrounded. Capt. Hank Fraser and a few others determined to fight as long as possible. The rest tried to get back to positions that could be held. Some made it, across 50 yards of open ground and 200 yards of wheat field, to a hedge where A Company was holding . . . Fraser, some other

Novas and Sherbrookes and machine gunners of the Cameron Highlanders of Ottawa took a huge toll of the SS but were finally overwhelmed and killed.[10]

A Company held out behind Fain, vainly hoping for B Company to come up on its left. German infantry gradually surrounded the company until by dusk there was no escape. They surrendered, and two Germans shot two of the Novas with their hands in the air. Private W.H. Gerrior who was still armed shot the two Germans and three others before pulling the bolt out of his rifle and throwing it away unseen. Then he too surrendered. But the SS were in a murderous mood and shot two more of the Novas on the way back to the hamlet. That mood boiled over when the smoke of battle drifted away and revealed all the Germans the Canadians had killed that day. Two more prisoners were shot out of hand. A Hitlerjugend riding in a staff car that came blaring its horn through the hamlet shot two more men. During the search of the prisoners, another Canadian was butchered for responding to the question of a friend. Trucks of German wounded raced through the town with their occupants waving their fists at the Canadians. One truck swerved out its way to run down two more men. In a sneer that epitomized German self-pity at its worst, a guard said, 'You bombed Germany. Can you expect mercy?'[11]

The impetus of the attack had pushed the rest of the 9th Brigade three miles back onto the town of Noyers-Bocage halfway down the main highway to Caen. Barely a squadron of the Sherbrookes had fought their way out of the fighting; the North Novas had lost 245 men. By nightfall the Germans were probing the Canadian lines outside the town. Division had hurried the 3rd Anti-Tank Regiment forward to thicken the defence. Survivors of the North Novas had rejoined their battalion one by one that night, some of them having escaped their SS captors at Fain. The word of the murder of prisoners was known quickly throughout the brigade. The men's hearts hardened. Now the Hitlerjugend would have the kind of war it wanted: no quarter. From that day, the Canadians never took an SS prisoner. 'Enmity,' wrote Ralph Allen, 'distilled out its last adulterant and left a pool of purest venom.'[12]

That kind of war was best described by the historian of one of the Canadian battalions who next day walked over the ruins of another village in the path of the battle where the 46th Royal Marine Commandos had stood their ground:

They fought like lions on both sides, so that the dead lay corpse by corpse. We searched every house, every courtyard, to avoid ambush. And here is the confirmation of how ferocious last night's battle must have been. The Commandos lie dead in rows beside the dead S.S. Grenades are scattered all over the road and in the porches of houses. Here we see a Commando and an S.S.-man, literally in each other's arms, having slaughtered each other. There, a German and a

Canadian tank have engaged each other to destruction, and are still smoldering, and from each blackened turret hangs the charred corpse of machine-gunner. Over here, are a group who ran towards a wall for shelter, and were shot down before they got there. And then, near the church, as the advance guard of C Company and the carriers turn the corner, there are three Germans. Only three. But one of them instantly draws his pistol, and hits one of our men. A Bren gunner kills two of the three S.S.-men, but the survivor does not surrender; he dodges us and gets away. Now, we understand with what kind of fanatic we have to deal.[13]

The direction of attack of the British 49th and Canadian 3rd Divisions in SPANNER had carried them in diverging paths that widened a growing gap between them. Into that gap rode the Panthers and 25th Panzergrenadier Regiment, wheeling around the fighting in Fain to hit the Canadian 7th Brigade coming up behind the 9th. The attack wiped out the three lead companies of the Winnipeg Rifles and rolled up the flank of the Canadian Scottish. The reserve battalion, the Regina Rifle Regiment, counterattacked and temporarily stabilized the situation, but only temporarily, until the next German lunge threw chaos into the Canadian ranks. Two of the brigade's three battalions had been mauled; the Winnipegs had only one company left. With the Reginas as the rearguard, the brigade retreated northeast. They too would be joined by escaped prisoners who reported the mass execution of Winnipegs and Highlanders. The Germans left a company to keep the pressure on the rearguard and swung forward towards its intermediate objective, the little crossroads town of Cheux, just three miles from Carpiquet Airfield. Using a tactic learned on the Eastern Front, the two leading Panthers fired their long-barrelled 75s straight down the road into the town and charged forward. The Panthers rode through the town, the panzergrenadiers behind them shooting up the rear service units. One company spread out over an airfield outside the town, blowing up clusters of fighter-bombers in revetments with that special glee only one who has been tormented from the air can know.

Kurt Meyer had jabbed his stick deep into the British hive. Now he would have to deal with swarms of stinging insects unleashed. More fighter-bombers, stationed at Carpiquet Airfield, were taking off to directly attack the SS only a few miles away. The Shermans of the 1st Hussars counterattacked as well as soon as they came up in a spirited assault on the town, ordered to be driven home regardless. Half a dozen tanks of A Squadron penetrated to the town centre but were hunted down by Panthers and panzergrenadiers with their panzerfaust antitank rockets. Twenty-three more Shermans were burning outside the town. The Canadian reserve, 8th Brigade, was hurried forward and counterattacked Cheux from the north, but the Canadian command had not timed them to go in with the tanks, allowing the Germans to fight off one attack at a time. Between attacks, though, the naval gunfire and massed artillery was making Cheux both a ruin and a dangerously exposed position for the Germans. Their successes that day had come from surprise and speed. They could not afford to nail themselves to one spot and allow the enemy's firepower superiority to grind them to dust. Witt reluctantly ordered the battle group to withdraw from Cheux and take up dispersed positions a half mile southwest. His own self-propelled artillery was close enough, though, to keep Carpiquet Airfield under fire, forcing the fighter-bomber squadrons to relocate to other fields.

By nightfall, estimates of the day's losses within 3rd Canadian Division headquarters were over four thousand killed, wounded and missing. While many stragglers would come in the next few days, the horror of Dieppe had been surpassed for the Canadians. Two infantry brigades had been given a severe working over, and one battalion in each had been practically wiped out. The 2nd Canadian Armoured Brigade had been similarly mauled, the Sherbrookes and 1st Hussars losing between them sixty-eight tanks. One of the Hussars' tank commanders recalled:

> The morale of the men was very low indeed. So many of the long-time comrades had stayed behind on the battlefield, the battle itself had been so savage, so furious, that every man felt that the 12th S.S. Panzer had a personal grudge against our tanks. Silently, grimly, we were looking at each other, knowing exactly what was in the other man's mind. They simply lay there, not sleeping, eyes opened, just staring into space. A poet or a writer would have found the proper words to describe this vacant look and what was going through their minds, but other than a few comforting words from the Padre, Major Creelman, not much was said. Mostly, everyone was rather vindictive, and silently swearing revenge. Had they met 12 S.S. Panzer again, immediately, they would have been very hard to control. The Padre did his best to get this feeling out of them, but was not too successful. Had any young subaltern said the wrong thing that day, the men would have been put up for court-martials, they were in such a mood.[14]

Only 8th Brigade and the tanks of the Fort Garry Horse were in still in fighting shape, and they were covering the SS battle group that had withdrawn out of Cheux. Their losses had been heavy as well. The two battered brigades were withdrawn north to tie in with the 8th on a line from Tilly to Cheux. Second Army was rushing in reinforcements all night, especially antitank regiments to strengthen the two brigades. The newly landing 154th Brigade of 51st Highland Division was diverted to the Canadian sector as well. Major General Keller and his staff spent a sleepless night pulling out every last resource to make sure the division presented a solid front the next morning. By shortening the division front and pulling it northwest, however, both Keller and Dempsey, had failed to see the gap opening up between the Canadians and 3rd British Division that was badly overextended in the deep Orne Salient.

If Keller was reeling from four thousand casualties, Meyer was worried by the losses among his Hitlerjugend. The little hamlet of Fain had been a slaughter pen for his teenagers, and the 26th SS Panzergrenadier Regiment had been as badly gutted as 9th Brigade. His tank losses had been crippling: twenty-three Mark IVs and sixteen Panthers. He was down to one third of his tank strength. Not even in Russia had he seen the enemy as individually tough and capable as these Canadians. He had also been incensed early in the fighting when he had been shown the bodies of a group of German soldiers that had obviously been captured and executed by the Canadians. His division had fought hard and bled profusely. It was now exposed deep in the centre of the British lodgement and could be in serious difficulties in the next few days. But he had accomplished his mission, to drive such a jab into the British line at this point that all attention would be riveted there.

The American Sector

Carentan

Rommel's removal of Witt's battle group from les Forges forced the contraction of the remaining German forces in the area to just north of Carentan. Von der Heydte's paratroopers abandoned their hold on the southern two beach exits and dug in around Ste.-Marie-du-Mont and St. Côme-du-Mont, only two miles north of Carentan. On their heels were the American paratroopers of the Screaming Eagles. General Taylor had pulled together the scattered battalions of his 101st Airborne Division, and had been ordered to take the city. For three days the German and American paratroopers struggled for Carentan's outskirts.

On 8 June Taylor threw four paratrooper and glider battalions at St. Côme-du-Mont. Two battalions of the 506th were to break into the town while the other battalions encircled it. The blow fell mostly upon the German 3/1058 Regiment and several companies of 3/6 Fallschirmjäger. The American artillery battalion fired 2,500 rounds of 105mm high explosive in support of the attack, and by mid-morning the men of the 1058th were straggling out of town as the battalion's command and control broke down under the shelling. Von der Heydte had no reserves left, and ordered the position evacuated. Most of the Germans escaped despite a nasty brush with one of the encircling U.S. battalions.

Von der Heydte had to pull back his whole line under American pressure. One battalion easily disengaged and followed the others streaming out of St. Côme-du-Mont. The other in St. Marie-du-Mont was not as lucky. A German historian described the breaking point of one battalion on 9 June:

During the night of 9 and 10 June the remnants of the 1st Battalion, a mere twenty-five men, twenty-five of 700, had found their way back to regimental headquarters and reported the annihilation of their battalion. It had been surrounded in Sainte-Marie-du-Mont, attacked by enemy forces, split up into separate groups, and literally wiped out. One-third of its men had been killed or drowned in the swamps. The rest, nearly all of them wounded, had been taken prisoners.[15]

Despite their élan and skill, the Germans were ground down by the enemy's unremitting firepower and the attacks of the American paratroopers, every bit their equal. The Americans, with three regiments in the attack and one in reserve, forced the barrier of the Douve River, one mile from the city. Von der Heydte's shrunken command was now fighting in the Carentan's gardens and suburbs.

On 10 June, an American officer under flag of truce delivered General Taylor's demand, written in German, that the 6th surrender. Von der Heydte replied, in English, 'What would you do in my place?' The colonel's gallant words masked an alarming weakness. He now had only two battalions left of his original four; the rest of the line was held by his heavy weapons and support units. His ammunition, especially for machine pistols and mortars, was dwindling fast. The only ammunition he had plenty of was artillery, but the guns had already been destroyed. An emergency delivery of mortar ammunition was in the wrong calibre, but the paratroopers wrapped the shells in blankets and shot them off. Finally, the Luftwaffe made an appearance on the night of 10 and 11 June and dropped canisters of mortar and machine pistol ammunition.

It was still not enough to counter odds of four to one. Von der Heydte made a personal reconnaissance of the high ground to the west of Carentan for alternative positions. The city was going to fall within hours and his regiment with it if he did not get them out. On the road, he met the commander of the 17th SS Panzergrenadier Division, Brigadeführer Ostendorff, and his operations officer, Obersturmbannführer Konrad. Ostendorff informed him that his regiment was now attached to the 17th and that he would counterattack on 12 June; 'We'll get that little job cleared up all right.' Von der Heydte insisted that it was now or never. The 6th could not hold out until tomorrow. Ostendorff was astonished; 'And surely those Yanks can't be tougher than the Russians.' 'Not tougher,' replied Von der Heydte, 'but considerably better equipped, with a veritable steamroller of tanks and guns.' Ostendorff was now curt. 'Herr Oberstleutnant, no doubt your parachutists will manage till to-morrow.'[16] But Von der Heydte was not giving up. 'You must send reinforcements in now, or I guarantee you the city will fall today. And no amount of fight-to-the-last bullet nonsense will avert that fate.' Ostendorff's face turned red as if he were going to shout. Then he pursed his lips and said,

'Konrad, hurry up the assault gun battalion and the panzergrenadiers, and let's get them into the town. Von der Heydte, let's go see about our problem.'[17]

On the Merderet

After the relief of the 82nd Airborne Division on 7 June and the arrival of the 325th Glider Regiment, Ridgway decided to make another attempt to seize a crossing over the flooded Merderet River. One of his battalions and a large number of individuals were trapped on the western side of the river. The paratroopers had held on to the eastern end of the bridge at la Fiere for two days under the command of Brigadier James Gavin, Assistant Division Commander, against determined attacks from the 1058th Regiment. Now with the glider regiment under his command, Gavin was ordered to secure the causeway and establish a bridgehead on the German side.

Gavin was worried that this was asking a lot of such a green unit as the glider regiment. Its commander wanted to try fording the river at night with his First Battalion and enveloping the German defenders from the rear. The ford in the river had disappeared under the inundation that made the water barrier five hundred feet across, but somehow the battalion made it across without being detected, wading chest-deep with their rifles carried overhead as in some training exercise. At daylight, they moved inland against minor resistance. The 1058th Regiment was alerted and responded quickly with a sharp, violent counterattack that sent the inexperienced glidermen reeling back towards the river. The Germans might have driven them into a slaughter in the water but for the self-sacrifice of Private First Class Charles N. DeGlopper. He stood up in the path of the German pursuit, firing his Browning Automatic Rifle into the enemy pursuers until they killed him. He had thrown his life away to stop them long enough to allow many of the glidermen to escape and for that was posthumously awarded the Medal of Honor.

By now the need to rescue the paratroopers trapped on the German side of the river was becoming desperate. Gavin decided to ram the 3/325th across the bridge in a straight run. The battalion commander begged off, saying he was too sick to attack. Gavin relieved him on the spot and appointed his executive officer to command the battalion. The supporting artillery fired, and the battalion dashed over the causeway right into the concentrated fire of the enemy.

At the moment for the 325th to go – they had all been instructed to run as fast as they could across the causeway – I gave them the signal, and from their positions, crouching along the side of the road, they began to run. At once many of them were hit and fell on the causeway, but some made it all the way across. After a few minutes of this, the first signs of a break occurred as we had expected. The overwhelming firepower of the Germans was just too much . . . It had been a costly affair, and many of the 325th men were stretched head to foot along the causeway . . .[18]

Gavin then sent in a company of paratroopers who followed their commander yelling over the causeway. More bodies tumbled into the heaps already littering the causeway, but most of the company made it across to attack directly into the teeth of the German defences. The artillery preparation had killed many of the defenders already. Most of the German artillery gunners were dead around their pieces along with their horse teams still in harness. Still the Germans had one more counterattack in them. The paratroopers made them pay for it, leaving rings of gray-clad bodies around each of the positions they had taken. The fighting became hand-to-hand as the paratroopers ran out of ammunition, then the Germans swamped them. A few survivors made their way back across the causeway. The 82nd had shot its bolt, and now forcing the Merderet would be up to the 90th Infantry Division, which had completed landing.

Azeville and St. Marcouf

After eliminating the last resistance within the lodgement area on 7 June, VII Corps organized a major attack to the north with four regiments abreast for the next day. On the left, the 508th Parachute Infantry and the 8th Infantry Regiments struck towards objectives between the Merderet River and Montebourg. On the right, the 12th and 22nd Infantry Regiments once again attacked the tough German naval battery at St. Marcouf and the equally obstinate inland battery at Azeville. Facing them were elements of three German divisions: 91st, 234th, and 709th, in three regiment-size battle groups with strong artillery support.

On the left the two regiments made slow but steady progress for the first day but at heavy cost. The already battered 8th Infantry bled even more. The leading company of 2/8th was badly cut up when caught in a hedgerow lane by concentrated mortar, machine-gun, and artillery fire. Charging across open fields against heavy machine gun grazing fire, L Company captured the German positions around the hangar at Magneville, losing many dead. The first battalion was luckier and outflanked the defenders at Ecausseville with two platoons of tanks. Firing into houses, they flushed out over a hundred prisoners. On 10 June both regiments came up against the defences the Germans had prepared after their failure to take Ste.-Mère-Eglise two days before. Resistance was so heavy that the Americans had to break off the attack and dig in.

On the right, the 12th and 22nd Regiments again beat themselves bloody against the two casemated German batteries held by the two German lieutenants. On 8 June Colonel Tribolet of the 22nd threw a battalion against each battery. Against St. Marcouf, Tribolet's 1st Battalion attacked with two companies behind a rolling barrage after two hours of softening up by the

Navy, field artillery, and mortars. Reaching the edge of the defences, the third company was passed through to attack the bunkers and casemates with poles carrying demolition charges. They used the pole charges so freely in the outer positions that they had none when they reached the strongpoint. As on 6 June, Lieutenant Kattnig turned his 100mm gun at Azeville on the St. Marcouf position. Its shells exploded among the scores of Americans standing on top of and outside the casemates, killing and wounding dozens including most of the officers as the rest of the Americans ran for cover. Then the German infantry company emerged from the bunkers and counterattacked. Struck off balance by the artillery then the counterattack, the 1/22nd hurriedly retreated out of the battery position. The attack on the Azeville Battery by the 2/22nd was almost an exact replay.

Another attack on St. Marcouf planned for that day came to nothing when artillery coordination broke down. All night the Americans poured a steady stream of 20mm tracer fire into the battery position to prevent repairs. With superhuman skill, the German sergeant-armourer repaired one of the guns inside the battery using parts from several other smashed guns. Then as the tracers continued to pour into the battery, the Germans fired into the beach-head so packed with disembarking supplies and new units, that every shell was right on target.

On 9 June, the increasingly frustrated Colonel Tribolet decided to concentrate on the weaker battery at Azeville while smothering St. Marcouf with artillery to keep it from supporting its sister battery. His Third Battalion infiltrated through the mine fields at the rear of the battery and entered the position easily. But seemingly, their effort was to no avail. Even the tank they had brought with them and the bazookas had no effect on the German bunkers. Having exhausted their explosives, the battalion withdrew. Tribolet promptly relieved the commander, but it was too late to get back in. Another attempt was met by heavy machine gun and mortar fire. Several German battalions had slipped forward to reinforce the batteries.

By the evening of 11 June, General Collins, commanding VII Corps, was feeling about as frustrated as Tribolet had in front of those infernal batteries. Compared to Omaha, VII Corps' record was a raving success. Compared to his objective to sever the Cotentin Peninsula and take Cherbourg, it was less appealing. True, the corps had averted the loss of the 82nd Airborne Division in a spirited action, but attempts to break out to the south, west, and north had run up against stone walls. Maxwell Taylor's 101st had been stopped within an ace of taking Carentan by the arrival of the 17th SS Panzergrenadier Division. The 82nd and the 90th Divisions had also failed, with heavy loss, to get across the Merderet. The 4th Division had just spent five days beating itself senseless against two German batteries that should have fallen on D-Day. If anyone should get a medal, it was the two Germans commanding them. The bright side was that he had two airborne and two infantry divisions safely ashore with the veteran 9th Infantry Division in the process of landing. He could feel the whole American chain of command breathing down his neck, from Bradley all the way to George Marshall, whose stern image reminded him that the graduate of the Virginia Military Academy did not tolerate failure.

Notes

1. J.B. Salmond, *the History of the 51st Highland Division 1939–1945* (Edinburgh: William Blackwood, 1953) pp.141–142.
2. Alexander McKee, *Last Round Against Rommel: Battle of the Normandy Bridgehead* (New York: New American Library, 1964) pp.71–72; British title: *Caen: Anvil of Victory* (London: Souvenir, 1964).
3. Richard R. Sedgwick, *The Scots Greys from Waterloo to Normandy* (London: Collins, 1954) p.131.
4. John Golley, *The Big Drop: The Guns of Merville, June 1944* (London: Jane's, 1982) p.20.
5. McKee, *Last Round Against Rommel: Battle of the Normandy Beachhead* (New York: New American Library, 1964) p.181; (British title: *Caen: Anvil of Victory*).
6. Homer, *The Iliad*, v, tr. William Fagles (New York: Viking Penguin, 1990) p.181.
7. Joseph Balkoski, *Beyond the Beachhead: The 29th Infantry Division in Normandy* (Harrisburg, PA: Stackpole, 1989) p.148.
8. Balkoski, ibid., p.179.
9. Reader's Digest, *The Canadians at War 1939–1945*, Vol II (Canada: Reader's Digest, 1969) p.471.
10. Will R. Bird, *No Retreating Footsteps* and *The Two Jacks*, quoted in *The Canadians at War*, Vol II (Canada: Reader's Digest, 1969) pp.471–473.
11. Ibid.
12. Ibid.
13. McKee, *Last Round Against Rommel: Battle of the Normandy Beachhead* (New York: New American Library, 1964) pp.87–88; (British title: *Caen: Anvil of Victory*).
14. Ibid., p.88.
15. Paul Carrell, *Invasion: They're Coming*, tr. E. Osers (London: George E. Harrap, 1962); (New York: E.P. Dutton, 1964) p.143.
16. Carrell, ibid., p.144.
17. Friedrich-August von der Heydte, *German Paratroopers: Crete to Normandy* (London: William Kimber, 1953) p.210.
18. James M. Gavin, *On to Berlin: Battles of an Airborne Commander 1943–1946* (New York: Viking, 1978) p.117; (London: Leo Cooper, 1978).

CHAPTER 7

Unternehmen ROSSBACH 12 to 13 June

Ultra Is Not Everything

Montgomery had not become visibly nervous about the failures of ROYAL OAK and SPANNER. He did snap at an officer on his staff who remarked that the codename SPANNER had described more what the Germans threw into the British plans than anything else. Only to himself, though, would he admit his worry. The Germans had not only shredded his grand plan for the campaign but had, with two blows at his centre, unravelled his attempts to repair the damage. Only the American V Corps had had any success in 2nd Army's sector, something the Americans were making all too much of considering it had stalled ten miles west of Bayeux. He was running out of fresh divisions faster than the landings could replace them. Between 7 and 11 June, he had lost the 1st Airborne and suffered the mauling of the 6th Airborne, 7th Armoured, and 51st Highland, and all save the 3rd Canadian and 6th were veteran units. His losses in tanks were easily made good. His losses in infantry were far more serious. He didn't have enough to begin with, and the replacements were about to run out. Then he would be faced with the necessity of disbanding battalions and divisions in order to keep others up to strength. The Americans had the infantry, but they were having trouble getting ashore in strength with the failure of Omaha.

His enemies were using these defeats to press for his removal. The Americans had been quiet since Omaha. It was his enemies among the British military leadership that were whispering to Churchill and Eisenhower. Air Marshal Leigh-Mallory was especially critical because Montgomery had gone to Eisenhower to override his objections to the drop of the 1st Airborne Division. He now had a bloody vindication to wave before anyone that would listen. Air Marshal Tedder, Eisenhower's deputy, was also no friend and was actively taking Leigh-Mallory's side. Montgomery's insistence that the air forces demolish every Norman crossroads town and village to impede German traffic had also been firmly rebuffed on the grounds of unacceptable casualties to the French population. The air marshals had a hand in this as well.

Of course, he could point to Eisenhower's unsatisfactory compromise on the air interdiction campaign that had left too many French bridges intact, all because General Spaatz could not bear to give up his air campaign over Ger-

168

many. Now the Germans appeared to be reinforcing the Normandy front as fast if not faster than the Allies. He could also point to the American failure at Omaha, but that would not endear him much to Eisenhower or the American Joint Chiefs who had arrived in Britain and were now waiting grimly in London. His political worries were as much a part of generalship at his level as his purely military worries. Success was the only thing that would alleviate both.

Offensive operations had bogged down in the close country of the hedgerows and the Germans' infernal ability to be one step ahead of him. After the dramatic success of the British divisions on D-Day, everything thereafter had been a cruel disappointment. One thing had been consistent, though. Rommel had come back punching, and every blow that he had laid on had been painful. This was Rommel's element, and he was playing right into it. Now Ultra had alerted him to a possible German offensive against the Orne Salient on 14 or 15 June. The chatter between OKW and Army Group B had been clear as to the date and place. That would give him time to tidy up the battlefield around 3rd Canadian and bring up a few surprises for Rommel. This wouldn't be the first time he had used Ultra to catch the Desert Fox on the point of his offensive.

Rommel's appraisal of the situation was much more positive than Montgomery's. Reinforcements were arriving faster than he had expected, though with the casualty rate he had expected. Divisions arrived piecemeal and needed a few days to pull themselves together after the ordeal of running the gauntlet of constant air attacks. Nevertheless, morale was good after the Americans had been thrown back into the sea near St. Lô. The British had been severely handled twice when they had attempted offensive operations. Now Hitlerjugend had done just what he had asked of it and jumped with both feet right onto the pivot point of the front. The British had responded with the expected alarm. Dietrich's I SS Panzer Corps staff had been augmented with assets from 7th Army to put together the plan that Rommel had outlined. With Kurt Meyer's 12th SS, Dietrich's corps would control four divisions in the coming attack: Panzer Lehr, 2nd Panzer, and 84th Infantry. Panzer Lehr and 2nd Panzer were two of the strongest panzer divisions in the German forces: together they had about 350 tanks and assault guns. Supporting the operation was LXXXI Corps, with three divisions east of the Orne and II Fallschirmjäger Corps, with four divisions west of the Vire, eleven divisions in all and one more than the British had in their lodgement. The operation was codenamed ROSSBACH, in memory of the lightning manoeuvre that Frederick the Great had used to rout a French Army in the Seven Years' War. Pleased with Panzer Lehr's victory, Hitler had even promised to add something special to the offensive from his bag of super weapons tricks.

The Luftwaffe's weather report delivered that morning had added a new and exciting element to ROSSBACH. The report predicted that a storm front had accelerated its movement and was veering over northwestern France. The next two days, 12 and 13 June, would have rain and drizzle with low cloud cover. Nature was offering him the perfect shield against Allied air power for two days, but it was two days before the scheduled beginning of ROSSBACH. He had planned on Hitlerjugend to resume the offensive and continue to draw off Montgomery's reserves. His own preparations were not complete. A number of rocket launcher and artillery regiments were still not in position, and a number of tanks were out of service due to lack of spare parts. Still, the basic elements of the operation were in place, and in the balance, the weather advantage more than outweighed the few pieces of his game that were not on the board. They would go the next morning.

When Rommel made his decision, a German intelligence officer offered a captured American lieutenant a cigarette in a French stone farmhouse. The young prisoner inhaled and then smiled nervously, the mirthless, submissive smile of a thoroughly cowed and frightened man. Captain Hartmann let the fine Virginia tobacco caress own his lungs also as he checked his notes and clarified a few things. 'Thank you, Lieutenant. You may go.' He made eye contact with the guard who took him out. How many times had he seen those hunched shoulders and bleak eyes after an interrogation. He had been lucky to find such a callow young prisoner, a boy really, totally without the tempering of combat. He broke down easily, and even before leaving the room, the shame of it began to eat at his heart. You could read it in his face that it would haunt him the rest of his life.

The lieutenant had just provided Hartmann with the last confirming piece of information that would pinpoint the *Schwerpunkt* of II Fallschirmjäger Corps' attack on the U.S. V Corps, the yawning gap between the 2nd and 29th Divisions. *Schwerpunkt* is a hard term to translate easily. The sense of it is best conveyed by the words, 'solar plexus', and the overwhelmingly ugly sensation of being struck there by a sledge hammer. Hartmann had found the boundary between the U.S. 2nd and 29th Divisions, that delicate place between units made vulnerable by often uncertain responsibilities. The join between the two divisions had stretched as they had moved forward on slightly diverging axes. General der Fallschirmtruppen Eugen Meindl, the German corps commander, shook his head in amazement at this priceless piece of intelligence. Rommel had just assigned his corps a supporting role in ROSSBACH, to tie down V Corps so that it could not reinforce the British to the east where the main blow would fall. With this knowledge in hand, he could do more to the Americans than just hold them.

The evening of 11 June found the U.S. V Corps well forward of its starting point after three days of combat. The 29th Infantry Division had pressed westward on to Trévières on the road to Isigny, the back door to Carentan. The 2nd Infantry Division had attacked southwest toward St. Lô and its forward regiments had reached the outskirts of Cerisy-la-Forêt and Balleroy. Between these regiments was the Forest of Cerisy which the division had decided to go around, rather than get bogged down in forest fighting. Meindl's Corps had its two Fallschirmjäger divisions in the line, the 3rd in front of the American 29th and the 5th in front of the 2nd. The 116th Panzer Division had been pulled out the line two days ago and hidden in the Forest of Cerisy. The 17th SS Panzergrenadier Division, fighting at Carentan, had left one regiment to hold the city with 6th Fallschirmjäger Regiment and deployed the rest of the division eastward in the night behind 3rd Fallschirmjäger Division.

Unternehmen ROSSBACH: Day 1

By 0600 the whole of northwestern France was socked in, grounding the ever present Jabos. Simultaneously the German guns east of the Orne bridgehead and south of the Orne Salient erupted. For half an hour the gun barrels thundered, eating up the piles of ammunition carefully assembled near each battery. Gunners worked their pieces with the sustained physical effort that concentrates explosive death on its targets. Rocket launcher regiments rippled with shrieks as their rockets disappeared into the low, dripping clouds. The bombardment would have been a full hour had the original timing been followed and all the ammunition delivered. It was bad enough. The German shells fell first with a sudden thunderclap on the forward infantry positions, catching many of the enemy off guard and eating breakfast. The German artillery had been especially reticent the last few days and had lulled the British into a cautious complacency. Now men were leaping back into slit trenches and foxholes amid heavy casualties. Then the drumroll moved into the rear, first targeting the infantry reserves, then deeper for tank concentrations, communications, and service units. Then it swept back and fell on the forward infantry again.

The Hard Luck Corps

Even as the barrage was falling on the Americans, the German Fallschirmjäger of II Corps rose from their positions and moved forward in the rain. They overran the surprised and dazed survivors of the forward companies in the first rush, and then began to infiltrate through the hedgerows to find the weak places between American units. In this they were helped by the steady rain which reduced visibility and muffled sound. The Americans had also learned a few things from their experiences and threw in sharp counterattacks in a dozen places where the Germans appeared. The 2nd Division's counterattack had thrown the 5th Fallschirmjäger back to their starting lines. The 2nd was a veteran division, while the Germans had barely filled their ranks by the time of the invasion. Here unit cohesion and experience told as the Indian Head's 38th Infantry Regiment was fighting on the outskirts of Cerisy-la-Forêt to the west of the forest. By the early afternoon all four divisions had sunk their claws into each other so deeply that it would take days to back off.

When the 2nd Division's commander committed most of his reserve around Balleroy in the hope of outflanking 5th Fallschirmjäger, Meindl threw his punch at the American solar plexus. Both 116th Panzer and 17th SS Panzergrenadier Divisions converged from south and north towards the taut and weakly-held boundary between the American divisions centred on le Molay-Littry. It snapped at the first contact. Within minutes almost sixty German tanks and thirty assault guns followed by three panzergrenadier regiments were pounding down the little Norman country roads and lanes due east towards Bayeux. The enemy infantry and antitank guns that could have made this patchwork of hedgerows and stone farmhouses a trap were not there. Meindl had split V Corps wide open and achieved a breakthrough.

Against the Orne Bridgehead

Colonel von Luck was watching the German hurricane on the outskirts of Ste.-Honorine, east of the Orne:

> For 12 June, division issued another order to attack: the village of Ste.-Honorine, lying on a commanding hill, was to be won back, to give us a view over the enemy battlefield and deny the British a view of our own positions. My combat group was to be further reinforced. A brigade of multiple rocket-launchers, 'moaning minnies,' with over 300 tubes 21cm and 30cm in caliber, was to support us. These launchers had a particular psychological effect: the projectiles flew over the battlefield with a loud, nerve-shattering whine and forced the surprised enemy to take cover immediately.[1]

The infantry of LXXXI Corps came in just behind the bombardment and struck the British all along the perimeter of the bridgehead. Von Choltitz's determination had spread to the whole corps. Within an hour, the Germans, especially Kreutz's 346th Division, had made so many penetrations that the 4th Armoured Brigade had to be committed by regiments and squadrons in half a dozen places. Colonel von Luck was again in the van with his battle group. Before the dust had settled he had chased the enemy out of Ste.-Honorine and then dug themselves in on the northern edge of the village. Now it was the turn of the Royal Artillery and the Royal Navy to speak. Von Luck was awestruck by the warships he could see for the first time.

> Then began the heaviest naval bombardment we had known so far. We could see the firing of the battleships, cruisers, and destroyers. The shells, of calibers up to 38cm, came whistling over like heavy trunks, to burst and rip vast craters in our lines.[2]

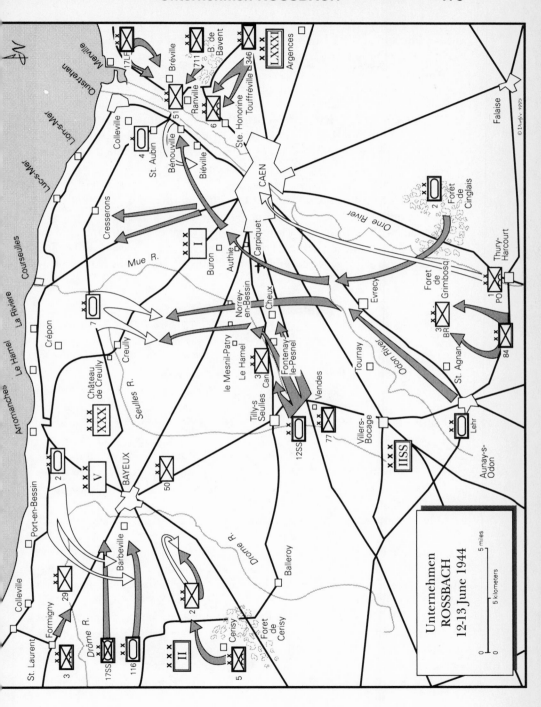

Unternehmen
ROSSBACH
12-13 June 1944

5 miles

5 kilometers

On the heels of the artillery came the enemy counterattack that broke into the smashed village. The fighting became hand-to-hand with many dead on both sides until the Germans were forced out. The focus of the battle shifted northward as the 346th was lunging up toward Ranville while the 17th Field Division was attacking towards the British headquarters from the direction of Bréville. Again and again the tanks of 4th Armoured Brigade had to counterattack German penetrations and help the infantry throw them out. It was becoming increasingly difficult to do. The Germans had learned, even the 17th Field Division, that the closer you got to the British the less able they were to use those big naval rifles. Fear had sharpened their infiltration skills considerably. By noon the two divisions had become so deeply inserted into the 6th Airborne and 51st Divisions' positions that the fighting broke down into disjointed fights around company strongpoints. A few German machine-gun teams managed to infiltrate to within a hundred yards of Ranville and take the main road under fire for half an hour. A 6th Airborne Division staff officer rounded up a few headquarters guards and flushed the Germans with the help of tank from 13/18th Hussars.

Against the Orne Salient

At the base of the Orne Salient, the *Landsers* of the 84th Infantry Division waited for their barrage to lift before attacking. Already the lead companies had crawled up to within a few hundred yards of the British. The 84th was a veteran division, with a good record on the Eastern Front, but like so many other divisions, it had been sent to the West as a burnt out husk and been rebuilt around its veteran core. Sergeant Willi Langenhaus was one such veteran. He had seen the spires of the Kremlin as a young private in the great drive to Moscow in 1941 and only survived the retreat by killing one of the tough Siberians and taking his padded winter clothing. There were enough men like Sergeant Langenhaus to whip the trainloads of young replacements into shape, and by any measure they had done a good job.

The division had slipped into the line quietly over several days and had quickly learned about their opponents in the 3rd British Division through aggressive patrolling and contests over minor physical features of terrain. Six British battalions in two brigades, 9th and 1st Airlanding were in defensive positions. Three more Polish battalions were holding the town of Thury-Harcourt. Behind the infantry, the British had one tank battalion. The 84th's mission was to fix the first two British brigades in place so that Panzer Lehr Division could sweep by their right flank. The division's six battalions would be attacking against equal odds. Langenhaus had lived through much worse in Russia, and his gruff self-assurance told his men that they just might do it here.

As soon as the guns stopped, the German companies started forward. In many cases they caught the enemy still trying to reorient himself from the shock of the artillery. Wherever they met opposition, they tried to slip around and penetrate behind into the depths of the enemy position. Sergeant Langenhaus led his squad between two strongpoints crawling through the hedges and tall grass. He positioned the squad MG-42 to rake both positions from the rear. The bullets laced into the backs of the South Staffords and they fell back into their trench or slumped over its parapet. The other position was alerted and started firing with its Bren gun. One of the Germans fell screaming into the hedge. The MG-42 returned fire and overwhelmed the Bren gunner with its firepower and kept the other men in the position down. Now Langenhaus led the squad in a rush onto the British, throwing potato masher grenades ahead of them into the trench. Another German fell, but the squad was on top of the British now. Langenhaus shot two of them, and the rest surrendered.

> We killed fifteen Englishmen and had seven prisoners and one of our own wounded to worry about. I sent Schmidt back to the company to tell them we had opened a gap in the enemy position. Before they arrived, the English counterattacked with a platoon, and we killed many more. My machine-gunner was another old hand from Russia, Johann Gottwald, and worth his weight in gold. I don't know how many men he killed that day, but there was a ring of bloody brown-uniforms in a semicircle around us.[3]

As the *Landsers* were taking a tight grip on British 3rd Division, Bayerlein ordered Panzer Lehr forward. His intermediate objective was Evrecy, and the division raced forward from its assembly area near Aunay in two columns on either side of the Odon River. The right hand column found 84th Division troops still attacking the flank of the British 1st Airlanding Brigade. Prince von Schönburg-Waldenburg waved the infantry aside and charged down the road at the head of his 2nd Battalion of the Panzer Lehr Regiment. The tanks fired on the move and sprayed the British with their machine guns, but kept on moving. One was hit by a 6-pounder antitank gun and started burning. The next tank in line duelled with the gun and won, and the column kept moving. Another mile down the road they ran into Shermans. A squadron of the East Riding Yeomanry had set up an ambush that destroyed five German tanks in its first salvo. Three more brewed in the next. The Prince pulled back down the road and sent a company to manoeuvre around the British. When they were in position, he attacked again. This time the British tanks were the ones caught by surprise, and they began exploding in line along the same hedge where they had been hidden, setting the hedge itself on fire. Corporal Georg Entemann was in tank 311 when it passed the flaming tank hedge. 'The English tanks roared with fire out of their hatches, so hot that it blew against the hedge and set it on fire even though it was wet with rain. The smoke from the fire went straight up through the rain and seemed to be sucked up into the low clouds.'

Major Markowitz's 2nd Battalion of Panthers was finding even less opposition on its move north up the Odon Valley. Occasional British reconnaissance vehicles fled or were destroyed as the Panthers lumbered down the road. The Germans were instinctively craning their necks to spot the ever present Jabos. It was slowly dawning on them that today they were fighting on more equal terms, but they still glanced nervously skyward. Outside of Evrecy they surprised a self-propelled artillery battalion firing in support of the brigades fighting the 84th Division. Markowitz's Panthers found the line of guns an easy target. The ammunition carriers exploded wonderfully. Most of the guns were destroyed in a few minutes. The tanks now began passing service units and supply points which they shot up without stopping. By ten in the morning, Bayerlein was in Evrecy, completely unknown to the three British brigades deep in his rear.

The guns of the 2nd Panzer Division had joined in the initial bombardment, but their targets had been the British strongpoints along the Orne opposite the Forest of Cinglais where the division had been assembled for the last several days. From Caen to Thury-Harcourt, the British had strung out 185th Brigade as flank guard along the river. The brigade had only one effective battalion left after the battles on 6 June, the Warwicks, and a company of the divisional machine gun battalion. The Norfolks and the Shropshires had been pulled back for reconstitution. Unknown to 185th Brigade, the bridging units of 2nd Panzer had been moved at night across the narrow fields that separated Cinglais from the Forest of Grimbosq that hugged the river for five miles. After the artillery let up, 88s and machine guns took the British strongpoints under direct fire as the engineers dashed their bridges down to the river in three places. One company's worth of Warwicks had been holding that three-mile stretch of river and was quickly wiped out by the concentrated fire. The tanks of 2nd Panzer were crossing within an hour. As Panzer Lehr captured Evrecy, a battle group of 2nd Panzer Division's 3rd Panzer Regiment and 2nd Panzergrenadier Regiment had made contact and was passing east of the town and crossing the Guigne River. The two German panzer divisions had deftly snipped off the Orne Salient within four hours. Caen lay only seven miles to the north. To the west of the city there seemed to be a yawning gap that led all the way to the sea.

The Cheux Breakthrough

Second Army was just beginning to realize the enormity of the situation when the two panzer divisions wheeled north from Evrecy. The attack which was not expected for two more days was suddenly ripping through their guts. Only the day before had tank and antitank units intended to blunt the attack been given their movement orders. Two antitank regiments, the 20th and 62nd, from 3rd Division and I Corps had assembled west of Caen near Carpiquet Airfield, together with 3rd Division's last brigade, the 8th. Stronger antitank forces had been brushed aside in Russia by these same oncoming panzer divisions. The antitank regiments were ordered to establish a defence in the villages and patches of woods along the banks of the Odon only a mile south of their concentration. This would put them straight in the path of the panzers. The nearest armoured force was the 7th Armoured Division at Crepon, as far away as the panzers. It would be a race to see which arrived first.

The atmosphere at I SS Panzer Corps headquarters was jubilant when the two panzer divisions closed the pocket at Evrecy. Dietrich was beside himself with the initial success of the operation. Now was the time to drive the spike home and watch the British lodgement deflate. Panzer Lehr's next objective was the crossroads town of Cheux, and 2nd Panzer's was Carpiquet Airfield. From there, I SS Panzer Corps would wheel across Highway 13 and strike north to the sea, isolating Caen and trapping the two British divisions east of the Orne. At the same time, Kurt Meyer's 12th SS Panzer Division would attack and destroy the Canadians and act as a flank guard for the rest of the corps.

The panzer corps flowed north, crossing the main highway between Villers-Bocage and Caen at three in the afternoon pushing ahead of it the armoured cars of the I Corps Inns of Court Regiment. General Crocker had committed his corps reconnaissance regiment, the only armoured force he had now within reach. They delayed where they could and kept the Germans under observation where they could not. They also carried the artillery spotters who were able to begin calling in effective fire on the panzer corps' columns clogging the roads to the south. If the weather had deprived the Allies of firepower from the air, it had not silenced the Royal Navy's big guns. The ships laid down patterns along those clogged roads that left nothing but twisted scrap and body parts among the craters where it struck. The rain and low clouds did hamper visibility for the spotters, though. What they could see they could bring down fire upon, but what they could see was much less than in dry weather.

As the British were scrambling to throw something in front of two of Germany's greatest veteran divisions, Kurt Meyer was giving his final orders before the attack to the commanders of the 12th SS Panzer, a division that in six days had established an awesome reputation. In front of him was the battered 3rd Canadian Division. If he could break through, he would be slicing across the rear of whatever forces the British had in front of Panzer Lehr and 2nd Panzer. It would be like severing the nerves and muscles of the enemy's raised arm. After that it would open running for the coast as the flank guard of the mighty German host. Better yet, once past the Canadians, his division would be out of the hedgerow country that so aided the defenders, an advantage the Germans had made the most of so far. Panzermeyer's attack was reinforced by the regiment of the 77th Infantry Division that had screened his front the day before. The *Landsers* arrived after a night's march along with a regiment of rocket launchers and a battalion of assault guns and another of 88mm antitank guns. These units he formed into a third battle group.

The Canadians had withdrawn the 9th Brigade to Cheux where it prepared to defend the town. The 8th Brigade was in Fontenay-le-Pesnel, closest to the enemy. The broken 7th was in reserve where the few surviving Winnipegs had to be attached to the depleted Canadian Scottish to even approach the strength of a weak battalion. General Keller was packing every other man in the division into the forward brigades. The Cameron Highlanders' machine gun battalion, the 7th Reconnaissance Regiment, 3rd Division Engineers, and the 4th Light Anti-Aircraft Regiment fighting as antitank gunners reinforced the depleted infantry. Service units were marched forward and attached to the brigades as infantry. His three artillery battalions were placed just barely two miles to the rear to form a last ditch direct fire antitank defence if it came to that. It would be all or nothing for the Canadians.

Panzermeyer was in the bell tower of the church in Vendes when he gave the order to attack. He could hardly see a thing, the drizzling clouds were so low. Across the division front, commanders shouted 'Panzer, . . . Marsch!,' setting in motion the young killing machine of 12th SS Panzer. The Panther battle group drove straight towards Fontenay and the 8th Brigade, as multiple rocket launchers shrieked their long, fiery rockets overhead like the arrowstorm at Agincourt six hundred years before. Division artillery and the numerous mortars every German unit seemed to have added to the weight of metal crashing down on the town. Buildings burst into the streets adding to the Canadian barricades. The Canadians hunched down in their cellars or hastily dug trenches awaiting the end of the storm. Antitank guns, trucks, tanks, and anyone in the open was rent and thrown about. Then the SS were almost to the town's edge before the guns stopped. Canadian artillery threw its own screaming steel directly on top of the Germans in several places. Elsewhere tanks and SPWs with their dismounted infantry were crashing through the surrounding gardens and orchards. The town was still wreathed in a cloud of dust when the SS penetrated into the streets in one or two places as the Canadians began emerging from their cellars. Then it was quick and violent death with no mercy. The Canadians were just in time to brew up three tanks a dozen yards from the town's entrance. The machine guns of the Cameron Highlanders were back in action in time to cut down the SS panzergrenadiers when they became separated from their tanks.

Where one German company had penetrated the town, a troop of the Fort Garry Horse supported a counterattack by the French Canadians of the Regiment de la Chaudière. The tanks rolled down the street shooting directly into each house with their 75mm guns as the Chaudière followed to clean out survivors. Panzerfausts exploded the lead Sherman, blocking the street. The tanks behind concentrated their fire on the houses from which the antitank rockets had come. The Quebecois broke into houses and fought the Germans room to room. The fighting coursed over the back gardens and across roofs.

Dead men lay among the spring flowers and tumbled into the streets off the tiles. It was like this where ever the Hitlerjugend and the Canadians fought in Normandy. As the Germans were forced back into the last few buildings on the edge of town, another battalion supported by tanks came out of the orchards to crash into the Quebecois. A Firefly Sherman destroyed the first Panther and then was turned into a torch by the next. Slowly the course of the fighting reversed, and now the Chaudière was being pushed back into the ruins. A similar struggle was underway on the other side of the town where panzer-grenadiers of the 25th had broken through the Camerons' machine guns at a terrible cost. They were counterattacked by the North Shore Regiment and tanks. The hard New Brunswicker lumberjacks and hunters threw the Hitler-jugend out in a litter of burning SPWs and bodies in camouflage smocks. The Germans came back twice more, and on the second try gained a foothold.

To the southeast of the town, the Mark IV battle group dashed for the open wheat fields that marked the end of the hedgerow country. At the last hedgerow that barred their path, they encountered a squadron of the Fort Garry Horse. The Canadians fired first and left three tanks burning and then pulled back at high speed into the rolling wheat. The Germans were after them, deploying across the fields where they widened out. The Garrys fell back in bounds, stopping only long enough to fire a few rounds, drawing the Germans along past the last heavy hedge line perpendicular to their advance. When dozens of tanks followed by SPWs and other armoured vehicles were flooding past, the hedge erupted with long tongues of flame. The Garrys had led the Germans into an ambush now sprung by a battery of antitank guns. Canadian artillery now fell among the surprised Germans milling crazily over the fields. Sturmbannführer Prinz's vehicle was one of the first to be struck. With the commander dead, the Germans took a few moments longer than usual to respond to a new situation, and more of them died as the 17-pounders found new targets. Finally the battle group extricated itself from the killing ground and fell back, leaving over thirty smoking wrecks of armoured vehicles. Had it not been for the mist and drizzle that limited visibility, the toll would have been much higher.

To the east again, the 77th Division's battle group attacked Cheux under the same searing barrage that had destroyed Fontenay. The *Landsers* followed the assault guns into the assault with the 88s firing over their heads in direct support. Then the big guns of the HMSS *Warspite* and *Ramillies* shouldered their way into the battle, dropping their fifteen-inch shells directly into the Germans. Assault guns were tossed into the air or flung onto their backs, and human beings simply disappeared. The lead assault gun company and infantry companies were wiped out. The battle group fled back to its starting point.

By noon, Kurt Meyer realized the battle still hung in the balance. The Canadians had traded him blow for blow and were still in the ring. They had even had a few nasty surprises for two of his battle groups. But the fighting in Fontenay was still raging, and his Hitlerjugend were slowly getting the upper hand. When the Canadians snapped, it would be like a damn bursting. The flood would carry him to the sea. Still, everything depended on how well the other two divisions were doing. If they failed, his division would be stuck in the middle of the British Army.

Those two divisions were at the same time crashing through the British antitank defence between Cheux and Caen. They had been aided by driving rain that hung over the area as the divisions approached. With engagement time reduced drastically and naval gunfire spotters equally limited, the panzers were breaking the barrier in a dozen places. Still the British antitank gunners stood to their guns, often getting kills at a hundred yards or less and dying with their guns as the panzers suddenly appeared with their panzergrenadiers out of the rain's cloak to cut down the crews. Here and there, the gunners wiped out small packets of German tanks and SPWs in antitank ambushes, but the integrity of the defence was broken as the Germans streamed through and out into the wide wheat fields beyond.

A company of tanks and a battalion of panzergrenadiers from 2nd Panzer overran Carpiquet Airfield, racing over the runways to shoot up an aircraft still on the field and driving the men of the 1st Battalion, the Suffolk Regiment back into the outskirts of Caen. The rest of 8th Brigade was withdrawn into the city as well. The Germans just bypassed the city and continued north to cut the Bayeux to Caen highway. At the opposite end of the breakthrough, a similar force cut behind Cheux heading north. On that five-mile sector, the German tide was rushing through the broken British barrier. Some units stood like rocks in the torrent that swirled past. The rest were gone.

The low wet clouds hung upon the day like some backdrop of doom. Normally, one could see for miles from a high window or bell tower in the Norman countryside, but today the weather was German. All it needed was the damned Valkyries to be riding in and out of the clouds. Static was also playing hob with radio communications so that the normal flow of information was spotty and broken. The static didn't help German communications either, but they knew where they were going and were high on aggressive action fed by success. All too often, the Germans were upon the British before they could react. For if the Germans were high on speed and success, the British were afflicted by the uncertainty of when and where the enemy would appear and all the fears of being enmeshed in the dark.

Second Army headquarters was held together in these hours by Dempsey's steely calm and firm self-control. Montgomery had swept all the reserves in the lodgement towards the breakthrough in a race against the Germans. It was Dempsey who was putting the pieces into action as expertly as possible when the world is coming to an end. He wondered briefly if this was how Gough felt when 5th Army was broken by the Germans in April 1918. The first report had just come in of Germans on the Bayeux to Caen Highway near Caen. Then Germans were reported to the rear of Cheux in the Canadian sector, but the Canadians were still holding on in a bloodbath at Fontenay. Where was 7th Armoured? They had been put on the road and should intercept the Germans somewhere along the highway. The 29th Armoured Brigade of 11th Armoured Division, just landed on Juno was also rushing towards the breakthrough. Even the U.S. 2nd Armored Division had been alerted to begin movement across the front, but then came the news of the breakthrough against V Corps. Montgomery was on the horns of a dilemma. Second Armored was the only complete armoured division left in the lodgement. It could restore the situation. But which situation? The breakthrough at Cheux or the one that split open V Corps. He understood von Moltke's principle, 'Order, Counter-order, disorder' well enough to know that timing was everything. The U.S. armoured division could not be put on the road for one fight and then diverted for another. Then it would fight neither. Nor could it be split up to fight in two places at once if decisive results were needed. The V Corps would just have to fall back on Bayeux and link up with the British 50th Division south of the city. There just wasn't much else in the reinforcement bag except 15th Scottish Division's leading brigade, the 44th Lowland, just landed and on its way to backstop the armour. One infantry brigade!

'Order, Counter-Order, Disorder'

General Gerow wasn't having any of Montgomery's icy patience. His corps had just been chopped in two by a strong armoured force that was heading straight for the corps rear. The only thing to stop it was 2nd Armored Division. Gerow exploded in rage when he heard the British order to hold for possible commitment between XXX and I Corps. The emergency was right on his own doorstep. He ordered 2nd Armored into battle to save V Corps.

At 1706, as the Hell on Wheels Division rolled west from its reserve location, 2nd Infantry Division was pulling back its open right flank all the way back to the outskirts of Bayeux. The 38th Infantry and its attached 15th Field Artillery Battalion found their retreat blocked by German companies that had infiltrated through the Forest. With 1st Battalion as rear guard, the 2nd and 3rd Battalions turned about and attacked supported by the 105mm howitzers firing over open sights. Private First Class Juan Mendez won the Distinguished Service Cross that late afternoon when his platoon was pinned down by a German machine gun and another scout was killed. Mendez raced across the fire-swept ground; his rifle was shot out of his hands, but he took another from a casualty and single-handedly attacked the German machine gun, killing three Germans and wounding two. His platoon advanced behind him. In dozens of small actions like this, the 38th broke out of the German trap and retreated in good order down the main road to Bayeux while its sister regiments pulled back as well under far less pressure. To the north the 29th Division also fell back towards Bayeux.

The 2nd Armored Division which was sweeping into the hole blown by the Germans in V Corps was a powerful creation of American industrial production and organization. Its two armoured regiments, the 66th and 67th, had three tank battalions each of more than fifty medium tanks. Its armoured infantry regiment, the 41st, had three infantry battalions in halftracks. The division's three artillery battalions were self-propelled. Like other U.S. armoured divisions, the 2nd was organized into Combat Commands A, B, and Reserve, the American equivalent of the flexible German battle groups. Combat Commands A and B were usually organized around two tank battalions from each of the tank regiments, one of the motorized infantry battalions, and one of the self-propelled artillery battalions. The remaining two tank battalions and one motorized infantry battalion were commanded by the commander of the armoured infantry regiment. The two lettered combat commands were also reinforced with companies from the armoured combat engineer company and attached 702nd Tank Destroyer and 195th Anti-Aircraft Battalions. This was the structure in theory. In reality the 2nd Armored Division was going into combat without most of its trains, which had not been landed yet. The combat commands would fight with what they had. If tanks and other vehicles broke down, they stayed broken unless the crews themselves could effect repairs. Supplies and ammunition were what they carried on board each vehicle. Fuel was what was in the tanks. Anything else would have to be jury-rigged from corps trains or from the two infantry divisions. Essentially, 2nd Armored had one good shot in it, and Gerow had decided to use it here. That shot was in the hands of Major General Edward H. Brooks, an old artilleryman and developer of the 105mm M-7 self-propelled howitzer.

Such was the force rushing to engage 116th Panzer and 17th SS Panzergrenadier Divisions west of Bayeux. In tanks, the Americans outnumbered the Germans more than three to one. Each combat command outnumbered both German divisions together, but in armoured infantry, the Germans had the same advantage with three panzergrenadier regiments. Hell on Wheels crossed the Drôme River a few miles north of Bayeux throwing out its 82nd Reconnaissance Battalion to find the enemy.

American scouts found the Germans packed along the highway that crossed the Drôme further south at Barbeville, itself only two miles from Bayeux. They were streaming east oblivious to the fact that General Brooks with three hundred tanks was poised to strike them in the flank from the north. With his reconnaissance elements spotting, the three self-propelled artillery battalions and attached corps artillery quickly began firing and walked their shells up and

down that road with an accuracy that only comes from having an old artilleryman as division commander. The effect was devastating on the 17th SS
Panzer Division's fleet of SPWs, flakpanzers, and support vehicles. When the
Shermans of the two combat commands burst upon the road, they found scores
of wrecked and twisted vehicles and hundreds of bodies along the road. They
had to drive over the debris or push it aside to get at the remaining Germans. A
few German antitank guns got into operation and fought back. One 88mm
gun knocked out three Shermans, and a few assault guns from the head of the
column doubled back to the rescue, but the numbers of Shermans that swarmed
over the area smothered German attempts to fight back.

Sending Combat Command R west to block the rest of 17th SS from pushing
forward again, Brooks continued the drive south, following Napoleon's advice
that if you are confused as to the enemy's situation, attack and you will surely
find out. The maxim was correct, but this time 116th Panzer had been alerted
by the 2nd's romp over the 17th SS only one-and-a-half miles to the north.
Their reconnaissance elements reported the American movement south. The
Germans put their tanks along the railroad embankment and behind hedgerows and waited. When the lead tanks of both combat commands came within
range, the Germans sprung their hasty ambush with a concentration of fire that
left eight Shermans burning. The panzergrenadiers poured their automatic fire
into the attack, killing most of the crews that managed to escape their stricken
tanks. Now the fighting became a race to find each other's flanks among the
sodden hedgerows, rain-choked streams, and stone farmsteads. Every attack by
the Shermans fell into crossfires of antitank weapons. The armoured infantry
now came into their own, slipping ahead of the tanks to attack the antitank
guns first and use their own tanks as mobile artillery. In this phase, Brooks
made excellent use of his artillery to counter the German superiority in infantry,
but nowhere could he find that advantage that would dislodge 116th Panzer.
One of the armoured infantrymen remembered:

> I'll never forget the soaking wet feeling and the inch by inch fighting back and
> forth over and through those damned hedgerows. My platoon was supporting a
> tank company, and we shrank hour by hour, a few men killed here by a German
> machine gun at the corner of some hedge or a Sherman turning into a torch
> around the next corner as some ballsy German gets up close to it with a pan-
> zerfaust, and then all that fire shooting straight up as the rain poured down.[4]

The scales were finally tipped by an accident. German patrols south of the
fighting ran into the 38th Infantry retreating in good order towards Bayeux in
the last of the early evening's gloomy wet light. The 38th hit back aggressively,
thinking this was another German attempt to cut them off, and pursued a short
way. As reported to the commander of 116th Panzer, an infantry division was

advancing upon his rear while he was decisively engaged. Nightfall gave him the opportunity to disengage and withdraw a few miles to the west.

Panzermeyer Tires of the Canadians

Panzermeyer decided Fontenay was not worth the delay and disengaged his battle group. In this case discretion was, indeed, the better part of valour. He had lost almost a thousand dead and wounded and would have lost even more to break the Canadians there. With the front breaking open, places like Fontenay could be bypassed and cleaned up later. His other battle group had already moved forward again across open country. The 77th Division battle group he also directed to bypass Cheux and leave it in the rear. The mass of vehicles now streamed between the two towns, overrunning the few troops of the Fort Garry Horse and antitank gun units that were in their way. A dozen little actions were fought against small groups of Canadians, leaving a trail of burning tanks and smashed guns that barely delayed the Germans. They dashed across the fields between the hedgerows. Meyer's division came in on the flank of Panzer Lehr in a mighty three division charge through the thinner than normal bocage country. Some units of 2nd Panzer, whose inner place on the three-division team that wheeled around Caen gave them the shortest distance, had penetrated across the highway to Authie and Buron. At that moment, five hundred German tanks were sweeping everything before them. The sea, barely ten miles ahead, beckoned. Victory herself seemed to be reaching out her hand holding a wreath.

The Highway 13 Meeting Engagement

Victory with her wreath suddenly faded into the mist as British Cromwell tanks emerged from it, speeding straight into the panzer swarm. The Desert Rats were in action again! First and 5th Royal Tank Regiments on line met 12th SS and Panzer Lehr head on. Not since Kursk had two such large armoured formations crashed into each other in such a meeting engagement. But at Kursk the Soviets and Germans had been fairly matched in numbers. The two British tank regiments had been issued new tanks and replacements and had absorbed the survivors of the County of London Yeomanry and now numbered almost 150 tanks. The two German panzer divisions numbered almost 200 tanks and assault guns, many of them clearly superior to the Cromwell.

The British tankers followed the Soviet example and drove at speed into the middle of the German formations to get the flank and rear shots that the Cromwell's underpowered 75mm gun demanded for a kill on the Panther and Tiger. The weather cloak had worked for the British this time by lessening the Germans' engagement range. The British were upon the Germans so quickly that few in the forward companies' tanks were destroyed in the initial rush. Wheeling through the German formation, the Cromwell's superior speed and manoeuvrability were an advantage as was the Cromwell's faster turret traverse speed. Captain Richard Parker recounted that moment.

> It was as if two Medieval hosts had levelled lances and crashed into each other, something out of the story books we all used to read. All semblance of man-oeuvre by unit was lost; each tank sought out its own opponent in the mêlée. The Germans were taken by surprise at first, and we brewed up a number of them in those few seconds. The Mark IVs were easy targets. You could kill them easily with a front shot, but it was the Panthers and Tigers that were the hard kills. My tank flew past a Panther faster than it could swing its turret. I traversed mine and put a shot up his arse and watched it fireball.[5]

Parker's time ran out just then as well. Another Panther was fast enough to put a shell through his tank and set it on fire. He and the crew scrambled out before it blew and threw themselves into a ditch, shared by the crew of the Panther they had just hit. All eight men, by tacit agreement, opted to be spectators only to the rest of the fighting raging around them. One of Parker's men had brought the medical kit with him and spent his time easing the pain of the badly burned German gunner.

Elsewhere the fighting swirled over the muddy fields and around the villages of le Hamel, le Mesnil-Patry, and Norrey-en-Bessin, just south of Highway 13. Tanks fired at point-blank range, ripping turrets off hulls to spin in the air before crashing into the trodden wheat. One 1RTR Cromwell and a 2/12 Panzer Panther fired simultaneously at twenty feet to kill each other in simultaneous explosions. Another Cromwell shook as a high velocity 88mm tore through it killing the men in the fighting compartment. The driver gunned the burning tank and sped straight for the Tiger that had shot it. Just as the German fired again, the wreck of the Cromwell collided with it and exploded, splashing the Tiger with burning fuel. Then another explosion rocked the Tiger, and the flames from both vehicles met overhead to form one pyre.

The infantry and antitank units from both forces had followed behind the tanks and now began to enter the fight. British 17-pounders and German 88mm guns were firing into the edges of the tank cauldron picking off tanks where they could. But the 7th Armoured's 131st Infantry Brigade was as outnumbered as the 22nd Armoured Brigade. Opposed to its three infantry battalions were ten German ones, and half of them in SPWs. But the British followed the tanks and got 1/6th Battalion, the Queen's Royal Regiment into Norrey-en-Bessin along with a company of the 65th Anti-tank Regiment. The guns and the infantry made the town a hedgehog of fire in the middle of the battle. Bayerlein threw attack after attack at it with 902nd Panzergrenadier regiment supported by assault guns and divisional artillery. But each assault was struck down by British fire, leaving smashed and burning vehicles and gray-clad bodies in arcs where their forward movement had stopped. A squadron of 5RTR broke out of the mêlée to the right of the town and broke up the last panzergrenadier attack. They were in position to slice into Panzer Lehr's rear, and now Bayerlein committed his reserve, the SS Heavy Battalion 101.

Lumbering forward, the thirty-four Tigers represented the single most powerful force on the battlefield in Normandy. The only other Tigers had been the few in Panzer Lehr's own panzer regiment. They were preceded by German artillery and rocket fire that drenched the town. Bayerlein watched the attack, 'The powerful Tigers spread out and headed straight for the British with my panzergrenadiers following as the rockets raced over them with their fiery tails. I shall never forget the sight.' This time the British had no advantage of surprise and tried to withdraw into the village, but the Tigers fired with cool precision and left half of them blazing wrecks before the rest could escape. The German artillery preparation had momentarily disorganized the British defenders of the town and allowed the Tigers to close the distance, even at their slow speed. A few hundred yards from the town, the 17-pounders went into action, picking off one Tiger after another, but the battalion kept coming. Return fire was just as deadly to the antitank crews who fell dead around their guns. Now they were through the beaten zone and breaking through the gardens and into the streets with panzergrenadiers swarming behind to shoot up the antitank guns and dig out the infantry. Michael Wittmann's Tiger 200 was in the lead of his company. Shot after shot from the Cromwells in the village broke up on Tiger 200's armour, leaving only scorch marks. The 88mm fired methodically leaving a trail of burning Cromwells behind. The fighting had spread to the whole town as the panzergrenadiers tried to root out the stubborn 1/6th Queen's, but the Cromwells and most of the antitank guns were finished as well. The Tigers began firing into house after house. The battalion commander ordered a retreat. He personally remained behind to help man the last 17-pounder to cover the escape. The Germans attested that this gun accounted for two Tigers and delayed them for half-an-hour.

As the end of day deepened the gloom, the battlefield stretching for four miles was illuminated by the pyres of hundreds of burning vehicles. The battle, though, was guttering out as losses, disorganization, and physical exhaustion overtook every other consideration. The Desert Rats had given everything and were spent. Almost a hundred of their tanks, two-thirds of their force, were lost that afternoon. The Germans' losses had been as great. But the 7th Armoured had done what had been expected of it. Its suicidal attack had broken the impetus of the German drive short of the last defensible line before the beaches, the Seulles River. The Desert Rats had given Montgomery one more day.

The Desert Rats pulled off the field and withdrew north to lick their wounds. The Germans hesitatingly followed. It was the shrunken remnants of 12th SS's Mark IV battalion that first crossed the Bayeux to Caen Highway in the early evening. Meyer felt a surge of exultation when the signalman read him the message after the day's slaughter. But darkness was covering the battlefield, hastened by the low clouds that kept out moon and stars. Before the gloom engulfed the armies, the tired pursuers of I SS Panzer Corps crossed Highway 13 and there were halted.

Suddenly released from action, the adrenalin pumps shut down in thousands of Germans finding resting places and hasty defensive positions along the highway. The sustained high of their whirlwind advance and the rush of the battle had utterly drained them and slipped into a sleepy exhaustion that turned eyelids to lead. A few men wolfed down cold rations; most were too tired and tried to find places to sleep sheltered from the dripping darkness. In half a dozen places, they were jerked awake and back to their vehicles and weapons by the sounds of battle: machine gun and tank fire, artillery and the cries of 'Alarm! Alarm!'. The reconnaissance battalions of the 7th and 11th Armoured Divisions were aggressively probing their lines. All night long, the 8th King's Royal Irish Hussars and the 2nd Northamptonshire Yeomanry, which had covered 7th Armoured's retreat, raided and drew out the Germans until most of 12th SS Panzer and Panzer Lehr stood to their arms all night.

Behind the Hussars and Yeomanry, the 29th Armoured Brigade of 11th Armoured Division was concentrating south of the Seulles River. Thus the Germans and the British found themselves on the long arms of a triangle that pointed toward Bayeux. The Germans were on the southern arm, the Bayeux to Caen highway or Highway 13. The British were on the northern arm, the Seulles River. The short arm of the triangle, running north and south, was the smaller Mue River. Between the Mue and Caen to the east was the 2nd Panzer Division, poised to complete the encirclement of Caen the next day. Into this gap, the British were bringing 4th Armoured Brigade out of the Orne bridgehead, leaving 6th Airborne and 51st Highland Division with only the 27 tanks of the redoubtable 13/18th Hussars and the 56 of the Scots Greys.

A Polish Anabasis

Far to the south, the bypassed brigades of 3rd British Division were still struggling with the German 84th Division when nightfall allowed some units to break contact. General Sosabowski was the first to abandon the bottom of the German prisoner of war bag and strike north with his 1st Polish Airborne Brigade. The Poles were under no illusions as to their status as prisoners of war. Along the way they picked up a few troops of the East Riding Yeomanry and some artillery and some lost companies of the King's Own Scottish Borderers and the Royal Ulster Rifles. Sosabowski put the tanks the head of the column. He was the unhesitatingly accepted leader of this growing anabasis. His objective was Caen, if the city still held. His radio was picking up all sorts of reports of catastrophe to the north. But he marched his column into the dripping night. There was nothing else to do.

He paralleled the river picking up stray Warwicks along the way. Just before the column reached the bend in the river opposite the Forest of Grimbosq, he was warned by some Warwicks that the Germans' crossing sites were just ahead with heavy bumper-to-bumper traffic. There was no way to slip across between convoys. Sosabowski listened intently while his blue eyes glinted in the beam of a flashlight. 'We will not sneak around these Germans. We will march over them and break their bridges. That way we can hurt them and do something for our forces fighting to the north.' He gathered his battalion commanders and the Yeomanry troop leaders and explained his plan.

At the first crossing site, a squad of German military policemen were shivering in the rain as they directed the convoy trains of 2nd Panzer Division and I SS Panzer Corps. They were not paying attention to the woodland trail that paralleled the river and cut across the road the convoys were taking. Out of the woods a troop of Shermans loaded with Polish paratroopers crashed onto the intersection. The first tank's main gun fired in the direction of the bridge and blew up the first truck. Its machine gun swept over the military police and left them a clutch of bodies in their wet rain gear. More tanks lumbered out of the dark onto the road shooting up and down at the crowd of trucks. From the backs of the tanks the paratroopers shot up anything they could. More Poles emerged from the woods on foot to seize the intersection as the tanks drove towards the river and the first bridge, their guns blowing trucks off the road. Soon the rainy night was illuminated by burning vehicles and exploding ammunition. The Poles were eager to slaughter Germans packed into their trucks and showed no mercy. The tanks slithered down the improvised roadway to the bridge and machine-gunned the engineers who were trying to set up a defence. Seventy-five millimetre high explosive blew the trucks off the bridge and then systematically blew the bridge itself apart. Within half an hour, the first German crossing point had been ripped apart and the roadway littered with burning vehicles and corpses. The tanks and their Polish riders then disappeared into the night towards the next crossing. The rest of the column followed past the intersection and a very Polish version of the Inferno.

They left each crossing site in the same condition on the march north in the dark and the wet. On his way out of the bag, Sosabowski rendered the Allies the greatest service they were to receive on that evil day. By slashing across the rear of the German communications and breaking 2nd Panzer's bridges, he raised an alarm in I SS Panzer Corps that was to divert their attention when they needed to concentrate single-mindedly on one great objective: the sea. By morning the column was five miles from Caen. Sosabowski sent out scouts in the few jeeps he had to make sure the way was clear and pushed the column forward until they reached the outskirts of the city. They were passed through and immediately guided by 3rd Division staff officers to places in the defence of the city. Sosabowski had brought over 3,500 fighting men to the city's garrison. He was none too soon. That afternoon, the lead elements of the German 84th Division closed in south of Caen driving ahead of them several hundred more survivors of the 9th and 1st Airlanding Brigades. The rest of their number were marching into captivity.

Marching Through the Night

Sosabowski had done more than play havoc with 2nd Panzer's trains when he broke their bridging over the Orne. He had halted one of the streams of the second wave of German infantry divisions marching south from the 15th Army. The 331st Infantry Division had intended to follow 2nd Panzer over its bridges but now had to mark time in the Forest of Cinglais as its own meagre bridging units were hurried forward from the rear of its extended column. Further south, though, the 85th Infantry and Luftwaffe 19th Field Divisions crossed the Orne and turned north in the night, marching on muddy country roads to come in behind the panzer divisions. Besides Sosabowski's column, those roads were also in use by British and Canadian soldiers isolated by the last two days' whirlwind of fighting. The Germans had been too busy and too few to saturate the bypassed areas and round them up. Singly, in small groups, and even in companies, they also headed north, hidden by the rain and pitch darkness of a night without moon and stars. Here and there they clashed with the Germans and then disappeared again into the blackness but always they kept moving north.

The front from south Tilly to Caen was full of moving men of both armies soaked to the skin, trudging down muddy roads. The Germans had the advantage of military police posts to keep them on the right paths north. On more than one occasion it was to enemy soldiers that they inadvertently gave directions. Outside the village of Orbais, three tanks of the Sherbrookes and a dozen trucks with Canadians cut off in the fighting two days before were waved through by German MPs who could barely see the outline of the armoured vehicles. Mostly the roads were filled with German infantry, marching with that swinging gait that ate up the miles in their long columns, glistening in the occasional light reflected off their slick rain gear and the metal of their helmets, their rifles slung upside down to keep water out of the barrels. Interspersed between the infantry columns were horse-drawn field artillery, self-propelled guns, rocket-launchers with their honeycomb tubes, low-slung assault guns, and the deadly 88mms, flak guns on halftracks, and all the assorted trains that keep every army alive and fighting. Closer to the front, there were recovery teams from the three panzer divisions searching for knocked out or broken down tanks to drag off the to the repair workshops that lit the darkness with the searing glare of acetylene torches.

To the west of Bayeux, similar columns were arriving from Brittany bringing reinforcements from 7th Army. The first to arrive, in truck convoy relays, were the remaining battalions and support units of 3rd Fallschirmjäger Division fighting the American V Corps. Behind them came the battalions of the 5th Fallschirmjäger Division and the II Parachute Corps headquarters to assume control of all the divisions engaged against the Americans in the British sector. The entire front seemed to be in motion towards the coast as German reinforcements began closing.

Rommel joined Dietrich at I SS Panzer Corps headquarters shortly after dark, this time with a company of panzergrenadiers as an escort. Also in tow was the still very confused American, Lieutenant Eberley, safely tucked away in an armoured car. Rommel had not spoken to him since the day he had been rescued, but Eberley's fears had been somewhat allayed by his decent treatment. He had turned up his nose at first at the German field rations until he saw his driver and the rest of the crew of the armoured car eating the same thing. They had been talkative and friendly and not unduly restrictive, but they kept a sharp eye on him and were anxious that he did not advertise his presence.

Right now Rommel had more immediate problems than worrying about one prisoner, albeit a special one. Rommel had become the de facto commander of 7th Army, controlling the main battle and the operations of I SS Panzer, II Fallschirmjäger, and LXXXI Corps, while the loyal Pemsel continued to act as Chief of Staff and control operations against the Americans in the Cotentin Peninsula with LXXXIV Corps. Rommel's Fingerspitzgefühl sense had unerringly brought him to the front's centre of gravity, the single spot were the enemy's balance could most easily be overthrown. He felt like a diamond cutter who had carefully aligned and measured a fine stone for the single deft blow with his hammer that would make a perfect cut. Dietrich quickly briefed him on the situation and the disposition of the panzer divisions. Second Panzer and Panzer Lehr were in good condition having suffered acceptable losses in their sweep into the heart of the British lodgement. Twelfth SS Panzer had been badly cut up in the last two days fighting with the Canadians. Kurt Meyer reported that he had lost almost 5,500 men. Most of his fighting battalions were skeletons, and he had barely fifty-three tanks and assault guns of the 149 the division had driven into Normandy a week before. Dietrich decided to move the corps Heavy Tank Battalion 101 from Bayerlein's to Meyer's division, and they had already begun moving laterally behind the front. He had also ordered the 77th Division battle group to move to cover Hitlerjugend's open flank on the west where the Canadians still might have some fight left.

'Now, Dietrich', said Rommel as he bent over the map, 'this is what we will do to the English in the morning.' Dietrich and his staff were listening in rapt attention when the signal officer interrupted with a message from the Führer. Rommel scanned it, and a wry smile crossed his face, 'Gentlemen, allow me to transmit the thanks of Adolf Hitler for your glorious victory today.' Then he drew Dietrich aside and showed him the message form; 'He is coming on the eighteenth to "view the ruin of England's treachery".' Dietrich read further; 'Now Germany will fight on to total victory.' He looked Rommel straight in the eye. 'I thought he would have sense enough to make peace. We don't have another such victory in us.'[6]

Breakout

The commander of the Canadian 9th Brigade put his last two troops of the Sherbrookes at the head of his brigade column. It had been an awesome sight late that afternoon to see the stampede of German vehicles sweep past Cheux half hidden in the rain and mist. That sight had left him in no doubt that his command had been isolated. Luckily, they had been almost ignored since then. He knew it would not last as follow-on units eventually closed to the front. He decided that he would not stick around for the inevitable. With darkness the brigade would strike out across the German rear to reenter Allied lines to the northwest across the wheat fields that would avoid most crossroads villages. The tanks were up front carrying infantry to batter a way through any opposition. Just behind them were self-propelled guns, and anti-aircraft vehicles. The rest of the brigade followed by the artillery and service units. With great luck they might slip through unnoticed in the confusion of the German breakthrough. For that reason nothing was to be done to attract the Germans' notice to them. The advance guard would hold their fire until the last minute to avoid contact.

The column crept through the night as the mist and drizzle played tricks with the eyes at only one or two vehicle lengths. Shapes loomed up out of the darkness and stopped hearts until they were seen to be abandoned cattle that scampered away, and once in a while broken down vehicles. Sergeant Danny MacPhearson was straining his eyes as he stood up in the turret of the lead tank. This was worse than walking through a graveyard on Halloween. The rain running down the back of his collar made him shiver, or so he explained to the Highland Light Infantry squad hanging on to his turret and back deck.

Then he thought he could hear engine noise ahead. A few more yards and a moving shape emerged out of the dark passing in front of him. MacPhearson's eyes grew wide, then he shouted to his gunner, 'Gunner, assault gun, battlesight, fire!' The gun roared and kicked, and the shape was struck by a hammer that sent sparks shooting into the mist. Fire burst from it, then ammunition exploded. Behind it another shape was veering in MacPhearson's direction as he was reporting the contact. The tank behind him came up on his right and fired first. The second assault gun stopped suddenly and began to belch flame and smoke. MacPhearson drove forward past the burning assault guns and saw dozens of German infantry scattering from his path. The rest of the column was behind him. Everyone was firing now at the fleeing figures in the newly illuminated night. German infantry seemed to be everywhere. His turret machine gun was spraying bullets in wide arcs to the sides and front through the wheat. The following tanks had their guns staggered to the left and right and kept up the fire. The anti-aircraft with their quad-fifty calibre machine guns were sending tracers through the wheat to the flanks as well.

Within minutes, the armoured advance guard was through the German column that had scattered in the darkness. The infantry followed quickly past the burning assault guns, but no more than the first two companies of the Highland Light Infantry had passed when the Germans rallied and began to counterattack the column. MG-42 grazing fire hit the third company, sending it to earth. A German platoon came out of the mist and entered the light of the burning vehicles and was promptly shot up. The column was at a dead stop now with Germans working around the edges trying to find its flanks. Engine noises in the dark and suddenly the squat shapes of assault guns waddled slowly into view with infantry walking behind. This was it. All the antitank weapons had been with the armoured head of the column that had shot ahead. The Highlanders aimed their fire to kill the accompanying German infantry, but the bulk of the vehicles protected most of them.

Then an assault gun was hit from behind and began burning. Two more were hit in quick succession, then a fourth and fifth. The German infantry scattered in panic running straight into the fire of the Highlanders. Past the burning assault guns drove the Sherbrooke's Shermans with MacPhearson at the head waving at the infantry. His tanks took up positions to the left and right of the column. He shouted to the Highlanders, 'Move on, move on, we'll stay until you all get by.' By the light of the burning vehicles, he watched first the rest of the Highland Light Infantry, then the Stormont, Dundas and Glengary Highlanders march past, then the trains with the wounded, and finally the sad remnant of the North Nova Scotia Highlanders as rearguard. He fell in behind them with his three tanks, his the last with its turret reversed to present its gun to the receding patches of fire in the wheat. The 9th Brigade had escaped, and as it turned out, marched over the German's 77th Division battle group to do it.

Unternehmen ROSSBACH: Day 2

Rommel arrived at Bayerlein's headquarters just before dawn, pleased to see one of his old Africa hands again. Bayerlein would have the critical mission of the day: to breach the line of the Seulles River and drive to the sea, cutting the British lodgement in half. Panzer Lehr had suffered badly in the previous day's final battle, and had lost almost seventy tanks and assault guns, leaving Bayerlein with only a hundred or so and however many the repair workshops could get into action. He made it clear that his division had only one more good effort left in it. His losses had shaken him, but with Rommel he could still admire their old desert enemy. 'Now, that is the 7th Armoured I remembered from Africa. Rarely have I seen such a spirit of self-sacrifice.'

Hitlerjugend had bled over the past two days. In the final battle the day before, it had lost over thirty armoured vehicles and was reduced to no more than fifty. Its mission was to guard Panzer Lehr's flank and assist in the breakthrough. East of the Mue River, 2nd Panzer's 120 tanks and assault guns would also strike north and then east to isolate Caen and cut off the British forces east of the Orne River. Should this happen, half the British lodgement would be chopped off into several large isolated pockets that the follow-on infantry divisions could finish off. As Rommel prepared to leave, Bayerlein urged him to stay at his headquarters out of the wretched weather. The field marshal suddenly became serious and stopped just outside the tent. He held out his hand to the rain, 'See, Bayerlein, our heavenly armour. Don't be ungrateful. The Luftwaffe says we have only this one more day, maybe less, before it moves off. Then the Jabos will be back.'

The Caen Pocket

The second phase of ROSSBACH was initiated by 2nd Panzer's attack north out of Buron in the early morning. At first the only opposition was from British line-of-communications infantry and anti-aircraft companies that quickly melted away as the panzers overwhelmed their light firepower. Here and there an artillery battalion stood its ground and fired directly over its sights. The ensuing duels were short as the unprotected gun crews fell around their guns. More of a hindrance to the advance was the flood of service troops trying to escape to the beaches. The area had been filled with supply, maintenance, and administrative units that simply abandoned their bases and camps. The German blow had fallen too quickly for any provision to be made for rear security. Now it was either surrender or flight. Flight was in two directions, either to the beaches where lay the hope of evacuation or into Caen. For the older German veterans, it was like the glory days in Russia in 1941 and 1942 when they had fallen upon masses of retreating Soviet troops. The results were the same: slaughter. Whole convoys were blown off the roads by the panzers who either drove over the wreckage or found it easier to go cross country. Corporal Willi Fleischer was driving one of the tanks.

> We drove past one truck convoy we had shot up from a distance. The trucks had been packed with troops, and the dead littered the road where they had spilled out, but the trucks were still packed with more of the dead, and they were burning. I will never forget the sight and smell of all that burning flesh.[7]

The field hospitals, still occupied by their staffs and patients, they passed without incident. German medical units drove right in, the officers coordinated with their British counterparts, and both groups seemed to merge into one as the wounded began to stream in. Thousands of the enemy's rear echelon troops began surrendering, abandoning their stalled convoys or coming out of the hamlets and woods to give themselves up. The panzers just bypassed them and told them to wait by the side of the road. The Germans rode past the hulks of 21st Panzer Division's tanks destroyed on D-Day and continued north in two columns. The left-hand column's objective was the sea; that of the right, the bridges over the Orne.

Just south of Biéville, 2nd Panzer met its first serious opposition in exactly the same place where 21st Panzer was first hit by surprise on 6 June. Corporal Jeremy Knowland, 44th Battalion, Royal Tank Regiment, was the best gunner in his squadron. He was sighting the 17-pounder on his Sherman Firefly on the lead Mark IV of the column speeding down the road straight into Biéville. The squadron commander had told him to strike the first tank just as it passed the closest German wreck from that earlier encounter. The rest of the squadron would fire after him on the following tanks. His finger gently squeezed the trigger, and the tank rocked backwards. He reacquired the target to see it stagger under the impact and lurch off the road. The crew leaped out and ran for cover as more British fire fell amid the rest of the German column. Three more tanks were picked off, halted, and burned. The 44th Tanks, like its sister unit, 3rd County of London Yeomanry (Sharpshooters) of 4th Armoured Brigade had been rushed out of the Orne bridgehead to be thrown in the path of 2nd Panzer. Second Army was in direct communication with 4th Armoured, the only significant force in front of a German lunge to the sea. The 44th Tanks' first good punch seemed to be a case of history repeating itself.

They overlooked one major difference. Second Panzer was not 21st Panzer. This mostly Austrian division recruited in Vienna had one of the best combat records in the German Army, acquired with Army Group Centre in Russia, and its commander, Lieutenant General Smilo von Lüttwitz, a craftsman of war. Corporal Knowland, for one, instantly recognized that the first round had only been that: the first round, as he watched the Mark IVs of the 2nd Battalion, 3rd Panzer Regiment shake out of their column and split left and right to encircle Biéville. Just about then, German artillery began pasting the village and dropping smoke to either side to hide its own tanks. Following each column was a battalion of 2nd Panzer Grenadier Regiment. Forty-fourth Tanks had been ordered to hold Biéville to the end, but the Germans seemed to make those orders obsolete by bypassing and isolating the battalion. The commander left one squadron to delay the Germans coming around Biéville from the west while he attacked the other group with his remaining three squadrons. As the Shermans surged out the village, the Mark IVs wheeled towards them in a contest of gunnery skills at 300 yards. Corporal Knowland quickly added two more German tanks to his record when his own tank was hit by a shot that passed through the turret in a blaze of sparks and metal shards. His tank commander slid dead in his seat, and the loader was a heap on the floor among the brass casings. Then fire was everywhere. Somehow he got out in the fastest two seconds of his life and leaped off the turret, his clothes on fire. He rolled through the puddles until the fire was out. The driver crawled over to him and pointed towards the town. Panzergrenadiers and antitank guns had rushed into the village as 44th Tanks was engaged with their tanks. From there they had shot up the Shermans from behind. One of their Pak-75 antitank guns had killed Knowland's tank.

The fight for Biéville lasted another half hour as the German panzer-grenadiers grappled house by house with the one company of the brigade's motorized infantry battalion. This time the Germans did not show the scruples of inexperience that the British had on D-Day by hesitating to destroy French houses with their owners inside. They were expert at demolishing houses with anything that came to hand. By noon the village was in their hands, and the remnants of 44th Tanks were caught in a vice as the other half of the German tank force hit it from the rear. In that crossfire 44th Tanks shrivelled and died.

To the west the Yeomanry had been beaten up and surrounded by the combined arms tactics of the 1st Battalion, 3rd Panzer, and the 304th Panzergrenadier Regiment. In two hours of combat, 4th Armoured Brigade had ceased to exist except for the Scots Greys still fighting east of the Orne. Now nothing blocked 2nd Panzer Division's drive to the sea. At 2nd Army headquarters, Dempsey and Montgomery were listening over the radio to 4th Armoured's death rattle. If thoughts of Tobruk and Singapore haunted their thoughts in those awful moments, they did not betray them. Montgomery's voice cut through the gloom like an icy knife. He was utterly in command of himself.

Gentlemen, this is the situation. In a few hours the Germans will have sheared off a quarter of our lodgement and isolated another quarter. Jerry's given us a hard knock, but his counterpunch is about to exhaust itself. All we have to do is hold the line of the Seulles for another eighteen hours, and the weather will clear. RAF promises clear skies beginning tomorrow morning, and, gentlemen, the Germans will be out in the open, fixed and overtextended.[8]

Struggle Along the Seulles

All we have to do is hold the line of the Seulles! As Montgomery spoke, the river line was the scene of some of the bitterest fighting of the campaign. Skillfully employing the high ground north of the river to fire down on the Germans, the British had stalled the rest of I SS Panzer Corps' increasingly desperate lunges at the barrier. In addition to the river with its antitank overwatch, the British had hastily prepared the three towns just south of the river: St. Gabriel, Creully, and Amblie, as heavily defended barbicans. Against the two panzer divisions, there were the remaining 50 tanks and infantry brigade of 7th Armoured, 150 tanks of 11th Armoured, and the three infantry battalions of 15th Scottish Division's 44th Lowland Brigade. Into the line had been thrown every line of communications infantry company, sappers, anti-aircraft and antitank battalions that could be moved in time. Every inch of ground south between the Seulles and Highway 13 had been put into a fire plan for British artillery battalions hub to hub behind the river and for the Royal Navy's gun crews besides themselves to have been impotent against the German advance on that terrible 12th of June. Artillery spotters had volunteered to stay behind in the woods and villages south of the Seulles to call in fire on every yard of the German advance. In the dark and rain of the night before, the sappers had laid hasty mine fields all along this front. All night as the mines had been laid, there had been a steady flow of service units and wounded from 7th Armoured heroic delaying action along Highway 13. There had been hundreds more casualties as lost units and stragglers wandered into the poorly marked minefields in the night.

But in the morning the British were ready. The Royal Artillery and the Royal Navy marked the German advance with trails of smashed vehicles and broken bodies. Almost every column was so tortured by the accurately delivered artillery that they were reeling by the time they approached the barbican towns. Without killing an Englishman, they had suffered several thousand casualties and lost hundreds of vehicles of all types. By late afternoon there were arcs of destroyed tanks, SPWs, and Flakpanzers in front of each of the towns and their vital bridges. A few tanks and panzergrenadiers bypassed the towns and reached the river only to be shot up by the fire from the high ground on the other side. The German artillery chimed in to drench each of the towns with high explosive. Finally, under cover of smoke and artillery, Panzer Lehr thrust a battle group into Creully. Captain Joachim Schindler led his shrunken Panther company down the mainstreet straight for the bridge. A pair of antitank guns guarding the approach to the bridge fired. Both shells struck the front slope and zinged off with a high-pitched clang of metal on metal. His machine gunner swept the crew off one gun while his gunner blew both gun and crew into the alley from which they fired. A Cromwell turned the corner and fired . . . and missed. Schindler's gunner did not. His driver gunned the engine and the Panther knocked aside the burning Cromwell and flew over the bridge so quickly that no other British guns could be brought to bear. Four more of his Panthers followed in quick succession. The sixth and seventh were caught in the antitank crossfire from the heights across the river. They caught fire and burned completely blocking the bridge. Unaware of this Schindler led his little force forward shooting up British troops in his path, then took a road to the right that led to a tall structure. Schindler realized immediately that he had struck gold.

I learned later after the war that the this place was the Chateau de Creullet, Montgomery's headquarters of all things, and that of the British forces defending the Seulles line. There were scores of vehicles parked around it – trucks, signal vans, staff cars, and armoured cars. There was only one thing to do – 'Panzer . . . Marsch!' We attacked right into the place. Our guns set the vehicles in a blaze as men scrambled everywhere to get away. We drove through their tents and into the Chateau's gardens firing away at anything we could see. Machine gun fire came from the upper windows, so we pumped a dozen rounds from the 75mms into the place and set it on fire.[9]

Behind him in Creully, the panzergrenadiers had fought their way to the bridge. They were setting up a base of fire over the bridge and calling in their own artillery to cover an assault. Two attempts were beaten back with heavy losses. Under intense fire a Panther moved onto the bridge and up to the first of the burning tanks. It slowly nudged the other till the burning tank slid sideways and through the balustrade to tip drunkenly and then pitch into the river. The Panther then repeated this bravura performance, and the other tank trailing fire fell into the water with an enormous sizzle. The Panther then sped across the last half of the bridge and found a spot from which it could bring the British antitank guns under fire. He knocked out three before four and five holed him in a gush of fire. By then the panzergrenadiers were crossing the bridge, first in sections then platoons with their heavy weapons. The concentration on the lone tank had distracted the British gunners long enough to allow a German company to cross the river and dig in.

Notes

1. Colonel Hans von Luck, *Panzer Commander* (New York: Praeger, 1989) p.148.
2. Ibid., p.149.
3. Dieter Paul Wölffer, *Die 84. Infantriedivision* (Breslau: Verlag Steiner, 1955) p.133.
4. Jonathan H. Miller and Paul Merchant, *The 41st Armored Infantry Regiment* (Washington: Infantry Journal Press, 1949) p.156.
5. Richard Parker, *Once More into the Breach: 7th Armoured Division in Normandy* (London: John Murray, 1950) p.173.
6. Sepp Dietrich, *With the I SS Panzer Corps in Normandy* (London: Hutchinson, 1949) p.187.
7. George R. Smith-Mitchell, *Caen Disaster* (London: Gale and Polden, 1956) p.169.
8. Francis de Guingand, *Memories of Montgomery* (London: Hodder and Stoughton, 1954) p.226.
9. Fritz Bayerlein, *Panzer Lehr: Erinnerungen* (Königsberg: Hindenburg Verlag, 1955); *Memories of the Panzer Lehr Division* (London: Cobden Sanderson, 1957) p.174.

CHAPTER 8

Starting Over and Operation TALISMAN 14 to 26 June

A New British Commander?

The morning of 14 June was bright blue, and the Allied air forces roared over the Channel at first light to deliver two days of pent-up fury upon the Germans. For the panzer divisions of I SS Panzer Corps it was the beginning of an ordeal that many would remember with more horror than the previous two days of battle. At least for them there would be the relative safety of stationary positions that they could camouflage. For the trains and infantry divisions strung out to the rear, it became a massacre of everything that moved. Rommel's warnings of Allied air power were manifested in miles of wreckage and slaughtered men and horses littering the roads and fields. They had suffered this gauntlet all along their routes of march, except for the last two days of rain. Soaked uniforms and soggy boots had seemed a small price to pay for such relief. But the Jabos were more than making up for lost time with every mile that brought them closer to the front.

But for all their fury, the Jabos could not undo the damage done to the British lodgement by ROSSBACH. Eisenhower was in Normandy almost ahead of the fighter-bombers to assess that damage. He had steeled himself to relieve Montgomery if necessary. Certainly the little man's enemies had whispered countless reasons why into his ears. Even the British Chiefs wavered in shock. All but Churchill, who was all courage to back his winner and see the thing through; but even he would accede to the military decision of the Supreme Allied Commander, if . . . Eisenhower's mission was to appraise morale at the front, but he also had a morale problem at the top. After two years of victory clawed up from the very bottom, the British had been thrown back down the hill again. There was too much talk by tired men of evacuating the lodgement and trying again, half-hearted talk in the latter case. The mechanism of evacuation was already being planned, and off Sword Beach the day before it had begun in earnest under conditions far more desperate than Dunkirk. Landing craft had been carrying off thousands of men all night until German tanks broke through to the beach. In all, seventeen thousand men had been brought off without equipment. Thousands more had fled down the shore

198

to Juno Beach spreading confusion in the darkness. That greatest observer of man at war, Homer, had smelled the reek of the scene some three thousand years before in the phrase, 'panic, brother to blood-stained route.' Dempsey had used his few remaining lines-of-communication battalions and called on the Royal Navy Commandos to get the situation at hand. The sight of the sky filled with fighter-bombers stacked up for their turn at the Germans and the steady roar of the Royal Navy's guns restored calm and discipline as much as the sight of any grim-faced Royal Marine ready to shoot some bloody cook or supply clerk who had shit his pants. Stragglers and service units with no mission were broken up and sent to the infantry battalions as makeshift replacements.

The hairsbreadth margin of 2nd Army's survival hit Eisenhower when he arrived at the Chateau de Creullet. The upper floors had been burned and shell holes pockmarked the walls. The wreckage of scores of vans, staff cars, and trucks turned the once elegant grounds into a junkyard. Most startling was the clutch of four burned-out Panthers and half a dozen Shermans where they had evidently fought it out to the death. Montgomery met him outside his personal van, the one British vehicle that seemed to have come through the storm of battle unscathed. 'Good God, Monty, why on earth didn't you move your headquarters back out of immediate danger? This is no place for an army group commander.' 'By the time the Germans got to the river down there, there was no more "back". Besides, Ike, the men needed to know that their commander was up front. I think Marlborough said something about, "I will not send troops to danger which I will not myself encounter."' He paused. 'Well, you are evidently here to look around. Come with me; you are just in time to see something.'[1]

He led Eisenhower to a small wood overlooking the bridge and Creully across the river. Mortars and artillery were stonking the area around the near end of the bridge, where a German company had secured a bridgehead over the Seulles the night before. As the stonk let up, tanks and infantry swarmed forward and overran the position. In five minutes it was over, and a few dozen German prisoners were quickly herded to the rear. The tank-infantry team then rushed the bridge and disappeared into the town accompanied by the sudden racket of small arms fire. German artillery belatedly fell in support of the wiped out bridgehead, and shells walked up the slope and into the wood from where the generals had watched the action. Exploding in the branches, the shells sent jagged wooden splinters as deadly as canister (shells packed with small steel balls) towards the observation party and sent half a dozen men writhing on the ground. Montgomery seemed not even to notice. He noticed out of the corner of his eye that Eisenhower had not moved either. He had always wanted to see how a five star reacted to his first time under fire. Montgomery could never quite overcome his disdain for a man who had missed service in France in World War I, though through no fault of his own, and then risen to his position by virtue of his excellence as a staff officer.

From their vantage point, Montgomery explained the sweep of the battle-field as calmly and as lucidly as if he had been leading a staff walk over the field of Agincourt. It had been the weather, he explained, that had come so brilliantly to Rommel's assistance. He pointedly compared Eisenhower's seizure of the 6 June weather window with Rommel's seizure of a similar weather opportunity on 12 and 13 June. If Eisenhower had had doubts about the seemingly flawed deployments that had led to the ROYAL OAK and SPANNER debacles, he did not raise them. The more Monty spoke, the more Ike became willing to write off the last two days as the hard fortunes of war and the more convinced of his soundness to set things right. The Germans had shot their bolt and come close, but not close enough. Montgomery went on that now was the time to tidy up the battlefield (that damned phrase of his again!), accelerate the landing of new divisions, and give the Germans a drubbing in the next round. That appraisal and optimism was the same he had been getting from Bradley who was telling him that the German grip on the Cotentin Peninsula was about to snap. He left that evening convinced that the situation had downshifted from desperate to merely difficult.

Many men might have disagreed. Montgomery had faced the dreadful reality that the already horrendous British losses might suddenly become much worse. Over fifty thousand men were dead, wounded, or missing. In Britain, they were speaking not of Tobruk or Singapore now but of the Somme. Of course, that most of those fifty thousand were prisoners was some comfort, but they were still as irreplaceable as if they had all been shot in the head. There were also two major pockets behind German lines that were packed with British troops. Caen, bypassed by 2nd Panzer, held upwards of twenty thousand men, mostly 3rd Division and I Corps service and support troops as well as 185th Brigade, 1st Polish Parachute Brigade, and fragments of other battalions. Sosabowski, as senior officer present, had forcefully assumed command and had quickly put the city in a state of defence just as the German 84th Infantry Division had arrived to invest it. The Orne River bridgehead held another sixteen thousand men of 6th Airborne and 51st Divisions, cut off when 2nd Panzer had broken 4th Armoured Brigade. Within the remaining lodgement, 2nd Army's order-of-battle had been shredded. I Corps had practically disappeared. British 3rd Division had been written off, and two divisions were trapped on the other side of the Orne. The only remaining division was the Canadian 3rd Division which could muster the strength of a strong brigade. XXX Corps was in better shape with 49th and 50th Divisions having played no part in the battle, but 7th Armoured had been fought out, and like the Canadians, was little more than a weak infantry brigade with tanks. U.S. V Corps' infantry divisions had reestablished a solid front a few miles west of Port-en-Bessin south around Bayeux and were still combat ready. The 2nd Armored Division had bludgeoned the Germans out of their breakthrough and still represented the strongest armoured force on both sides, but without its trains had little flexibility as a 2nd Army fire brigade.

Before Eisenhower left, Montgomery obtained his endorsement of the following priorities:

(1) Mass forces as quickly as possible for a major push to relieve the Caen and Orne pockets;

(2) Ruthlessly restrict landings to combat reinforcements and the supplies necessary to sustain 2nd Army's immediate combat needs;

(3) Resupply the Caen and Orne bridgehead pockets by air. In the case of the latter, prepare contingency plans for its breakout to the sea and evacuation;

(4) Redirect strategic bomber assets from continued strikes over Germany to total support of the ground campaign in France.

Montgomery was convinced that Rommel had won a Pyrrhic victory. He had gained much ground, taken many prisoners and much booty, but his best divisions, the panzers, had been bled white and were now largely out of hedgerow country and exposed to the endless hammering from the sky. The Germans had even come back into range of the Royal Navy's guns. He also fully concurred with Bradley that the Cotentin was about to yield its promised breakthrough and the port of Cherbourg. His grand strategic plan had been vindicated though at a terrible cost. The Germans had, indeed, thrown the full weight of their armour against the British and starved their forces fighting the U.S. VII Corps. Montgomery was equally convinced that this logic was meaningless in the light of continued heavy losses. The British public was war weary to the bone and had been badly shaken by the past week's setbacks. All of Churchill's political skill and capital had been expended in this final rally of support for him. There was far more at stake in his plan to relieve the pockets than expand the lodgements for continued operations and to keep the panzers off the Americans' backs. The rescue of the men in those pockets was the talisman of Britain's determination to forcibly prosecute the war. The relief would have to wait on the rebuilding of 2nd Army's offensive power, especially its tank arm, and the earliest that could be done was 20 June. The pockets would have to hold.

The Other Side of the Hill

Montgomery would probably not have been surprised to know that on the other side of the hill Rommel essentially shared his analysis of the situation: close but not close enough. At Evrecy he explained his conclusions to Dietrich, Bayerlein, and von Lüttwitz. The situation in his eyes was all too close to the

Luddendorf Offensives of March and April 1918 which had also pushed the British up against the wall. Even if the British had been knocked out of the fight, there were still the Americans with their endless numbers and material resources. Rommel suggested another similarity: Luddendorf had also refused to make peace at the crest of his good fortune. Lüttwitz was emphatic. His division was loyal and could be relied upon.[2] Dietrich took Rommel by the hand and shook it forcefully, 'You're the boss, *Herr Feldmarshal*, I obey only you – whatever it is you are planning.'[3]

Of immediate concern was the continued exposure of the panzer corps to air attack. By night, the 85th Infantry and 19th Field Divisions relieved Panzer Lehr and Hitlerjugend which dispersed to the rear to reorganize and rest. The 331st Infantry Division after finally crossing the Orne followed 2nd Panzer in holding open the salient between the Caen and Orne pockets. The infantry divisions made all the difference now. Had Case Three not released these solid infantry formations, the panzer divisions would have been burned out in the front line. Hitler had relented in their release, but it had been the Old Junker, von Rundstedt, who had thrown his sword on the scales. If anyone was to be thanked, it was the ancient field marshal, pruning his rose bushes at OB West.

Montgomery had also been correct in divining that Rommel's attention would stay fixed on the British sector of the front. German reinforcements even from Brittany were increasingly diverted to the British sector. The 353rd Infantry Division was diverted from LXXXIV Corps at the last minute to the new XXV Corps south and southeast of Bayeux (the weak 352nd, 77th Infantry Divisions). Even the panzer divisions from south of the Loire were earmarked for the British sector. Only a few battle groups stripped out of coastal defence divisions were sent to shore up LXXXIV Corps.

On the afternoon of 17 June, a long stick with a white flag was poked out of a hedgerow on the German side and waved vigorously. A voice shouted in good English, 'We are coming forward under flag of truce.' Then a German officer emerged carrying the flag and stepped into the sunken lane. The Bren gunner and riflemen of a squad of the Green Howards were too much taken by the surprise of the moment to think of firing. An officer was called forward and stepped into the lane and walked forward to meet the German. They saluted and shook hands. The German came to the point. They had a prisoner they wished to return, a special prisoner carrying a personal message for General Montgomery from a high German authority. He emphasized that the message was to be delivered in person only. The German waved his hand at the hedge behind him, and an American lieutenant stepped out and blinked in the sunlight.

A month ago Lieutenant Eberly would have been nervous if he had been addressed by his battalion commander. Now he was waiting for the commander of the 21st Army Group to return. He had been frisked and questioned by some tough customers in the last two hours. They were as mystified as they were impressed by the photograph he showed them of himself and Rommel. His battalion commander who had once seemed so important had been flown down to identify him and was visibly agitated over the whole thing. After that, his treatment improved but not the barrage of questions. He stuck to the facts of his capture. Finally, he was ushered into the august presence, an officer on either side. The little, thin-faced man put him at ease immediately but obviously wanted to get to the point. The photo lay in front of him. 'Sir, I gave my word that the message would be for your ears alone.' Montgomery waved the two officers off. 'Yes, now, what is it?' 'Sir, Rommel wants an armistice.'[4]

American Breakthrough

On 16 June, VII Corps' go-for-broke offensive was kicked off. The day before a windfall had come Collins' way when the 22nd Infantry discovered that its nemeses, the German forts at Azeville and St. Marcouf, had been evacuated. Unrelenting naval and field artillery attacks had finally rendered them useless. With the forts no longer a factor, the attack would have nothing so solid to break its impetus. At 0530 the 82nd Airborne, 9th, 90th and 4th Infantry Divisions attacked behind a heavy bombardment. General von Schlieben's defence disintegrated within a few hours. The battle groups from the over-aged and underequipped coastal defence divisions has simply been worn down and exhausted by full infantry divisions of fit, young men. Every division had its own supporting tank battalion, it seemed, and together they had the strength of a strong panzer division. The only German tanks had been some obsolete French models captured in 1940 and older German models that they dared not use on the Eastern Front. None were a match for the Shermans. The 82nd Airborne attacked at the hinge of the German line, where it dog-legged south to run along the Merderet, and smashed it off its frame in a few hours' fighting. The 9th Division shot past and reached the coast in two places within thirty-six hours.

The German collapse had been so sudden that Collins had no need to commit the newly arrived 79th Infantry Division. The 9th Division's slice to the coast had been so swift that most of the German LXXXIV Corps, 32,000 men, had been trapped to the north with only fragments of miscellaneous units escaping south. Von Schlieben was attempting to withdraw his broken battle groups into the defences of Fortress Cherbourg when he received a Führer Befehl (Order) ordering him to stand fast and hold as much ground outside the fortress as he could. Collins pounced on this gift and was upon the Germans with the 9th, 79th, and 4th Divisions before these fragments of units could properly man the outer defences. The Führer Befehl cost von Schlieben another 23,000 men in under a day. He retreated with the remainder into the fortress itself, which is what he had wanted to do in the first place. As a result of this catastrophe, the last wave of Case Three reinforcements coming from south of the Loire, including 9th and 10th Panzer Divisions, were diverted to this new hole torn in the front.

Calm Before the Storm

As the VII Corps' siege of Cherbourg ground on, the Allies began to breathe far easier. Second Army was being steadily reinforced, though the restricted size of the lodgement placed definite limits on the forces that could be put ashore. The original landing schedule had been thrown out the window; 2nd Army was far behind in the number of divisions it had expected to have ashore by this time. But, at least, the missing elements of 2nd Armored Division, and all of the U.S. 30th Infantry, British 15th Scottish, and 11th Armoured Divisions had been landed by 16 June. The 30th joined V Corps, and the two British divisions were put under the newly landed British VIII Corps which took stricken I Corps' place in the line. XXX Corps was also strengthened with the newly arrived 43rd Wessex Division and 7th Armoured rebuilt around 33rd Armoured Brigade. Since the terrible losses of 12 and 13 June, both the British and the Germans had been too exhausted for major operations and had been content, with some exceptions, not to engage in major operations.

The Germans had also been active in bringing reinforcements to the front. Both the 1st and 2nd SS Panzer Divisions, the infamous Leibstandarte Adolf Hitler and Das Reich had arrived on 15–16 June to relieve the 12th SS and Panzer Lehr for a thorough rest and refit. In a reorganization, Hitlerjugend was retained with the two new SS divisions in I SS Panzer Corps. Panzer Lehr and 2nd Panzer came under the new XXXXVII Panzer Corps. Case Three was steadily paying dividends all this time. The divisions released at the start of the invasion had given Rommel a superiority in divisions of three to two, nineteen to thirteen divisions, and in armoured divisions of seven to three in the British sector. Understandably, the German divisions were smaller than the Allied, but the tank strength was about equal at 700. The III Flak Corps had also been prised out of Göring's hands and was now bringing its 160 88mm anti-aircraft guns to the front. Although the flak corps could not drive off the Jabos, the troops were heartened to see so many more of them crash in flames. As Rommel ordered Panzer Lehr and 2nd Panzer to Lisieux for rest and refit, he pointedly ordered Bayerlein and von Lüttwitz to keep their division in readiness for a special mission.

Twin Plagues

The Retribution Weapon

The first Allied troops in Normandy to learn of the beginning of the V1 missile storm falling on British cities were the 13/18th Hussars in the Orne Bridgehead pocket.

It was one morning, about this time, the German aircraft dropped showers of propaganda leaflets to inform our troops that – 'London is in flames and rapidly being destroyed by our new flying bombs. If you do not believe it, you have only to make your way to a nearby hill whence you will be able to see, in the far distant sky, flames and smoke belching up hundreds of feet in the air from the doomed capital.' It was a crude form of propaganda and everyone laughed, although a trifle worried about the flying bomb offensive, which had been launched against England on the night of the 15th/16th June.

Several days later, early one morning, the troops were suddenly surprised by a very loud, low, raucous and vibrating noise in the sky. Thinking it to be a strange type of enemy aircraft about to dive-bomb them, they were ready with the Anti-Aircraft guns, but, as the object came into view, all held their breath. The noise was coming from what looked like a long and enormous bomb, with flames shooting out of its tail. Suddenly they realized that this was the flying bomb. How it came to be flying east towards German territory was not discovered, but luckily the Anti-Aircraft gunners missed their target.[5]

The Hussars had had reason to be 'a trifle nervous' about the V1 or *Vergeltung* (Retribution) weapon, although its initial salvo against London on 12 June was something of a dud. Only ten missiles had been ready to launch due to incessant Allied air attacks on launching sites and depots when Hitler ordered the attack to begin on 12 June. Of the ten, only four hit Great Britain, and only one was effective, killing six people and wounding eighteen. The Allied leadership which had been tensed for months for advent of the wonder weapon, now had reason to laugh. The propaganda leaflet picked up by the Hussars had more to crow about. On 15 June, seventy-three missiles struck London, and the British stopped laughing.[6]

Over the next ten days, two thousand missiles were launched and hundreds penetrated the massive air defence shield the British had moved to southern England within twenty-four hours. The Normandy lodgement was stripped of air defence weapons to man the barrier. Thousands of aircraft were diverted from supporting the ground campaign in France to hunting down the V1 launching and storage sites near the Pas-de-Calais. The only element of the air campaign against Germany itself that continued was the massive Bomber Command retaliation raids on Berlin which cost thousands of lives.

On 19 June, as a great Channel summer storm was brewing, Hitler rewarded Rommel's successes on the ground by sharing a few of his wonder weapon toys. He allowed one quarter of the missiles to be diverted from shuddering London to the south English ports of Dover, Folkestone, Margate, Portsmouth, and Southampton, the logistics terminals supporting the Allies in Normandy. There the missile storm was far more lethal than in London simply because the air defence barrier could only take them under fire over the Channel as they were falling on their targets rather than passing overhead. A far larger proportion of

V1s aimed at the Channel ports hit these cities than those aimed at London. Port operations were badly disrupted, especially after ammunition ships exploded in Portsmouth and Southampton.

Now there was no end to Hitler's generosity as he again became drunk on real victories. Half a dozen launch sites that were not completely fixed, had been adjusted to aim southwest down the Norman coast. What the Hussars saw flying east towards the Germans was one of the missiles that had gone off course after actually reaching the front. Others worked more predictably and began landing in and around the British and American lodgements. The accuracy of the V1 left much to be desired, but it was effective against large geographic targets such as London and the two chunks of Normandy held by the Allies. As any hit on a city will cause death and destruction, so almost every hit within the lodgements, especially the much smaller British one, was a potential disaster. That potential was soon realized. A newly landed company of the 43rd Division was practically wiped out in its assembly area by one missile. That same afternoon two fell on Bayeux, wrecking several blocks of that old city, and a third fell into an assembly area for the U.S. 2nd Armored Division, killing and wounding over two hundred men. The next day an ammunition dump near Arromanches suffered a direct hit.

When the Germans had cut the lodgement area in half, the Allies had lost much of their carefully dispersed ammunition stocks. New stocks had been rushed ashore, but the constriction of the lodgement and the chaos within it had kept the ammunition dangerously concentrated around Arromanches. The resulting detonation spread to the whole complex of ammunition dumps near by. The explosion was later compared to a small nuclear weapon and was heard in both London and Paris. All across the front, men on both sides remembered the gigantic crack of the greatest explosion they had ever heard and suddenly turning in that direction to see nature's storm blown aside and an enormous cloud rise through the rent in the sky. The area had been packed with service units and thousands of men who would have been working on the Mulberry artificial harbours but for the storm. Everything within a mile radius was knocked flat and within another mile badly damaged. The human toll was sickening. Over 2,600 men were killed and wounded. Bodies and other debris were tossed over great distances and rained down amid the ships riding out the storm and on both sides of the front. All the myriad things that are used and consumed by an army: helmets, weapons, fragments of ammunition cases, ration cans, pieces of vehicles, shredded canvas and uniforms, and worst of all, bits and pieces of human beings fell into the fields, and trenches, or splattered on tanks and guns. For many British and German soldiers, the most grisly memories of the battle were of the body parts hanging from the trees and hedges, the *Fleischregen* or meat rain, as the *Landsers* called it. The medical system completely broke down in trying to deal with so many casualties in one small area in the midst of the great storm. Even the Royal Navy found grisly or strange souvenirs, discovered days later. One cruiser was struck by the largest recorded piece of metal ever to hit a ship – and survived to tell how the turret of a Sherman tank crashed through its bridge.[7]

The Great Disaster

The mid-month spell of good weather in the Channel followed on the heels of the disaster of 12 and 13 June and seemed like a godsend to the British. Just when they needed to push reinforcements into the lodgement, the weather had turned fair. On 17 June, Admiral Ramsey authorized the movement of the final and most sensitive components of the two Mulberry artificial harbours from British ports. Already parts of the great concrete piers and massive floating rubber breakwaters were in place at Arromanches. The failure to take Omaha Beach had moved the American Mulberry from its intended site at St. Laurent to its alternate site within a mile of the British Mulberry site. Neither site was as fully completed as had been hoped. The loss of Omaha had dangerously reduced the over-the-beach area that could be used for ship-to-shore landings. Pushing a second Mulberry into that same space had cut down that capability even more.

On 19 June, every available tug from Britain and the east coast of North America began pushing the first two-and-a-half miles of seven miles of floating roadway across the Channel to the half-built harbour sites. These most delicate of all the Mulberry components would compose the flexible wharfs along the inner harbours. As they approached the Norman coast, offshore winds began to drive the waves into a fury. The greatest summer storm in forty years had begun to flail the Channel. The roadways quickly foundered as the storm heaved up six- to eight-foot waves that reached force eight on the Beaufort Scale. The rubber breakwaters were broken loose and thrown up onto the shore as the sea rushed into harbours whose very flexibility was their undoing. The waves and wind tore and twisted them until even the mightiest steel joints failed the incredible stresses. Massive concrete boxes, the size of five-storey buildings sunk into the sea, slipped their moorings under the force of the tidal scour, and most of the blockships were driven up onto the sand. Hundreds of small craft within the harbours were dashed like rams into the already buckling flexible wharfs, doing more damage to them and holing themselves. When the storm subsided, over eight hundred small craft had been wrecked. Many of them had been thrown up upon the beach and lay like beached herds of whales. Five times the number of ships and amount of stores were lost during the storm as on D-Day itself.

The storm raged for four days, and reinforcements shrank to a trickle, barely 1,500 men and 500 vehicles coming ashore at Utah Beach. The two-day storm had already put back the landings of three divisions by a week or more over the surviving British beaches. The explosion at Arromanches had practically strangled logistics. As the storm lifted, the British and Americans realized that two years of massive effort and their hopes had been twisted and torn as badly as the broken Mulberries. The weather had dashed Montgomery's plans for an early rescue attempt, aided by the 'V1 from Hell' as the troops were calling it. Putting the logistics back together again had been a minor task after the storm compared to the dealing with the numbing demoralization that set in. He had physically exhausted himself visiting every unit in Normandy to infuse them with some of his optimism. That Cromwellian certitude and drive worked its magic one more time.

During the storm, the Germans had four free days of unhindered movement to push more reinforcements to the Norman front. Even after the storm subsided on 23 June, mist and rain hung over the Norman countryside for two more days. In that time II SS Panzer Corps, commanded by SS Obergruppenführer Paul Hausser and consisting of 9th and 10th SS Panzer Divisions, arrived in Normandy despite the delays and claw marks left by the French resistance. The corps relieved 2nd Panzer and moved into the salient between the British and their two pockets. Second Panzer joined Panzer Lehr in reserve. Rommel now had the luxury of a large operational reserve in the form of XXXXVII Panzer Corps. From south of the Loire were arriving the 11th Panzer and 265th, 266th, 275th, 276th, and 277th Infantry Divisions to reconstitute LXXXIV Corps facing U.S. VII Corps. Although these divisions were essentially battle groups, made up of the most ready elements of the divisions, they were enough to fill in the open flank. On top of the early execution of Case Three, the six days of bad weather were, indeed, a godsend for the Germans. By 26 June they would have twenty-five divisions in Normandy against the Allies' nineteen.

The Last Throw: Operation TALISMAN

For four days, 14 to 19 June, the Allied air forces had flown a ring around the two pockets to break up any German attempt to break into them. The Royal Navy's guns also added to the rings of giant craters that surrounded the beleaguered pockets and to the casualties of the besieging German infantry divisions. The arrival of the masses of 88mm anti-aircraft guns of the Luftwaffe III Flak Corps had torn scores of airplanes out of the sky, but the bombing and resupply drop flights continued without pause. Then the six days of bad weather completely cut off the two British pockets from resupply by air. Caen, which had been a major resupply point for the front, easily subsisted on its own stores and the airdrops. The presence of a number of hospitals gave decent care for the large numbers of wounded. The bulk of the city, much of it in ruins, also provided a ready-made fortress that was easier to defend. The forces in the Orne Bridgehead quickly felt the pinch of their circumstances. As a force in the field, they had depended on daily resupply from a centralized supply system that was now cut off. Their meagre stocks were maintained by air drops through the morning of 19 June when the great storm began to ground everything with wings. The Germans of LXXXI Corps were emboldened by the prospect of inflicting a Tobruk on the British, and their attacks resumed on 23 June with great ferocity.

One delay after another brought the pockets to the end of their tether. The two divisions in the Orne Pocket did not have the supplies to sustain themselves. The two plus brigades in Caen had the supplies but not the numbers. But Montgomery had moved mountains and overcome disasters to put his final offensive effort into place by 25 June. The man he chose to command the attack was Lieutenant General Sir Richard O'Connor, Commander of VIII Corps and an old friend and classmate. O'Connor had been the executor of the destruction of the Italian armies in North Africa in 1940. Captured by a fluke in Rommel's first offensive, he had escaped when the Italians changed sides in 1943. Operation TALISMAN would use VIII Corps (11th Armoured and 15th Scottish) reinforced with the U.S. 2nd Armored, the U.S. 120th Infantry Regiment (30th Infantry Division), and the partially rebuilt 3rd Canadian Division in corps reserve, to cut its way to the relief of the Caen and Orne Pockets. In the process, VIII Corps would turn a trick on the Germans and trap much of II SS Panzer Corps north of Caen and west of the Orne. The two armoured divisions would attack side by side with five hundred tanks in one great battering ram aimed southeast at Caen. The 11th Armoured would attack across the Seulles and southeast to cross the Mue at Cairon, to Buron and Authie, just outside Caen. The 15th Scottish with several attached antitank regiments would act as the flank guard for 11th Armoured. The 2nd would have the sea flank and strike south directly from the Douve area to the northeastern suburbs of Caen. The attached 120th Infantry would clear the coast and then attack south to take Bénouville and open the Orne Pocket. The forces in both pockets would play a role in their own rescue as well. As the armoured divisions got within three miles of the city, the garrison would attack the Germans from the rear and break through to Buron and Authie. Similarly, the forces in the Orne Pocket would attack across Pegasus Bridge and drive to meet 120th Infantry. British XXX Corps would launch a strong diversionary attack with 43rd and 49th Infantry and 7th Armoured Divisions from the direction of Bayeux to tie down I SS Panzer Corps.

Paul Hausser's II SS Panzer Corps was all that stood in the way of this juggernaut. Its two panzer divisions, 9th SS 'Hohenstaufen', and 10th SS 'Frundsberg', had both been in the process of reequipment in northeastern France and Germany when Case Three set them on the road to Normandy. The first battalion in each division's panzer regiment had been in the process of receiving their new Panthers at Camp-en-Mailly. They had barely joined their

divisions in Normandy. They nevertheless arrived short of their full comple-
ments. The second battalions were also short of Mark IVs and had to substitute
assault guns. Even the corps Heavy SS Panzer Battalion 102 was short of one
company of Tigers, leaving it with only twenty-eight. The 238 tanks and
assault guns in the corps were outnumbered by the almost 300 Shermans in
2nd Armored Division alone. Each division had slightly more than 110
armoured fighting vehicles almost evenly divided among Panthers, Mark IVs,
and assault guns. The number of tanks was not everything. The corps had come
fresh from victories over the Soviets at Lemberg and Tarnopol. Obersturmbannführer Otto Meyer, commander of 9th SS Panzer Regiment, had just
been awarded the Knight's Cross of the Iron Cross on 2 June for his leadership
at Tarnopol. Now Meyer was located with his regiment between Douve and
Bénouville. The 21st SS Panzergrenadier Regiment was in support, and the
20th had sealed off Pegasus Bridge. On its left flank was 10th SS Panzer
Division with its left flank on the Mue. In effect, the whole corps was in the
path of 2nd Armored Division. To the west of the Mue, the Seulles River line
was held by 85th Infantry and 19th Field Divisions. Behind Highway 13 lay
much of 1st SS Panzer Corps (1st, 2nd, and 12th SS Panzer) with another 320
tanks and assault guns. Much would depend on XXX Corps drawing them off.

Opening Moves

At first light on 26 June the Allied air forces came in wave after wave to bomb
and strafe the Germans from Bayeux to Caen. Next the two Allied navies took
up where the airplanes left off. At 0700 XXX Corps launched a sharp attack on
the 19th Field Division which was just staggering out of its positions, stunned
from the bombardment. The division crumbled as the two larger British
divisions hit. They had penetrated two miles before 12th SS Panzer counterattacked. Rocket-firing Typhoons circling the battlefield swooped down on the
Hitlerjugend tanks, hunting them down one by one while the Desert Rats and
the 49th West Riding battered them from the front. The Germans fell back
into a string of rubbled villages, turning each one into a small fortress that
quickly absorbed the strength of both divisions. But XXX Corps was accom-
plishing its mission. Already one panzer division had been drawn into the
fighting, and now Das Reich was moving forward from corps reserve, and the
more they moved, the more they were hunted from the air.

At 0930, VIII Corps attacked out of the villages it held south of the Seulles
preceded by an intense thirty minute artillery stonk of every known and suspected German position. The German main defence belt occupied the belt of
ruined villages and splintered woods a mile south of Creully. The 85th Infantry
Division was made of sterner stuff than the 19th Field to its left, and emerged
from its holes to stop the inevitable attack. 11th Armoured struck straight
south out of Amblie across the two-mile-wide wheat fields, hoping to skirt east

around the strongest of the 85th's defences. At the same time, 15th Scottish attacked directly into the teeth of them with 46th and 227th Highland Brigades. If the 15th Division didn't breach this barrier, there would be no flank guard for 11th Armoured's thrust to Caen. But Major General G.P.B. 'Pip' Roberts' 11th Armoured had barely made several hundred yards before resistance sprang to life at the two German anchor posts at either end of the wheat field: Pierrepont and Fontaine-Henry. Carefully concealed antitank and machine gun positions began raking the outer tank columns, but the range was extreme, and few vehicles were lost. Roberts had anticipated that enough Germans would survive to throw a spanner into the works (they always did). The artillery began firing smoke which drifted quickly over the German positions. 11th Armoured flowed through the gap. The first German barrier had been breached.

To the east, 2nd Armored Division's attack immediately ran into both 9th and 10th SS Panzer Divisions. Combat Command A attacked across open fields towards Columby-sur-Thaon with more tanks than a normal panzer division. But Frundsberg was rich in tough panzergrenadiers with fine antitank weapons. They were dug in from the Mue to Columby to Mathieu. An attempt to bypass the village to the west broke up in a deadly crossfire that left thirteen tanks of 2nd Battalion, 66th Armour Regiment, smoking in the high wheat. The Panther battalion emerged from the village and attacked into the flank of the Shermans, their long-barrelled 75mms brewing up one tank after another. The Americans withdrew under cover of smoke and artillery. Combat Command B was luckier at first. Its use of smoke got its 1st Battalion, 67th Armour Regiment, past Cresserons and the antitank nest in its ruins. The 2nd Battalion was stopped as the smoke cleared, and the Germans found their targets. The 1/67th struck out for the open wheat fields between the next two villages, Mathieu and Périers-sur-le-Dan, but entered the intersection of antitank fires from this second line of defence. The Americans had been glad not to be fighting in the hedgerows and had thought this area with its wide wheat fields land villages was perfect tank country. It was also perfect antitank country. The villages were the little forts in which the antitank weapons sheltered, and the wheat fields were the broad clear fields of fire around them. And out of the villages, the panzers would issue to counterattack. Caught in the antitank fire and counterattacked by tanks, the 1/67th and its attached halftrack company from 2/41st Armored Infantry was steadily being whittled down. Finally they withdrew into a small wood half a mile to the north where they were pounded by German artillery.

The 120th Infantry with the attached 3/66th Armor advanced easily against minor opposition down the fringe of ruined villages above the beaches. The Germans had preferred to keep their strength a few miles inland and left the miles of wreckage and abandoned equipment largely alone. The attacks by the

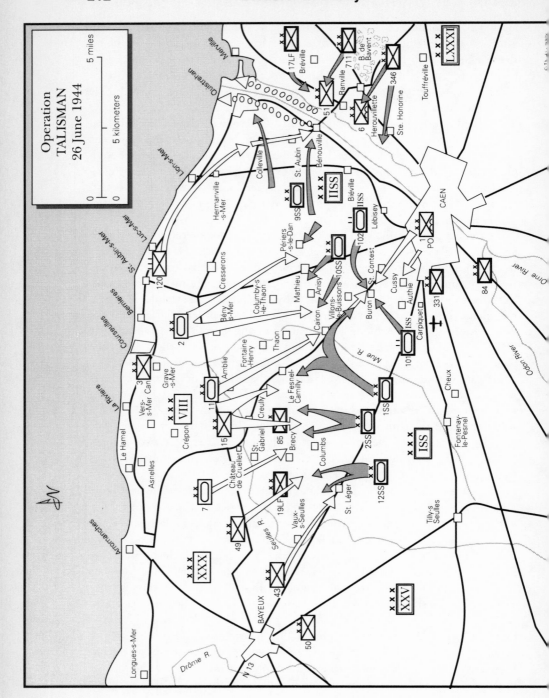

Operation
TALISMAN
26 June 1944

two combat commands had fully engaged the attention of II SS Panzer Corps as well. So no one was more surprised than the panzergrenadier company in Colleville-Montgomery when American tanks and infantry swept through them from the direction of the sea. Caught from the flank, most were either killed or captured. In Ouistreham, another German company was fighting a delaying action against a battalion of the 1/120th but was also quickly overrun. The 120th was mopping up separate companies of the 2/20th SS Panzer-grenadier Regiment of 9th SS Panzer which had been positioned to prevent a breakout from the Orne Pocket. A third company was forced out of the next town, St. Aubin d'Arquenay in the same way. For a green regiment, the 120th had had a great piece of luck to take such a dangerous enemy piecemeal by surprise. But the men of the 120th, North Carolinian National Guardsmen, had been together for almost four years, and the incompetent had been weeded out long ago. Green they may have been but these Tar Heels were equally a well-trained, well-led, and cohesive regiment.

When the Americans reached St. Aubin about noon, the tanks of the Scots Greys came charging over Pegasus Bridge. The first one reached the middle before two antitank guns turned it into a flaming wreck. The next tank crashed into it, pushing it over the side and continued on until it too was holed almost at the end of the bridge. Tank fire, artillery, and smoke now blanketed the German defenders of 1/20th Panzergrenadiers in Bénouville. A third tank pushed the second burning tank aside and drove off the bridge, followed quickly by the rest of the squadron and then the 1st Battalion of the Black Watch. The Germans were quick to counterattack with assault guns and panzergrenadiers, and a nasty pounding match flared up on the edge of the town as more of the Scots Greys and 154th Brigade stormed across the bridge. From St. Aubin, the Americans began attacking south behind their tanks, and by noon were within half a mile of Pegasus Bridge. The Orne Pocket was within a hairsbreadth of relief.

To the east, 11th Armoured Division's tanks had become enmeshed in the part of 85th Division's second line of defence in another clutch of villages around le Fresne-Camilly. There, wheatland was broken up by a few hedgerows that concealed more antitank guns and machine guns. Again 29th Brigade used smoke and artillery to suppress the Germans in order to slip by to the east. Twice the tanks and armoured infantry had to assault diehard nests that could not be avoided. Each time, the Germans extracted a higher cost than they paid, but the Brigade resumed the attack with little lost time. The follow-on infantry of 159th Infantry Brigade would have to clear out the bypassed Germans this time. A spotter aircraft then reported the approach of several dozen tanks from the south. General Roberts realized immediately that the arrival of German tank reserves in the path of his division's advance would eat up the clock and prevent a timely breakthrough to Caen. He threw out the 23rd Hussars to hold the German counterattack whilethe rest of 29th Armoured Brigade cut across the Mue River at Cairon. Finding it undefended, they drove on towards Buron two miles away.

TALISMAN in the Balance

By 1300 Operation TALISMAN appeared to be working. Two panzer divisions from I SS Panzer Corps had been drawn off by XXX Corps' attack. Second Armored's combat commands had not broken through II SS Panzer Corps despite serious losses, but they had fixed it in place so that other arms were reaching around it to the south. 11th Armoured was within four miles of the outskirts of Caen, and the U.S. 120th Infantry was about to link up with the British forces attacking out of the Orne Pocket. As Montgomery had planned, II SS Panzer Corps was about to find itself in a pocket. At this time, the garrison of Caen attacked from the opposite direction.

Captain John Heath's battery of 6-pounder antitank guns opened the breakout by taking the Germans in Cussy and St. Contest under direct fire. The Poles and the Yeomanry's tanks had assembled in two battalion groups in the streets of Caen, the tank engines idling and the Poles crouched atop them and in companies behind them. Heath could see one group.

> I have never seen more desperate and determined men than those Poles. For them it was literally victory or death. They burst out the street riding atop the tanks of the Yeomanry, and dashed across the few hundred yards before the Germans could react. We had kept their heads down, and I think they got into those villages with small loss. We limbered up the guns and followed the Poles into St. Contest. Just outside the village, there was a burning Sherman and a dozen dead Poles flung all about. The first few houses were burning, their front walls spilled into the street with dead German machine gunners. A Pak-75 anti-tank gun had been run over by a tank, its shield crumpled like cardboard, and its gun twisted at a strange angle. The crew were dead in a bloody clump. The Poles ahead were moving methodically down the street using the Shermans as mobile artillery to demolish one house then another. I found the battalion commander, a big, blond man, Count K———ski or something, and offered my guns which he was glad to have. A file of terrified German prisoners was rushed back past us. All the time I was with the Poles, I never saw them mistreat a prisoner. And I never knew men with more reason to do so.[8]

Sosabowski's 1st Polish Brigade had punched its way through a battalion of the Austrian 331st Infantry Division. Ahead of St. Contest was the village of Buron, through which the Canadians had passed on the night of D-Day, and where the link-up was planned. Two-and-a-half miles separated the Poles and 29th Armoured Brigade approaching from the northwest.

Colonel Hammond D. Birks was with the van of his regiment as they struck south from St. Aubin just after 1330. Birks had been at eighteen the youngest company commander in the American Expeditionary Forces in World War I. The Army had given him the 120th Infantry, a National Guard regiment, during the beginning of mobilization in 1940, and he had trained these lean North Carolinian Tar Heels hard for four years. Now he was leading these men in a desperate adventure. He could hear the fighting ahead around Bénouville which was on fire, the flames and smoke visible above the line of trees ahead. The regiment would be just in time.

The same thought was in Otto Meyer's (unrelated to Panzermeyer) mind at much the same time. His Panther battalion had just shot to pieces the last tanks of the enemy force that had penetrated past Cresserons. The Americans had taken refuge in a small wood which had been splintered by artillery. When they tried to make a break for it, they were picked off by the Panthers hiding behind a tree line. The woods in which they had sought refuge first were on fire, ignited by burning Shermans. More burning tanks and half-tracks trailed off to the north dwindling as the last of them had died. Now Meyer was answering the desperate appeals of the panzergrenadiers at Bénouville. Meyer ordered the battalion to the rescue. The Panthers sped southeast using as concealment the same long row of trees over which Colonel Birks had seen the flames of Bénouville.

Obersturmbannführer Bollert's tank was first in the column. Standing up in the turret, he spotted the head of the American column cutting through the tree line ahead on its way to Bénouville and ordered the battalion to deploy and attack. As he moved to the centre of the formation, an antitank round hit the side of the turret next to him. The clanging impact and shower of sparks two feet away from him alone might have been fatal, but the shell penetrated the turret and tore off his legs. Colonel Birks had left a small insurance policy on his flank, an antitank battery which now began to pick off the Panthers, offering more vulnerable side shots at close range. Even the U.S. 57mm antitank gun was effective under these conditions. The German attack faltered then collapsed as the Guardsmen picked off five more tanks. The rest retreated into the safety of woods to the south.

East of the Mue, Obersturmbannführer Jochen Peiper's 1st SS Panzer Regiment was in the van of the counterattack of 1st SS Panzer Division 'Leibstandarte SS Adolf Hitler', the infamous and lethal death's head division suckled out of Hitler's own bodyguard. Peiper's mission was to eject the British from defences of the 85th Division, barely holding on at le Fresne-Camilly. Given his record, there was no reason to expect anything but success. On 27 January he had been awarded the Oak Leaves to his Knight's Cross after chopping a bloody lane through four Soviet divisions. Another honours graduate of the Eastern Front school of war, he brought to battle experience and skill matched by hardly a single Allied contemporary in Normandy.

His mild features and appearance of being a well brought up young man belied a considerable reputation for toughness. Every move that he undertook had the prospect of success – even those that looked hopeless from the start – for, like Michael Wittmann, his decisions were based on a sound grasp of military principles.[9]

One of those principles being foresight, he had dispatched reconnaissance forward that now told him a large armoured force had passed through Cairon while British infantry were in force in le Fresne-Camilly. Strong infantry forces had also broken through 85th Division's positions just south of the Seulles as well. The front was now fluid, he thought, the perfect conditions to find opportunity. He instinctively went after the armour kill and sent a Panther company and attached panzergrenadiers up the concealed wooded road paralleling the Mue to burst into Cairon and hold it. The rest of the division was advancing north to meet the oncoming 15th Scottish Division. The Leibstandarte and the Scottish collided to the west of le Fresne-Camilly. The Germans had the advantage of over forty assault guns to support the SPW mounted 1st and 2nd SS Panzergrenadier Regiments. The British, however, had their antitank guns up forward with the advancing infantry. For the rest of the day the two divisions fought back and forth over a few square miles of villages, hedgerows, streams. But Peiper withheld his Panther and Mark IV companies. As soon as his Panthers were lodged in Cairon, he attacked with the rest of his force. He caught the 23rd Hussars by surprise. They had been facing south in his direction until the clamour of shooting in Cairon startled their commander. His whole mission had been to guard this flank of 11th Armoured, and somehow the Germans had slipped in and grabbed the division by the jugular. He acted decisively by counterattacking with his whole regiment. As his tanks pulled away, Peiper's tanks came into view racing towards the suddenly denuded line of trees behind which the Hussars had stood.[10]

Zusammenbrechen

At the same time 29th Armoured Brigade pushed on to Buron where the Poles were already fighting with a German infantry battalion. The German defence collapsed when the tanks of 3rd Battalion, Royal Tank Regiment crashed into the opposite side of the town. Taken from front and rear, the Germans surrendered, some 433 Austrians of the 331st Division. Generals Sosabowski and Roberts met in the centre of the town with hearty handshakes. The message was sent to VIII Corps that the relief had been effected. The Poles and tankers of 3RTR were more restrained than the headquarters staffs of VIII Corps and 21st Army Group who spontaneously cheered the news that had broken the awful tension. The second half of TALISMAN had locked in. This news had fallen on the heels of the message that the Americans had linked up with the

Scots Greys and 51st Highland Division and that 2nd Armored was pressing successfully down on Buron from the north. Not only had the two pockets been relieved, but the tables had been turned on the Germans who now had a panzer corps cut off in its own pocket.

Second Armored Division pulled its reserve combat command into line between Combat Commands A and B for one more big effort. The fighter-bombers circled over Columby-sur-Thaon, Anisy, Mathieu, and the woods along the Mue, diving for any tank or infantry that showed themselves. Then followed the father of all artillery stonks as the field and artillery regiments of both armies and the guns of the Royal Navy raked and hammered the town into fine rubble. As the tanks moved forward the artillery continued then shifted to smoke. The Americans swarmed over and around Columby before the few dazed survivors of 10th SS Panzer could stagger out of their holes much less man their smashed weapons. The masses of tanks continued on past Mathieu where 10th SS seemed to have come back to life. A few antitank guns began to pick off tanks and halftracks until the U.S. self-propelled batteries began firing direct over the sights support to silence them. At Anisy Combat Command B found even more opposition; the fabric of the defence had survived and was hitting back.

Unterscharführer (corporal) Willi Pohl now commanded the Pak-75 antitank gun section; the sergeant commanding the section was dead in the bombing. It wasn't the first time command had fallen to him; at Tarnopol he was just a loader when his gun chief was killed and the other men too. He had served the gun alone for an hour, knocking out four T-34s, and earning himself the Iron Cross First Class to wear below his blouse pocket. Like so many front line veterans he also wore the red, black, and white ribbon of the Iron Cross Second Class in a blouse button hole. Now he was finding out these American Shermans brewed up even faster than the Russian tanks. There were still three guns left in the section, and they had scored seven kills in fifteen minutes. The American counterbattery fire was intense and accurate. The gun on his left took a direct hit and flew into jagged pieces along with its crew. Two minutes later, the gun on his right was silenced by a shot that killed or wounded most of its crew. The tanks had forced their way into the village with a battalion of armoured infantry. Pohl knocked out one more tank before ordering the crew to drag the gun back to its alternate position covering the town square. They were there barely seconds before tanks drove into the square, their turrets sweeping back and forth. 'Feuer!' Pohl shouted, and the first tank became a fireball. The second fired in their direction, spraying them with stone and brick fragments. A machine gun to their right kept the American infantry at bay for a while until bazooka fire silenced it. Pohl disabled another tank working around the square. Then Americans were firing into them from the rear. He tried to slip his submachine gun off his shoulder, but felt a blow to his chest that staggered him, and he fell to the pavement. He was barely alive when the Americans turned him over. One ripped the ribbon off its blouse button-hole. Pohl heard him but didn't understand, 'What the hell is this ribbon; it ain't no iron cross. Hey, this one's still breathing. Medic!'

But TALISMAN was not quite yet a done deal. The team of Rommel, Dietrich, and Hausser were experienced players in the game of guile and riposte. Already Peiper's tanks had broken through the tree line and destroyed the single squadron of the Hussars left behind. They wheeled for Cairon and trapped the rest of 23 Hussars against the German company in the village. They must have hit twenty tanks from the rear before the rest realized what was happening, but by then it was too late. The crews of the few surviving tanks abandoned their vehicles to either surrender or run for the patches of woods to the north. Peiper had no time for prisoners. They were machine-gunned down as they stood in a group by the road.

Rommel had anticipated the risk of an armoured thrust to relieve Caen but thought its opportunities more important. It was a chance to snap off the enemy's spearhead which Peiper had just done. With such subordinates, a German commander could do miracles. They had been raised on risk, daring, and a taste for the main chance. No army in modern times had fielded so many such gifted officers at every level. Time and time again, these human dynamos overcame incredible odds to hunt down victory. Because of them, German units were at the right spot at the right time more often than their enemies. Because of them, German units were tactically employed more effectively on a whole than their enemies. The art of German generalship anticipated the intelligent and aggressive actions of subordinates, and nowhere was it more true than in TALISMAN.

Dietrich now ordered the commitment of his corps reserve, Heavy SS Panzer Battalion 101, in support of Peiper. At this point the cascading effects of actions by men of initiative and daring, men like Peiper, were paying dividends. Peiper's regiment attacked the rear of 29th Armoured Brigade. General Roberts' attention was immediately pulled backwards. Half of the 2nd Fife and Forfar Yeomanry and a company of the 8th Battalion The Rifle Brigade (Motor) were run down and shot up as they tried to turn around off the road. It was then that the thirty Tigers of Battalion 101, supported by the two reserve battalions of 331st Division, crashed into Cussy. The troop of Yeomanry tanks were brewed up in minutes. The Polish battalion resisted to the death, but 6-pounder antitank guns were crushed under the Tigers which demolished house after house with their 88mm guns as the Austrian infantry followed. From the north, Hausser committed his corps reserve, Heavy SS Panzer Battalion 102. The twenty-eight Tigers crossed the wheat fields to intercept 3rd Royal Tank Regiment as it was trying to change front to meet Peiper's attack. Battalion 102 ploughed through the confusion, two companies abreast shooting up everything in their path. The puny British 75mms bounced off the Tiger's heavy frontal armour. They would fire away getting repeated good hits that only dented or scorched the German armour. Then they would explode as a slower German Tiger fired its great killing 88mm.

Sosabowski realized that this was one trap his Poles were not likely to survive, as he watched the Tigers savage the British relief column. More Tigers were coming up from the south where they had just wiped out one of his battalions. His second battalion was now fighting off German infantry attacking St. Contest. His remaining battalion and Captain Heath's 6-pounder antitank guns were with him in Buron. Twenty-odd British tanks had retreated into Buron to escape the slaughter by the Tigers roaming the wheat fields. General Roberts had tried to rally his forces and had disappeared in the confusion. Sosabowski could see scores of funeral pyres billowing black smoke on the road outside Buron and on to the northeast towards the Mue.

If he had looked to the north, he would have seen even more such columns of black, oily smoke. Second Armored Division had finally come to a halt outside of the next town, Villons, a little more than two miles north of Buron. It was here that Frundsberg's commander committed his understrength 10th SS Panzer Regiment and his last battalion of panzergrenadiers. His assault guns had already taken up position behind the tree line that ran from the river to Villons. Combat Command A had lost a dozen tanks there but was breaking through. Accurate tank gunnery had left as many of the assault guns burning, their flames whipping up through the trees, catching some on fire. Accurately called-in artillery was also shredding 10th SS Panzer's last barrier before Buron. Combat Command R was fighting its way into Villons. The panzer regiment struck between Anisy and Villons taking Combat Command R in the flank with seventy tanks. As they crossed the road, they caught an American column nose to tail in a deep cut on the road from Columby. The Panthers fired into it destroying the first several tanks and halftracks, trapping the rest. Then they passed on. Two platoons of Mark IVs lingered to shoot up the rest of the trapped Americans who by now had abandoned their vehicles and were fleeing back down the road. The panzergrenadiers and a few more tanks attacked into Anisy just as the Americans were about to wipe out the last defenders. It was a new ball game and one that the Americans started to lose.

Willi Pohl remembered the American aid station where they had treated him. Morphine had dulled the pain in his chest. He could hear the noise of firing outside as if it were a thousand miles from there. Then a few Germans burst into the house. An American doctor stepped forward and was shot dead. Willi raised his arm,and they swung at the motion, almost shooting him. An officer followed them in, saw the wounded from both sides being treated side by side, and pulled his trigger-happy men out. He was followed in by a German medic team carrying in three more wounded men.

Second Armored was halted in its tracks by the counterattack. Most of Combat Command R's 3/67th Armor had died in the road cut. Combat Command A's 2/67th was trying to pass through the tree line with 2/41st Armored Infantry. 10th SS Panzer Regiment's attack hit the following 1/67th in the flank. The Americans recoiled as their tanks began to brew up. The whole command pulled back, running the gauntlet of German tanks. The Shermans' faster speed gave them just enough edge to escape the German attack aimed at their rear. One Sherman company, obviously a rear guard, hung back along a row of trees. Their 75mms may not have been good enough to kill a Panther easily, but they were more than good enough to stop the Mark IV battalion before pulling back. Seven burning Mark IVs marked the furthest point of the German pursuit.

Horatio at the Bridge

Colonel Birks was bent over a map with the commander of 154th Brigade organizing the route of evacuation for the men of the Orne Pocket now streaming over Pegasus Bridge. It was almost two in the afternoon. The Germans on the other side of the Orne had launched another big push and were breaking into the pocket in half a dozen places. At the same time, the commander of 9th SS Panzer Division was now turning his undivided attention on them now that 10th SS had stopped 2nd Armored's attack. He still occupied Cresserons and Hermanville-sur-Mer with most of the 19th SS Panzer-grenadiers and assault gun companies. The 20th had been driven out of Bénouville but was regrouping south of it in Blainville. Most of 9th SS Panzer Regiment was directly west of the town. The commander realized what a thin cord the enemy dangled from. Leaving only a company in Cresserons, he attacked with the entire 19th Regiment and the assault guns into Colleville-Montgomery. The rifle company and antitank guns left behind by Colonel Birks were overwhelmed. The Germans sent a battalion towards Ouistreham but were stopped outside it by a tank platoon and another rifle company. They next moved St. Aubin and were engaged by another small force left behind by Birks.

By now Birks and the British knew that the Germans were charging down their escape route. Birks turned the rest of 3/66th Armor around and sent it back to St. Aubin with the 1/120th to hold the Germans there. At the same time, he sent the 2/120th back to Ouistreham to hold their last bolt hole. The Scots Greys were down to eighteen tanks from lack of fuel. Birks recommended that they load up with infantry and get to Ouistreham fast. If the Germans held Colleville, then the land route back was gone. But the Royal Navy could still bring some men off from Ouistreham at the mouth of the Orne. In fact, the Navy had had a force of ships and landing craft waiting off the beaches as a contingency. As they disappeared up the road, Brigadier Hill's 3rd Parachute

Brigade made its way across the bridge with some of the tanks of 13/18th Hussars. But they were the last. Heavy German artillery began falling on the bridge on both approaches and on the Orne River Bridge to the east of it. 5th Parachute Brigade was badly hit as it concentrated between the bridges to cross Pegasus. They had been the escort for the large number of wounded who had been loaded aboard the few vehicles that had fuel only to fall victim to the same German artillery. Immobile in their vehicles, they almost all perished. That left only 6th Airlanding, 152nd and 153rd Brigades as an increasingly desperate rear guard around Ranville. German LXXXI Corps was breaking into the town already.

The last act began when 9th SS Panzer and 20th SS Panzergrenadiers counterattacked once more straight for the approach to the bridge, half of which had already fallen into the water. Birks formed a rear guard of his third battalion and the half dozen Shermans of the Hussars. He sent 3rd Parachute Brigade, which had shrunk to the size of a battalion, on ahead. They were nearly out of ammunition in any case. The SS closed on Bénouville and the ruins of the bridge just moments after Birks abandoned them. He marched at the rear of the column until one of the Hussars invited him aboard his Sherman, the rearguard tank. They then passed a line of trees at right angles to the road. This gave them concealment from the Germans who were pressing north after them. Quarter-of-a-mile further on they passed the ruins of a Roman military camp, carefully preserved as an archaeological site. Birks pulled out a few antitank guns and the Hussars and put them among the ruins. They were just in time. The Germans burst through the tree line and sped up the road. One hundred and fifty yards from the ruins, Birks sprung the ambush and two Panthers were left dead in the middle of the road. The Royal Air Force made a timely appearance with flight after flight of fighter-bombers that gave the two German regiments on his tail a lot more to worry about. He then pulled out for Ouistreham, at the same time ordering his two battalions in St. Aubin to pull back as well.

By the time Birks entered Ouistreham, the Royal Navy was already embarking 154th Brigade on a line of landing craft in the Orne Canal. More landing craft were lowering their ramps on the beaches. All vehicles were ordered abandoned whether jeeps, trucks, or tanks. The beach was quickly littered with the last of the Scots Greys' chargers as the crews waded through the surf to scramble aboard the landing craft. The 3rd Paras were next and then any other stragglers who had lost their units. Before the Paras were off, Brigadier Hill sought out Birks on the firing line which wasn't far; the firing line was altogether too close to the beach. Hill extended his hand. Birks never forgot the strength of that grip nor the hard blue of the man's eyes. Then Hill took off his red beret and pressed it into Birks' hand. 'From the Paras to their friends!'[11]

The last of the British loaded quickly as the 120th held a strong perimeter against increasingly strong attacks by elements of all three regiments of 9th SS. Air cover and the naval gunfire were throwing a wall of fire around the town.

General Gale was nearby at 1502 when Pegasus Bridge fell into the canal with a great scream of torn metal. His last hope to bring out the entire force in the pocket had just fallen into the water with the bridge. Any hope to jury-rig rafts or let the men swim across faded when 9th SS's general counterattack kicked off a few minutes later. He signalled to the relieving force to escape, and turned to the last slim chance to get at least some of men still left in the pocket out. That chance would evaporate in the next hour. Now minutes were everything. Ammunition was practically exhausted, and some of his men were using German weapons now. The Germans were closing for the kill from the east. He turned to Lord Lovat of the Commandos and the commander of the 5th Paras. The two units would have been next to cross the bridge and were now suffering under the artillery that was hitting the few hundred yards between the bridges. 'Your only chance now is to escape down the finger of land between the canal and the river. Once you get opposite Ouistreham, there is a chance the Navy can pick you up. Hurry now, before the Jerries knock down the other bridge.'[12]

Gale had been prophetic. The Germans found the range of the river bridge as the last of the Commandos hurried across. The 5th Paras had already moved out as Lovat pushed his command after them. They immediately ran into their first piece of luck, an embankment that ran down most of the finger and offered perfect cover and concealment for the columns of red and green berets. The move was slow because the Paras and Commandos were bringing along all of their wounded that could be moved. No one who could survive the march was left behind. Their path paralleled the road to Ouistreham across the canal. They watched the 13/18th Hussars rear guard at the Roman ruins give the pursuing Germans a bloody nose, and hurried on. The three-mile march to the converging mouth of the Orne and the canal took hours because of the wounded, none of whom were left behind. After the Commandos came several hundred men from anti-aircraft batteries stationed between the bridges and anyone else that had happened to be there. The first of the Paras to reach the end of the finger, the Pointe du Siege, found a company of Royal Marines covering the landing craft embarking troops across the canal at Ouistreham. Within half an hour a procession of landing craft entered the canal and began loading the first of the wounded that were being carried to the front. The Navy, with its usual efficiency in these things, had planned to evacuate the entire pocket by sea if that contingency had been necessary and so had more than enough landing craft for the few that actually made it.

Lovat was among the last to leave the Pointe du Siege and could see the flames of Ouistreham across the canal and an occasional American as their rear guard pulled back deeper into the town. Despite the naval gunfire and the air support, the 19th SS Panzergrenadiers had followed the 120th into the comparative safety of the built-up area of the town with some of Meyer's assault guns. Colonel Birks was trying to conduct an operation rarely taught at the U.S. Army's Command and General Staff College at Fort Leavenworth: how to evacuate by sea a regiment locked in decisive combat with a redoubtable enemy. The tanks of the 3/66th Armor had been their saviours. Their guns repeatedly made the difference as the Germans pressed one determined attack after another while he pulled the regiment back company by company closer to the busy landing craft on the beach. By early evening, he had shrunk the pocket enough to squeeze his 2nd Battalion out of the line and down to the beach for evacuation. Two hours later, the 1st battalion and half of the tank crews were embarked and whisked to safety, but the German artillery had found the range to the beach and had killed or wounded two hundred men and sunk three landing craft. As he pulled the 3rd Battalion and his last tank company into a tight perimeter within the last row of buildings from the beach, the Germans slipped machine-gun crews into position further down the row of buildings to cover the beach with fire. They caught the first company of Tar Heels to run for the landing craft in converging fire that left half of them on the beach and the rest running back to the town.[13]

Notes

1. Francis de Guingand, *Memories of Montgomery* (London: Hodder and Stoughton, 1954) p.265.
2. Erwin Rommel, *Kriegstagebuch*, Band III (Potsdam and Leipzig: Verlagshaus Hindrichs, 1963) p.349; (London: Greenhill Books, 1964) pp.332–3.
3. Max Hastings, *Overlord: D-Day & the Battle for Normandy* (New York: Simon & Schuster, 1984) p.176; (London: Michael Joseph, 1984).
4. Charles Eberly, 'My Mission from Rommel,' *Harper's Weekly*, 28 August 1944, p.33. Eberly related that Montgomery was intrigued by the photo of Rommel and called in a photographer so that the lieutenant would have a picture of himself with Montgomery as well. In 1993 Sotheby's auctioned off the twin autographed photos for £22,000.
5. Charles H. Miller, *History of the 13th/18th Hussars (Queen Mary's Own) 1922–1947* (London: Chisman, Bradshaw, 1949) p.108.
6. Anthony Cave Brown, *Bodyguard of Lies* (New York, Toronto, London: Harper & Row, 1975) p.720; (London: W.H. Allen, 1976).
7. Bruce W. Watson, *Disaster at Arromanches* (Annapolis: Naval Institute Press, 1977) pp.192–193. The author likened this disaster to the explosion of an American freighter carrying mustard gas munitions at the Italian port of Bari in 1943. The explosion spread the mustard throughout the port and harbour, causing thousands of casualties.
8. John Culbertson Heath, *The Siege of Caen* (London: Collins, 1958) p.212.
9. Eric Lefèvre, *Panzers in Normandy Then and Now* (London: Battle of Britain, 1983) p.129.
10. Jochen Peiper, *My Honor is Loyalty* (New Delhi: Star of India, 1964) p.325.
11. Paul H. Vivian, *Covered With Glory: The 120th Infantry Regiment in Normandy* (Washington, DC: Infantry Press, 1952) p.192. Brigadier Hill's red beret now rests on Infantry blue velvet, the prize possession of the museum of the North Carolina National Guard's 30th Infantry Brigade, which carries the lineage of the 120th Infantry Regiment.

12. R.N. Gale, *Red Devils and Winged Pegasus* (London: Collins, 1950) p.322.

13. Vivian, *Covered With Glory: The 120th Infantry Regiment in Normandy* (Washington DC: Infantry Journal Press, 1952), p.215.

CHAPTER 9

Vae Victis? and Unternehmen TEUTOBURGER WALD 27 to 30 June

At first light, General Gale sent an officer down the street to the firing line with a white flag. The firing fell silent as he walked down the street to meet a German officer stepping out from a ruined house. Salutes, and the two officers disappeared into a side street.

Twenty minutes later, Gale was introduced to his captor, Lieutenant General von Choltitz, LXXXI Corps commander. With him was the commander of the 346th Division, Lieutenant General Oscar Kreutz, Gale's chief antagonist. For a moment, he and Gale measured each other up. Then Gale introduced the two Germans to Brigadier Brown, the senior surviving officer of the 51st Division. Brown looked as if were ready for the earth to swallow him up. He would be remembered as the officer who had led into the POW cages the remnants of the Highland Division, surrendered once already four years before. Risen Phoenix-like from the ashes, the 51st had once more been swallowed up by the flames. For Gale to see his Paras throw their weapons into heaps and be searched by the Germans was worse than death. They had been picked men, in the most glorious sort of way: they had picked themselves. Some of them had fought to the end with knives and bayonets. At least he would share this coming ordeal with them. Von Choltitz at least was decent if not chivalrous about the whole wretched business, and his men behaved well.[1]

The Poles had died almost to the last man at Buron but not before tearing the guts out of the Austrians of the 557th Regiment. Somewhere among all the corpses lay Sosabowski. Michael Wittmann's Tiger 200 was one of the twelve Tigers from the 101st SS Heavy Battalion that lay burnt out amid scores of British tanks around the town. At the personal direction of the Führer, Sepp Dietrich visited him in the field hospital to present him the Swords to his Knight's Cross. Caen also fell that morning. The four remaining infantry battalions, even reinforced with gunners and engineers, were not enough to man the entire perimeter which the Germans penetrated in half a dozen places, reaching the centre of the city in half an hour. There was hardly any fighting as the thousands of service troops began giving themselves up.

On the beach at Ouistreham, Colonel Birks surrendered his last three hundred men to the commander of the 19th SS Panzergrenadier Regiment. The German congratulated him on his gallant action to enable the rest of the force to get away. He could not resist chiding a tight-lipped Birks on how America again had paid a bloody price to do England's dirty work. Then he strode down onto the beach to look at the more than seventy tanks abandoned on the sand.[2]

At the Château de Creullet, Montgomery waited for the inevitable relief. Over 12,000 dead and wounded men and 30,000 more just surrendered was more than even his self-assurance could bear. In twenty-one days, he had lost almost 200,000 men, seventy percent British and Canadians. TALISMAN had broken all hope. As in the First War, the general two- to four-mile advance of Allied forces was in real terms a waste. To be sure, the destruction of two German infantry divisions south of the Seulles was a trophy, but it paled next to the utter exhaustion of Allied strategic options and the loss of so many lives. The good news was sad by comparison. XXX Corps had broken 19th Field Division and given those young thugs in Hitlerjugend a good thrashing; 15th Scottish had only let Leibstandarte go from its gory embrace in the night. If that had been all, it would have counted as a substantial accomplishment. But that was not all. The main show had been a debacle. VIII Corps' two tank divisions were wrecked with a loss in excess of four hundred tanks. Eleventh Armoured had lost its complete tank brigade, and 2nd Armored had lost over half of its tanks, not even counting all those abandoned at Ouistreham. Worst of all, their sacrifice had been in vain.

Now the Germans had sent another white flag through 50th Division and delivered a letter for Montgomery. Montgomery took it knowing that it contained better terms than he had intended for Rommel. He stared at the single page.

27 June 1944

Dear General Montgomery,

My terms are still the same as those transmitted by Lieutenant Eberly.

Rommel

TALISMAN had thrown the entire Allied leadership into shock. Even Churchill seemed at a loss. President Roosevelt was sending General Marshall to London. Britain was in mourning for her lost army, and for the first time, the Americans were unsure of the future. The success of VII Corps seemed less hopeful now that Rommel could transfer a score of divisions to contain it. On

27 June, Eisenhower and Alanbrooke flew over to the lodgement finally to relieve Montgomery. When they arrived, he showed them the letter.

At that moment Rommel was on the phone to a wildly exuberant Hitler. He would break England; he would deport its male population to rebuild Europe. Rommel invited him to view the spectacle of England's second and final ejection from the continent. And for the first time since shortly after the fall of Stalingrad, the Führer was persuaded to come close to the front to see his staggering victory, the masses of war booty and the hordes of prisoners paraded before him.

Unternehmen TEUTOBURGER WALD

In the city hall of Caen, five German general officers met behind closed doors on the morning of 28 June. Rommel reviewed the plan for Unternehmen TEU-TOBURGER WALD and each man's role. He reminded them first that the name of the operation had been chosen to signify a blow for German freedom and honour, when Arminius (Hermann) had united the Germans to destroy the instrument of Roman tyranny, the three legions of Publius Quintilius Varus. This operation would strike a blow against their own tyrant. Speidel's role was to welcome Hitler to Army Group B headquarters and explain the route of his procession to the front in Normandy. Bayerlein and von Lüttwitz with Panzer Lehr and 2nd Panzer Divisions would be across that route at Lisieux.[3]

Two days later Speidel was waiting on the steps of the Château La Roche Guyon when the Führer arrived. The entourage was huge, and would crowd even this great house. Hours before, a security battalion of SS Begleit (Escort) Brigade had arrived to secure the headquarters of Army Group B for the Führer's arrival. Jodl had hinted broadly that the Führer would be pleased if the Duke de La Rochefoucauld, the owner of the chateau, were present to greet him. The gentleman had been horrified when Speidel raised the issue and tactfully suggested that he would probably be indisposed. Speidel suggested that Hitler did not forgive such slights and to see it through. There would be no further call on his dignity. Now as the second escort battalion entered the grounds, the old man was standing next to him, elegantly turned out, stiff with the dignity of an ancient French house, and seething in his mortification. The convoy of sedans seemed endless. Jodl had warned Speidel that Hitler was bringing half of Berlin to help him exult in his moment of triumph. And many of the great men of the Reich brought their own entourages. Who would dare miss sharing the moment? The Führer stepped out his car and instantly, it seemed, was joined on one side by Reichsführer Himmler and Reichsmarshal Göring on the other. He was met by Speidel who welcomed him to the headquarters of Army Group B in Rommel's absence at the front. Then he introduced the duke who flawlessly offered the hospitality of his home. If he flinched inwardly, it did not show.

That night at dinner in the great hall of the chateau, Speidel was far from a conspicuous place of honour at the table. Hitler was droning on again in one of his monologues. Speidel was not sure which had been more painful, the monologue or Hitler's bland vegetarian menu that everyone had been forced to endure. There was a utility to the menu; Hitler brought his own kitchen staff and waiters. Speidel could see there were no members of his own staff in the hall. Then on cue, a staff officer approached with a message that he was wanted in the signals office. His departure was not noticed. There were two cryptic messages. The first was simply 'Pour-le-Mérite': Rommel and Dietrich were at that moment meeting with Montgomery and Eisenhower as the German armistice delegation. The second message read 'Hermann': Bayerlein and von Lüttwitz were in position with their divisions where they would block Hitler's escort and arrest him. Hitler was to be arrested, Rommel had insisted. Only if the escort resisted, would force be used. Then Speidel went to his own office and found Major Kaltenbrunner waiting for him with a small briefcase.

They went for a walk in the garden surrounding the chateau, passing half a dozen SS guards, until they were in sight of the great hall on its third floor. Another man approached, the duke who stopped to greet them. Hitler had been gracious enough to allow him the freedom of his own grounds. Having not been invited to dinner, he had the time to take advantage of it. He glared up at the well-lit windows. Speidel nodded to Kaltenbrunner who twisted a knob on the briefcase. The windows of the great hall burst outward, spraying shards of glass, chairs, bodies, tableware, and masonry. The thunderclap seemed to follow by a split second. The great stone wall of the building cracked and sagged, and then broke, spilling out the contents of a dozen rooms on four floors into a pile of broken stone and timbers. Half of the west wing of the château was gone. It was a few seconds before anyone spoke. In that time, the noise seemed to float away, leaving only the dust of the explosion lingering in the evening air. Then Speidel noded to the duke and said, 'My apologies for the damage.'[4]

Notes

1. R.N. Gale, *Red Devils and Winged Pegasus* (London: Collins, 1950) p.340.
2. William J. Patterson, *Leap Across the Channel* (Washington: Office of the Chief of Military History, 1951) p.411.
3. Hans Speidel, *Unternehmen TEUTOBURGER WALD* (Potsdam and Frankfurt: Altstein Verlag, 1957); *Objective Hitler* (London: Collins, 1978) p.209.
4. Ibid., p.310. Rommel was incensed over Speidel's disobedience of his orders to take Hitler alive. It was not until Rommel retired as Chancellor in 1962 that Speidel and he were reconciled.

Postscript

The late great science fiction writer, H. Beam Piper, wrote a delightful novel, *Lord Kalvan of Otherwhen*, in which history had taken a different path. In his world, the Aryans migrated east across Asia to cross the Aleutians and people North America. A shaman had awoken with a hangover one morning and pointed his people east instead of west and south. Piper's point was that a random change can snowball over time into a fundamental change of human history.

Disaster at D-Day does not draw so deeply upon 'the willing suspension of disbelief', but the premise is still valid. A few small changes at the beginning of the Allied landings in Normandy begin changing actual history by geometric leaps and bounds. There is no deus ex machina that drops the victory in one piece into Hitler's hands. Instead these small changes rely upon the variability of human reactions. Would you react the same if you were presented with the same set of circumstances more than once, especially if they were in the midst of crisis, stress, and danger? What is predictable is that old saw that fortune favours the bold. Better yet, 'Fortune favours the prepared mind'.

The 'alternate reality' described in *Disaster at D-Day* is based then on different but equally plausible decisions made under crisis situations. Each significant change pivots on decisions or events that were at the time the subject of heated disagreement or have emerged subsequently as questionable or controversial. In the following paragraphs I describe the interplay of the controversies between the historical reality and our alternate reality.

'In reality' Rommel wanted three panzer divisions directly behind the coastal defence divisions to throw a landing into the sea before a toehold could be secured. They were 12th SS Panzer, Panzer Lehr, and 21st Panzer Divisions. Instead, Hitler authorized the deployment of only the weakest of the three, 21st Panzer. In *Disaster at D-Day*, Hitler relents and allows Rommel to move a second panzer division, 12th SS Panzer, behind the front. The division deploys to just the area behind Omaha Beach that Rommel had in reality intended it to occupy. The division moves to Normandy just before D-Day, and Allied intelligence fails to detect the move, a believable failure since 'in reality' just such a move of a first class infantry division, Kraiss' 352nd, to just the same area a full three months earlier also went undetected. Adding to the Allies' misfortune, Rommel in our alternate reality travels to Normandy the night of 5 June to inspect the newly deployed 12th SS Panzer. 'In reality' it was his method to spend as much time as possible with the troops, especially when they were deploying to a new sector. The opportunity to do so is provided by the alteration of his plans to stop home in Herrlingen for his wife's birthday on 6 June en route to a meeting with Hitler. Frau Rommel takes to her bed with the flu and asks that her husband see her when she's better, the day *after* he visits the Führer. Thus, he is not absent on the day of the invasion but actually behind the critical hinge of the planned Allied lodgement. It is his presence as the commander at this critical moment that sets in train the events leading to the failure of the American landings at Omaha Beach.

The next link in the chain of events in our alternate reality is the dropping of the British 1st Airborne Division in Operation ROYAL OAK on 7 June, the day after the landings. Montgomery 'in reality' intended to use the Red Devils in just such a move but was thwarted by Air Marshal Leigh-Mallory. In our 'alternate reality' Montgomery wins this argument in his ongoing feud with the air marshal. The resulting resounding British defeat is coupled with von Rundstedt's decisive intervention with Hitler to activate Case Three, the immediate dispatch to the invasion front of all theatre reserves. Hitler is finally convinced that Normandy is the invasion and not a great deception by the combined effect of the drop of the 1st Airborne, the capture of the operations orders for both U.S. corps, and von Rundstedt's remonstrations. Case Three puts twenty-three German divisions on the road to Normandy beginning on 7 and 8 June, whereas, 'in reality', German reinforcements were fed in piecemeal and burned up. Case Three provides in the 'alternate reality' the large number of infantry divisions that the Germans sorely missed in the actual battle.

The loss of the Omaha Beachhead now emerges as the great disaster of the invasion. The loss deprives the Allies of the opportunity to link up and form one cohesive lodgement and thereby dissolves the foundation of Montgomery's grand strategy. That strategy in both our realities was to draw the bulk of the German panzer forces upon the British sector while the Americans expanded their sector and built up for a major break-out. That break-out would then swing around and envelop the German panzer forces fixed in place by the British. Now the British 2nd Army is on its own; the surviving American VII Corps is not big enough to expand the American sector as Montgomery needed.

From this point on, the accumulating changes push history off into a completely new direction. The situation deteriorates as the Germans match the Allies in the race to build up forces in Normandy. Despite massive Allied air power and naval gunfire support, the Germans bring enough forces into Normandy to give scope to Rommel's superior generalship in Unternehmen ROSSBACH which nearly destroys the 2nd Army. Misfortune is heaped upon the Allies by the great storm that destroyed both Mulberry artificial harbours and by the rain of V1s on the English Channel ports and the British lodgement itself. Gorging on success, Hitler graciously accedes to Rommel's request to strike both ends of the Allies' logistics pipeline with the new wonder weapon. Montgomery tries once more to rescue the situation with Operation TALIS-MAN to relieve the more than thirty thousand British troops trapped in Caen and east of the Orne. The operation is a catastrophe that should presage another Dunkirk and Montgomery's relief.

Instead, the German plot to remove Hitler in order to secure peace intervenes. 'In reality' the anti-Hitler plotters fully intended to remove Hitler, hopefully before an Allied invasion, and offer generous armistice terms. The invasion intervened, but in the 'alternate reality' Rommel's successes highlight Hitler's intentions to keep on fighting. Rommel proceeds with the plot now armed with the prestige of his growing victories and the tacit support of most of his major subordinates, including the SS General Sepp Dietrich. Rommel, however, only intends to arrest and try Hitler before a German court as the Führer travels to the front to witness the spectacle of England's reckoning. Speidel, more politically practical, arranges Hitler's assassination before Rommel can have him intercepted and arrested. At the very moment Hitler goes to meet his Maker, Rommel and Dietrich are meeting with Eisenhower and Montgomery to discuss the armistice.

To lend a touch of historical authenticity, the text contains a number of fictional endnotes, some of which are hints at the nature of the postwar world. Had events gone the way described here, Rommel might well have survived to become chancellor of a de-nazified Germany, the very role the anti-Hitler plotters envisioned for him. To help the reader wend his way between fact and fiction (and to avoid many fruitless searches for fascinating but fictional titles) a list is provided of the not so authentic endnotes.

Chapter 1:   3,7
Chapter 2:   6
Chapter 3:   1,9,10,15
Chapter 4:   13,16,17,18,25
Chapter 5:   1,3,4
Chapter 6:   3,17
Chapter 7:   3,4,5,6,7,8,9
Chapter 8:   1,2,4,7,8,10,11,12,13
Chapter 9:   1,2,3,4

The story required a further liberty of fiction with the photographs used to illustrate the book. A number have been taken out of their original historical contexts to some extent with captions that follow the fictional plot. They are photographs 4–6, 10, 12–18, 20, 22–3, 26, 28 and 29.

In writing this book, I found the analyses of the Normandy Campaign by

Major-General David Belcham in *Victory in Normandy*, Max Hastings in *Over-lord*, John Keegan's *Six Armies in Normandy*, and Carlo d'Este's *Decision in Normandy* to be most useful in identifying the controversial aspects of the Normandy Campaign. Eric Lefèvre's *Panzers in Normandy Then and Now* and Paul Carrell's *Invasion* were invaluable guides to the German forces and prominent personalities at division level. The best American unit history was undoubtedly Joseph Balkoski's story of the National Guard's 29th Infantry Division, *Beyond the Beachhead*. G.L. Verney's *The Desert Rats*, the account of the 7th Armoured Division, and *By Air to Battle*, the story of the British airborne divisions, filled that bill on the British side. The works and archival holdings of the Department of War Studies at the Royal Military Academy Sandhurst, the U.S. Army's Center for Military History at Carlisle Barracks, and the U.S. National Archives in Washington, D.C. were invaluable in the preparation of this book. I am also indebted to Charles Messenger and Kenneth Macksey for their review of the manuscript and their expert and insightful critiques. Any shortcomings in *Disaster at D-Day* remain obstinately my own.

I wish to acknowledge the enthusiastic and invaluable help of the following friends: Captain Frank Shirer and Lieutenant Colonel Jay Zoellitch, without whom I would not have achieved an understanding of D-Day (their knowledge, on the other hand, approaches the metaphysical); Major Paul H. Vivian, North Carolina National Guard, who offered encouragement at my numerous crises in writing this book and who proved a patient sounding board for all sorts of ideas; Major Werner Saemmler Hindrichs, who was a great help in things German and military; to Bob Ralston and Lieutenant Colonel 'Grozniy' Bob Freeman, for their good advice and selfless concern for their subordinates; and to Colonel Bill F. Scott, USAF (ret) (lucky husband of Harriet Fast Scott), for whose graphic account of the initial air operations I am indebted. I also wish to thank the National Guard Bureau for permission to use the beautiful print of the 120th Infantry in Normandy by Keith Rocco.

To my late friend and mentor, Bruce W. Watson, I owe an imperishable debt for his faith, support, and comradeship. God bless you, Bruce. I will miss you. Your memorial is a lifetime adorned with good deeds and kindness.

My profound respect I extend to the British, Canadian, and American fighting men who suffered, endured and triumphed in this great battle and who ensured that *Disaster at D-Day* remains only fiction.

APPENDIX A

Division Strengths

To help the general reader visualize what is meant by the term 'division', the strengths of the various types of divisions are shown here. The German divisions, except for the elite SS panzer and Fallschirmjäger divisions, were rarely at full strength. Replacements for German casualties were also much slower in arriving than for Allied units.

	Men	Tanks/Assault Guns[1]
British Army		
Armoured Division	10–14,000	200
Infantry Division	18,000	
Airborne Division	12,000	
U.S. Army		
Armored Division	11,000	320[2]
Infantry Division[3]	15,000	
Airborne Division[4]	8,400	
German Ground Forces		
Army		
Panzer Division	15,000	162/21[5]
Infantry Division	11,000	
Coastal Defence Division	8,000	
Waffen SS		
Panzer Division	20,000	162/61
Panzergrenadier Division	17,000	/42
Luftwaffe		
Fallschirmjäger Division	16,000	
Luftwaffe Field Division	11,000	

Notes:

1. Both sides employed self-propelled artillery; however, only German assault guns had both the gun and armour to be more properly grouped with tanks.
2. A few U.S. armoured divisions such as the 2nd Armored were considered heavy divisions because they were given two tank regiments instead of only one. Most U.S. armoured divisions would have only half the tanks shown here.

233

3. Although not part of its table of organization and equipment (TO&E), a tank battalion was often attached to U.S. infantry divisions.

4. The two U.S. airborne divisions were almost doubled in size with the addition of more units for the D-Day operation.

5. The figures for the army and SS panzer divisions reflect the number authorized under the new TO&E issued on 1 April 1944 by the organization branch of OKH. In reality, army panzer divisions seldom had more than 110 tanks and SS panzer divisions 130.

APPENDIX B

Allied Order of Battle

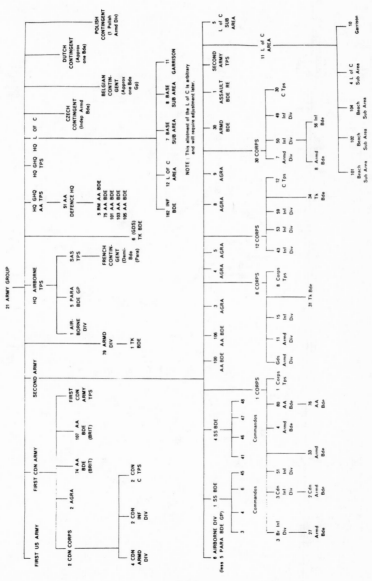

Omaha Beach

	EASY GREEN	DOG RED	DOG WHITE	DOG GREEN
H-5			◊◊◊◊ ◊◊◊◊ ◊◊◊◊ ◊◊◊◊ Co C (DD) 743 Tk Bn	◊◊◊◊ ◊◊◊◊ ◊◊◊◊ ◊◊◊◊ Co B (DD) 743 Tk Bn
H HOUR	Co A 743 Tk Bn	Co A 743 Tk Bn		
H+01	Co E 116 Inf	Co F 116 Inf	Co G 116 Inf	Co A 116 Inf
H+03	146 Engr CT	146 Engr CT Demolitions Control Boat	146 Engr CT	146 Engr CT Co C 2d Ranger Bn
H+30	AAAW Btry — Co H HQ Co E Co H — AAAW Btry 116 Inf	HQ 2d Bn Co H Co F Co H 2d Bn 116 Inf	AAAW Btry — Co H HQ Co G Co H — AAAW Btry 116 Inf	Co B HQ Co A Co B 116 Inf AAAW Btry
H+40	112 Engr Bn	Co D 81 Cml Wpns Bn 112 Engr 149 Engr Beach Bn	149 Engr Beach Bn 121 Engr Bn	HQ 1st Bn 116 149 Beach Bn 121 Engr Co D 116 Inf
H+50	Co L 116 Inf	Co I 116 Inf	Co K 116 Inf	121 Engr Bn Co C 116 Inf
H+57		HQ Co 3d Bn — Co M 116 Inf		Co B 81 Cml Wpns Bn
H+60	112 Engr Bn	112 Engr Bn	HQ & HQ Co 116 Inf	121 Engr Bn Co A & B 2d Ranger Bn
H+65				5th Ranger Bn
H+70	149 Engr Beach Bn	112 Engr Bn	Alt HQ & HQ Co 116 Inf	121 Engr Bn 5th Ranger Bn
H+90			58 FA Bn Armd	
H+100			6th Engr Sp Brig	
H+110	III FA Bn (3 Btry's in DUKWS)	AT Plat 2d Bn AT Plat 3d Bn 29 Sig Bn		AT Plat Cn Co 116 Inf 1st Bn
H+120	AT Co 116 Inf 467 AAAW Bn 467 AAAW Bn	AT Co 116 Inf 467 AAAW Bn 149 Engr Beach Bn	467 AAAW Bn	467 AAAW Bn
H+150			HQ Co 116 Inf 104 Med Bn	
H+180 to H+215		DD Tanks 461 Amphibious Truck Co	Navy Salvage	
H+225	461 Amph Trk Co			

Legend:
[I] LCI [M] LCM [A] LCA ◊ DD Tank
[T] LCT [V] LCVP [D] DUKW

Note Plan as of 11 May

The British defeated at Dunkirk. As June 1944 approached, the question of 'would D-Day be a replay of Dunkirk?' was a growing hope for the Germans, as seen in this *Signal* cartoon, and a nagging dread for the Allies. *U.S. Library of Congress*